Sport in the Global

General Editor: J.A. Mangan

AMATEURISM IN SPORT

SPORT IN THE GLOBAL SOCIETY

General Editor: J.A. Mangan

The interest in sports studies around the world is growing and will continue to do so. This unique series combines aspects of the expanding study of *sport in the global society*, providing comprehensiveness and comparison under one editorial umbrella. It is particularly timely, with studies in the political, cultural, anthropological, ethnographic, social, economic, geographical and aesthetic elements of sport proliferating in institutions of higher education.

Eric Hobsbawm once called sport one of the most significant practices of the late nineteenth century. Its significance was even more marked in the late twentieth century and will continue to grow in importance into the new millennium as the world develops into a 'global village' sharing the English language, technology and sport.

Other Titles in the Series

AMATEURISM IN SPORT

An Analysis and a Defence

LINCOLN ALLISON
University of Warwick

FRANK CASS
LONDON • PORTLAND, OR

First published in 2001 in Great Britain by
FRANK CASS PUBLISHERS
Crown House, 47 Chase Side, Southgate, London N14 5BP

and in the United States of America by
FRANK CASS PUBLISHERS
c/o ISBS, 5824 N.E. Hassalo Street
Portland, Oregon 97213-3644

Website: www.frankcass.com

British Library Cataloguing in Publication Data

Allison, Lincoln
  Amateurism in sport : an analysis and a defence. - (Sport
  in the global society ; no. 21)
  1. Professionalism in sports
  I. Title
  796'.042

ISBN 0-7146-4969-4 (cloth)
ISBN 0-7146-8030-3 (paper)
ISSN 1368-9789

Library of Congress Cataloging-in-Publication Data

Allison, Lincoln.
Amateurism in sport : an analysis and a defence / Lincoln Allison.
p. cm.–(Sport in the global society, ISSN 1368-9789 ; no. 21)
Includes bibliographical references and index.
ISBN 0-7146-4969-4
1. Professionalism in sports. 2. Sports–Social aspects. I.
Title. II. Cass series–Sport in the global society ; 21.
GV733 .A44 2001
796.04'2–dc21
2001002916

Typeset by Jo Edwards in 10.75 Times New Roman
Printed in Great Britain by MPG Books Ltd, Bodmin, Cornwall

Contents

Series Editor's Foreword

Amateur: A person who practises something, especially an art or game, only as a
pastime.
                                    The New Shorter Oxford English Dictionary[1]

My ramifications stretch out into many sections of society, but never, I am happy to
say, into amateur sport, which is the best and soundest thing in England.
                    Sir Arthur Conan Doyle, *The Return of Sherlock Holmes*[2]

As professionalism prospered, Canute-like, G. Lacy Hillier[3] at his
'argumentative, ideological, pro-amateur best', in *The Bicycling News and
Tricycling Gazetteer* no less, in May 1892, mounted a spirited, forceful,
righteous defence of amateurism:

> Sport is amusement solely, but different amusements please different
> minds ... If it amuses a man to play at soldiering, volunteering is a sport
> for him, as much as cycling, or yachting, when they amuse their
> devotees. The essence of sport is relaxation. Sport is when we disport
> ourselves from labour and our usual daily work. Any pursuit followed
> regularly as a means of livelihood is no longer a sport ... the paid
> athlete is not a sportsman whether he be runner, cricketer, or cyclist;
> these pursuits are trades for the professionals, ... They must be
> followed for pleasure to be sports.[4]

He added:

> The sportsman, then, is the man who has an amusement which may cost
> him something, but which must not bring him in anything, for an
> amusement which brings him in anything is not a sport but a business ...[5]

Hillier is not dead! He lives again – in Lincoln Allison, an equally apodictic,
undaunted and self-confessed 'luddite' in terms of contemporary sporting
trends. Allison has set himself the self-appointed task of saving amateurism
'from any rejection to an historical dustbin' (p.5). He offers a most readable
apologia for amateurism at an early twenty-first century moment of rampant
commercialism, consumerism and professionalism in sport. Brave spirit.
Moments before I began to write this Foreword Jona Lomu appeared before

me stripped (to the waist) promoting the Barbarians against Scotland in a television commercial – and lo and behold, he appeared again later the same evening (clothed this time) promoting the advanced communications technology Lincoln Allison seemingly repudiates or, at least, shies away from. A double whammy!

This is a lively book full of strong and confident assertions: 'Amateurism in one respect was the creation of a sector of society which protected the individual and the group from both the market and the state' (p.5). It also protected, of course, highly privileged individuals and groups from the hoi-polloi, embarrassing defeats by them and consequent destruction of amour-propre. Allison thrusts, with a sharpened quill, into the tender parts of the modern politically correct body other writers dare not touch: 'it is ... possible to pick out ... considerable evidence of the cultural masculinization of women, particularly through sport ...' (p.5). Quite so.[6] If he is bluntly assertive as above at times, equally pleasingly, he can be delicately balanced in his judgements at other times. In general terms, he remarks, modern sport may have caused general gender confusion but its social consequences are clearly a great deal more egalitarian than the Victorian social system which gave it birth.

Allison in *Amateurism* travels down a philosophical lane with many turnings. Among other things he deals with amateurism as an ideal, as an ideology, in hegemonic decline, in a hostile contemporary culture. To enliven his philosophy he juxtaposes theory with experience. With justification, like many others, he is especially concerned about amateurism and the future. He asks, will a society without amateurism – and not only in sport – all things being equal (they seldom are, of course), result in a less free and less happy society? What would be the meaning and purpose of sport without amateur ideals?

Will such things come to pass? We must simply wait and see.

Lincoln Allison's *Amateurism in Sport* has much in common with Roger Scruton's *England: An Elegy*. There is little doubt that Allison would endorse Scruton's comment, 'it is only at the end of things that we begin to understand them. And understanding them, we know they are lost ... often it seems that we kill things by examining them; and then again, that understanding is a way to keep what we value, when all other means have vanished.'[7] He would certainly cheer Scruton to the echo for this remark: 'English society was a creation of amateur initiatives, its most valuable institutions were the result either of private patronage ... or of people making common cause and clubbing together.'[8]

Allison is a little unkind to social historians (and sociologists but then who is not!) who, he claims, are concerned 'only trivially about doing things for love or as ends in themselves' (p.6). This is not entirely accurate. Some are well aware of the need to take these things into account but Allison has a point up to a point. These elements in social history do require more attention. Oddly he seems unaware of 'new historians' who use, sometimes with considerable success, the conceptual equipment of social historian, sociologist and social anthropologist. Despite this he carries no bouquets for them.

Allison suffers moments of lancinating pain and seemingly most acutely, when he regrets the fact that many social historians and sociologists (he does seem to view both as a pustulant lot) philosophize insufficiently. One reason that they eschew (his term) philosophy could be because it is unhappily too often obtuse, obfuscatory, indigestible. It is not only the effective historian who must devote as much care to transmitting information as to collecting and shaping it. As Norman Davies remarks both laconically and sardonically, 'the value of unreadable academic papers ... is exaggerated'.[9] It must be said, however, that the author has the remedy. He is lucent, engaging, absorbing.

Allison also complains that too many books about sport are not about ideals or ideas but about contexts and experiences. In fact, the best histories of sport are about ideals and ideas *in context*.[10] Contextualization is invariably preferable to reification. By way of example, many English middle-class grammar schools – north, south, east and west, in the late nineteen and early twentieth centuries, could not wait to ape, and even become, public schools and replicate rather than confront their products,[11] and social control rather than social ethics determined the emphasis on 'fair play' in crucial mid-Victorian public schools![12]

This is an invigorating cold soak in philosophy. To use Allison's own terms, if he philosophizes to good effect rather than contextualizes with attention to detail, he has produced a timely, stimulating, provocative and readable 'apologia pro vita sua'.

J.A. MANGAN
International Research Centre for Sport,
Socialisation, Society
University of Strathclyde
June 2001

Preface

'What is it you are writing a book about? ... Oh yes, amateurism ... well I'm sure you'll make a very professional job of it.' Thus the normal, jovial, collegial response. But it does serve as an introduction to what must be an ever-widening circle of academic debts and friendships. There are those at the centre of the circle who are studying sport and whose critical reaction to a book on amateurism might be to express reservations about the size of the task rather than amusement. This list must start with my close colleagues at the Warwick Centre for the Study of Sport, Ken Foster and Terry Monnington who have offered assistance and encouragement. I am grateful also to graduate students at the Centre for the interplay of ideas between us, but especially to Kyle Philpotts and Hiroyuki Ishii who have done work themselves on aspects of amateurism. I have also had a number of useful interchanges with people involved in the academic study of sport at Leicester and De Montfort Universities.

But, just as helpful, in the end, have been the reactions of those who were initially amused. The response of many colleagues who are not involved in the academic study of sport has often started with intrigue or bemusement, but then moved on to a making of connections and suggestions for new directions in reading and thought. I would especially like to mention Wyn Grant, Peter Burnell and Tim Sinclair in this context. In most cases the realization came quickly that to study amateurism is also to study aspects of commercialism, coercion, civil society ... and that is only the Cs! It is interesting to note that, presumably as a consequence of what I have always called the myth of the autonomy of sport, few people have previously thought of amateurism in these regards.

Gratitude is also due to the nine people who were formally interviewed for Part II of the book and the 36 who responded to my survey on changes in English cricket. Beyond them there are hundreds of people with whom I have held discussions, both formal and informal, on the issues in this book, on five continents. I have been particularly gratified by the enthusiastic interest shown by many audiences in ideas which were assumed to have had their day. If I could single out two countries in which this was particularly true it would be the United States and Pakistan. In the American case I confess to a mental habit of equating the working of its society with the model of commercial society, but many of the people I talked to reminded me that one should not equate models with reality.

It was extremely useful for me to be able to travel widely as I prepared and wrote this book. In many cases I lectured on the work in progress and, even where I did not, I was often able to 'piggy-back' research interviews on to travel for lecturing or attendance at conferences. I am grateful to those who funded such travel, including the University of Warwick, the British Council, the educational funds of the European Union and an American academic foundation which does not wish to be named. I am also grateful to members of the younger generation who enthusiastically helped out an amateurish old technophobe who still likes to write with a pen; these are Mike Allison, Jim Allison and Alexander Roper.

Finally, a note of gratitude which is also an important assertion about the nature of this book. To put it in the conventional terms of contemporary academic bureaucracy, this is an 'interdisciplinary' work. You cannot write about amateurism without studying things that are called 'politics', 'education', 'sociology', 'history', 'philosophy', 'economics' and 'law'. (Perhaps this applies to any interesting subject.) The arguments at the core of the book are actually drawn from a certain tradition of economic and political philosophy, but they do require some knowledge of social history (because I have not dealt with the history in any normally accepted sense I have included a chronology as one of the appendices). In theory, 'interdisciplinary research' (as a genuine thirst for knowledge is bureaucratically categorized) is considered a good thing. But this consideration remains what Bertrand Russell called a 'Sunday truth', acknowledged in principle, but not in practice. University departments, 'research assessment exercises', degree courses and (therefore) academic publishers are organized as if knowledge were divided into rigorously separate categories. It is even a bit 'amateurish' to cross boundaries. A Senior Academic Figure was kind enough to take me aside during the early stages of the writing to warn me that what I was doing amounted to wasting my talents on a run-down backwater of an academic suburb. So I must also express my gratitude to everybody, including family, department and publishers who were prepared to tolerate this particular amateur.

The book falls into three distinct parts. Part I can be considered as a set of analytic essays on aspects or dimensions of amateurism. In respect of these essays I would remind the reader of the observation (most often attributed to either Dr Samuel Johnson or the first Duke of Wellington) that easy writing makes for hard reading, with the usual addendum that nobody is saying that the reverse is true. This was hard writing and probably makes hard reading. The second part, with some irony called 'The Lived Experience' (it is a common expression amongst ethnographic sociologists, but how could an experience not be lived?), is much less about the idea of amateurism and more about the experience of it. The third and final part takes the idea of amateurism as it is now and might be in the future. The three appendices grew almost into a separate part of the book. One covers a chronological list of events in the history of amateurism to complement the discursive treatment of history in the text. The second offers a broad range of definitions which it could have been cumbersome and tedious to include in the text. The third offers examples of verse referred to in the text with themes relating to amateurism.

Finally let me acknowledge an element of pragmatic contradiction in the existence of this book. It would follow from what I have to say about amateurism that I would have been better leaving questions of sport and amateurism as an 'other' and not letting them get mixed up with my work. Well, it is too late now! And I shall also argue that the idea of amateurism is, at the time of writing, in too poor a condition to be left unanalysed.

Lincoln Allison
Leamington Spa, 2001

PART I

Aspects of Amateurism

The Idea of Amateurism

Amateurism my be variously considered to be about doing things for the love of them, doing them without reward or material gain or doing them unprofessionally. It is a development of the idea of the *amateur*, a French word primarily indicating action or consumption arising from taste rather than instrumental self-interest. The appendage of an '-ism' to amateur indicates (as with 'racism' or 'capitalism') either or both of a belief or a doctrine which stresses the role of the amateur or a tendency to act as if the distinction between amateur and non-amateur were important. The earliest references to amateurs in English were in the eighteenth century, but it is only in the second half of the nineteenth that the word amateurism (as opposed to amateurship) comes into common use.[1] Amateurs and amateurism can exist in a wide variety of human activities, but it is only in sport that amateurism has been carefully defined and redefined and aroused social and political emotions of an intensity that has led non-amateurs to be described as 'vermin' and 'performing monkeys' and non-amateurism as the ethical equivalent of 'touching pitch'. However, although what follows is about amateurism-in-sport, I shall argue that not only are there important parallels with amateurism in other fields (such as sex, gardening and music), but it is the general principle of amateurism which poses an interesting and neglected ethical and political issue for the twenty-first century, and not specifically amateurism-in-sport.

The concept of amateurism is the product of a society (and later other societies) which aspire in varying degrees to the conflicting models of commercialism and professionalism. It is thus a reaction, an 'other' or at least a critical complement to the main forces of society. The origins of amateurism can be seen in reactions in England in the eighteenth century to a society which was commercial and post-religious (in so far as religion was no longer seen as the sole determinant of political legitimacy nor even of ethical guidance). The unrestricted power of money was a constant theme of eighteenth-century philosophy and literature. Oliver Goldsmith reflected that 'honour sinks where commerce long prevails'.[2] Edmund Burke's famously overblown response to the humiliations of Marie Antoinette in 1791 suggests almost a caricature of eighteenth-century reactions to the decline of aristocratic values:

> I thought ten thousand swords must have leaped from their scabbards

to avenge even a look that threatened her with insult. – But the age of chivalry is gone. – That of sophists, economists and calculators has succeeded, and the glory of Europe is extinguished for ever.[3]

But even Adam Smith, the apostle of commercialism, expressed his concern that a commercial society in which men are trained to the specific pursuit of interest, to the norm of rational exchange for mutual benefit, would lack the 'military virtue' to defend itself.[4] In short, the world of commerce threatened to be a world of greedy, selfish and unmanly men. Aspects of this charge were welcomed by some, as in the statement by Harriet Taylor in 1851:

> In days not far distant, men found their excitement and filled up their time in violent bodily exercises, noisy merriment and intemperance. They have now, in all but the very poorest classes, lost their inclinations for these things and for the coarser pleasures generally; they have now scarcely any tastes but those which they have in common with women, and for the first time in the world, men and women are really companions.[5]

As I read this passage a century and a half of roaring crowds and crunching tackles flashes across my mind. Like Dr Samuel Johnson in the eighteenth century asserting that the trade of advertising had developed as far as it possibly could or Norman Angell arguing in 1910 that global commerce had reached such a level of interconnectedness that war was now impossible, Harriet Taylor is so gloriously and interestingly wrong.[6] Much traditional country sport (both plebeian and gentrified) was in decline and unfashionable, certainly in any circles in which Taylor would move. The new cult of organized games was only just beginning to spread from the public schools and universities to the professions and the provinces. If Harriet Taylor failed to notice it or to give it any significance she was no different from virtually every other leading intellectual figure of her time.

The vision from the middle of the nineteenth century of a refined and non-macho future does concentrate our minds on the question of why modern sport happened. Surely it happened, not only because there was a taste for it, but also because there was a belief in it. A variety of western social critics from English Christians (such as Thomas Arnold) to French aristocrats (such as Pierre de Coubertin) believed to different degrees that commerce and reason were not enough. The world of men required also the ideas of prowess, loyalty and chivalry, reborn as modern sport and sportsmanship. De Coubertin's enthusiasm for the organized games of the

English public school was that of the aristocrat who finds that ancient virtues he had considered dead have been reborn in a new and vigorous form. It must be understood in relation to the broader and more profound concerns of his compatriot and fellow aristocrat Alexis de Tocqueville, about the general direction of modern society.[7]

Modern sport thus comes with the idea of masculinity built into it. What the success of modern sport does for femininity and feminism is an important question but not the concern of this book. Whereas it is still possible to point to examples of feminization and demasculinization in contemporary societies, and thus erect some kind of support for a belated and partial version of Taylor's thesis, it is equally possible to pick out evidence which points in the opposite direction and also to considerable evidence of the cultural masculinization of women, particularly through sport but also through changing sexual practices.[8] The general social outcome might be described as confused though it is clearly a great deal more egalitarian than the social system to which Taylor and John Stuart Mill were attached even though it has developed in very different ways from the progress they envisaged.

Far more importantly for my purposes, the cult of organized games as sport had to be essentially amateur. It was about gentlemanliness, leisure, loyalty and decency. It had to eschew the vulgar gladiatorialism of the Romans in favour of the religious athleticism of the Greeks if it were to play the moral role which its proponents hoped it would. In the context that meant that sport must be barricaded from vulgar commerce; there were also the more pressing considerations that the sports and games which had developed commercially – principally cricket, horse racing and pugilism – had been laced with gambling and corruption and offered what seemed extremely unfair competition to amateurs.

Thus the 'hegemony' which, I shall argue, amateurism established over the development of modern sport and which then collapsed in the last quarter of the twentieth century. But I am not a historian and seek above all to save amateurism from any rejection to an historical dustbin. My argument is that the concept of amateurism raises issues for the future in at least these two important ways: first, that it not clear what is the meaning and purpose (and possibly, in some circumstances, even the appeal) of sport without the ideals of amateurism. There is a serious question about whether mere performance or 'gladiatorialism' are sustainable. Secondly, there seem to me to be good arguments that the decline of the amateur sector in society (and here I am not referring particularly to amateurism in sport) will, *ceteris paribus*, bring about a society which is both less free and less happy. Amateurism in one respect was the creation of a sector of society which protected the individual and the group from both the market and the state.

Philosophizing and Contextualizing

There are two distinct ways of discussing a concept such as amateurism; they have separate purposes and different rules. For my current purpose I will call them Philosophizing and Contextualizing while having to admit that these names are contentious, not least because many people who practise contextualizing would argue that they are thereby philosophizing in the only legitimate way.

If you philosophize in my sense, you would ask of (the concept of) God, 'What could it mean to say "God"? Is there (in any of these senses) a God? What do you have to assume in order to infer the existence of God? What follows from the proposition that God exists?' If you contextualize you ask, 'Under what circumstances would people believe in God? In what sort of God would they believe in a society with such-and-such characteristics? Whose interests might be served by this or that conception of God?'

The dominant disciplines in the study of sport so far consist almost entirely of contextualizers. In different ways sociologists and social historians redescribe and explain events; '*deconstruction*' runs the two together. In their lights, amateurism is quite properly seen as an ideology which must be understood in terms of the class system. It is to be analysed (in the terms of traditional logic) by its connotations rather than its denotations. For them it is only trivially about doing things for love or as ends-in-themselves. It is significantly about maintaining the dominance of the already dominant classes within the institutions that constitute sport. For the philosopher (in my sense) it is only trivially about class, etc. and is more interestingly about doing things for the love of them, without payment and so on. The social context in which amateurism evolved in the nineteenth century is only mildly interesting, but the ways in which we might understand or prescribe amateurism for the twenty-first century are really important.[9]

The equation of sociology and social history is an odd one: only from the vantage point of someone who wants to philosophize do they have much in common. Sociology is highly abstract, concerned with restructuring our thought about society in terms of concepts which are not part of the common discourse, though they may become so if very successful. As a discourse it confers redescription with explanation as a kind of redescription-as-explanation. Social history, especially in Britain, has been much more empirical, concerned with the details of sporting development. On the one hand, a broad historical view of the civilizing process; on the other a close-up of whippet breeding in Northumberland or the earliest Afro-Caribbean football clubs. Many interesting ideas and many fascinating stories, but different weightings of description and explanation, to be contrasted with the conceptual analysis and prescriptive ethics which the philosopher wants to attempt.[10]

I do not think one can exaggerate this difference or overestimate its importance. Sociologists and social historians eschew philosophizing with a thoroughness that I find strange. One explanation must be the division of labour in professional academic life. Another must be the kind of project for the abolition of ethics inherent in Marxism and post-Marxism in which debate about virtue and the good life is undermined and replaced by consideration of context and the direction of 'the forces of history'. As a substitute for ethics this seems to me to have two grand weaknesses: first, it suggests (wrongly) that we do not have free will nor make choices which might affect history, and, secondly, that it simply hides a covert ethical core. Much contemporary 'critical' thought seems, to the reader at least, to contain a hidden ethical doctrine based on the 'enlightenment' values of equality and human rights. The trouble with hidden ethical doctrines is that they do not have to be clarified or defended. I shall stress later that I am highly sympathetic to the glimmers of a serious ethical view which are to be found in the writing of Karl Marx, but they are merely glimmers.

For example, much in the sociology of sport *seems* to be critical of the role of sport, at least as presently constituted, in fostering forms of inequality, most of all the inequality of sex. But there is no attempt to argue the merits of equality or inequality: the 'wrongness' is merely assumed.[11] By contrast, I shall examine sport from a liberal utilitarian point of view, descended from that of J.S. Mill, who subjected his passion for the reform of relations between the sexes to a rigorous ethical test, demanding,

> What good are we to expect from the changes proposed in our customs and institutions? Would mankind be at all better off if women were free? If not, why disturb their minds and attempt to make a social revolution in the name of an abstract right?[12]

All of which suggests an explanation of a mystery: Why are there no books on amateurism?[13] There are now many academic books on sport and amateurism has been a dominant ideal in sport. But books on sport are not about ideals or ideas, they are about contexts and experiences. Thus the tension between amateurism and commercialism is a major theme of much excellent historical writing about sport, but the *concepts* of commercialism and amateurism, their 'essences' in Aristotelian terms, are not discussed. Adam Smith and John Stuart Mill are conspicuous by their absence as are their more contemporary inheritors in economic philosophy, such as J.K. Galbraith, Tibor Scitovsky and Fred Hirsch.[14]

It is these writers who will furnish the bias of an argument about the possibility of good living and the part that amateurism would play in that possibility. The 'field' is perhaps best described as economic philosophy,

with close relations to ethics, political theory and political economy and
analogies (at least) to theology.

But to go beyond those disciplines and to incorporate some of the
considerations which arise from the writings of sociologists and social
historians poses problems. They, after all, are primarily concerned with
what we might call 'real' explanations, with producing forms of a
'plausible story' about why society is as it is. We (so to speak) are
interested in what Robert Nozick calls 'hypothetical explanations' about
what societies would be like if people had a full understanding of rights (or
were completely rational or had a coherent understanding of happiness).[15]
Why not just construct a model which explores the implications of an idea?
In this case develop the idea of amateurism and outline the possible
working of amateur institutions. Why would one read historians, let alone
interview practitioners? The two discourses are irrelevant to one another,
are they not?

In strict logical terms, I accept that they are and that a purely
philosophical treatment of amateurism (as Nozick treats the individual–state
relationship) might be possible. There is no single, grand reason for rejecting
this possibility, though several substantial ones. In terms of mere intellectual
curiosity the connotations as well as the denotations of a word are
interesting. Experience is a source of ideas, a kind of lode for the theorist.
But perhaps most of all, as a conservative as well as a liberal utilitarian, I
consider what has been a serious constraint on what might be.

Amateurism as a Difficult Concept

The idea of amateurism is complex, though no more so than other words
which abstract the features of human relationships and carry some sort of
appraisal. The complexity begins with quite separate criteria for defining,
including definitions based on the idea of payment – a 17- page version from
the National Collegiate Athletic Association in the United States and a one-
liner from the Rugby Football Union – and the full *Oxford English
Dictionary* version which does not mention payment. Much more interesting
than the observation that there are alternative definitions is the possibility
that the essence of the thing lies in the tension between the alternatives. With
'democracy' a minimal understanding of the concept begins with an
appreciation of the tension between 'majoritarian' democracy, defined as a
procedure in which the will of a majority can prevail, and 'liberal'
democracy, defined as an equal distribution of political rights (including
rights to be protected from the will of the majority) to all citizens.

A common-sense approach to language might suggest that if words are
so confused then one should abandon their use or, at least, attach extra labels

to them: always refer to 'liberal democracy' or 'majoritarian democracy', for example. But according to one theory of concepts, that would entirely miss the point of a certain kind of theoretical discourse. W.B. Gallie suggested that in terms such as 'democracy' (his other principal examples being 'art' and 'a Christian life') the real meaning of the term is the 'contest' over its use. These are 'essentially contested concepts', to be contrasted with 'essentially straightforward concepts' such as several million terms in such fields as biology and engineering with precise, agreed meanings and, on the other side, with 'radically confused concepts'.[16] It is more difficult to give an example of a radically confused concept presumably because if it becomes widely accepted that it is radically confused then it tends to drop out of use; but the 'aether' would serve as a case from the history of physics.

With amateurism the tension at the core is between the criteria of payment and the idea of loving or liking on activity (and doing it because you love it or like it). It is at least possible, but, I shall argue, quite difficult, to love an activity that you are paid to do, at least in the same way that a true amateur does. The idea of payment for certain economists may suggest confusion or triviality. Human beings never really do things as ends-in-themselves: actions are generally instrumental in terms of pleasure, status or self-esteem which can be given 'shadow prices' or other sorts of monetary value. Scratch the amateur and you find the 'shamateur' if you are determined to do so.

In Gallie's terms certain conditions must be met if a term is to be classified as 'contested' rather than 'confused'. There must be an 'original exemplar' uncontested as a member of the category and 'progress' or 'development' must take place as a result of the contest. A modern Christian, for example, might mean something very different by 'a Christian life' from Thomas à Kempis or St. Augustine, but the connection might be traceable back to them and might be properly understood only as a development of an ancient idea. 'Sport' itself seems a fairly classic example of an essentially contested concept with broad similarities to 'art'. We might construct a core that 'conceptual art' is a (perhaps even *the*) contemporary development of the idea of art, but some would argue that it is not art at all. In the same way, hunting and boxing may be seen as original examples of sport, but some would say are not sport at all, usually because they fail to live up to an ethical standard which 'sport' suggests. The idea of 'original exemplar' seems weak here, as in all Gallie's examples, but the ideas of contest and development remain important. We can and must continue to argue about the nature of 'sport' and 'art', not least because we have appropriate councils which seek to foster and develop their institutions. It may not even matter that they are in many respects 'radically confused': I am reluctantly convinced by the argument that 'sustainability' or 'sustainable development' *is* radically confused but is a necessary concept for continuing to debate and evaluate the relationship between eco-systems and development at the international level.

Amateurism is a less obvious (or perhaps less established) example than sport. What I am saying here is that if you want to take it seriously you must treat it as something like an essentially contested concept. In the last section of the book especially I shall propose the necessity of developing and debating ideas about amateurism for the future. As such, it has one unusual feature: although 'appraisive' (one of Gallie's criteria) it has been used from the start as both negatively and positively appraisive. There has always existed both the amateur ideal and mere amateurishness.

Conceptual contest allows of many different kinds of definition including those which report natural language and those which appeal to authority; in this case what is understood by amateurism in the public bar and in the rules of the International Olympic Committee. But the most important form of definition is the *stipulative* form in which the author recommends an interpretation or development of the idea for future use. My own definition of amateurism for prescriptive purposes is: 'a human activity is amateur in so far as it is chosen in order to enrich experience and that choice is not coerced by economic or social forces'. Of course, it will turn out to be a definition which generates much in the way of paradox, but that is the nature of the concept.

The Englishness of Amateurism

The concept of amateurism in its modern form is of English origin and evolved in specifically English conditions. So did sport in its modern sense and most individual sports. But it would be wrong to suggest that Englishness is an important attribute of these institutions. Cricket may be an English game to many Americans, but it certainly is not to Indians. Rugby is a Welsh game to the Welsh and a South African game (or should it be Afrikaaner – a delicate point) to South Africans. It could now be highly polemical to call (Association) football an English game and pedantic to describe baseball in that way, though it is as English as the rest in origin. Amateurism, it might be argued, is only English in a trivial sense: the idea was almost immediately taken up by the French, the Americans and others and spread throughout the world. It is as universal a church as football, no more English than democracy is Athenian.

But I think this argument is incorrect in significant ways. I shall argue throughout that amateurism in various senses is more rooted, more easily cultivated in English soil than in any other. It fits into an English form of civil society which has analogues and imitators elsewhere, but no exact parallels. The most important part of this civil society is the vast range of clubs, societies and associations with their own budgets and committees, many of which perform functions which are performed by states elsewhere. Indeed, perhaps the key is the weakness of the English concept of the state, replaced in most formal functions by the Crown. Only in England is it possible to ask the student of a university whether he is at a state institution or not and be faced by puzzlement and an equal division of opinion. In another dimension of amateurism, only in England are more than 90 per cent of criminal cases heard by unpaid magistrates, the Justices of the Peace, an institution which has served the Crown for more than six centuries. Only in England is there a tradition of 'amateur' civil servants at the highest level, well paid admittedly, but educated and capable of taking the broad view rather than that of the professional or the specialist. All of this is analysed fairly thoroughly in political science, but it is nowhere better described than by George Orwell when he discusses,

> [an] English characteristic which is so much a part of us that we barely notice it, and that is the addiction to hobbies and spare-time occupations, the *privateness* of English life. We are a nation of flower-lovers, but also a nation of stamp-collectors, pigeon-fanciers, amateur carpenters, coupon-snippers, darts-players, crossword-puzzle fans. All the culture that is most truly native centres round things which even when they are communal are not official – the pub, the football match, the back garden, the fireside and the 'nice cup of tea'. The liberty of the individual is still believed in, almost as in the nineteenth century. But this has nothing to do with economic liberty, the right to exploit others for profit. It is the liberty to have a home of your own, to do what you like in your spare time, to choose your own amusements instead of having them chosen for you from above. The most hateful of all names in an English ear is a Nosey Parker. It is obvious, of course that even this purely private liberty is a lost cause. Like all other modern people the English are in the process of being numbered, labelled, conscripted, 'co-ordinated'. But the pull of their impulses is in the other direction, and the kind of regimentation that can be imposed on them will be modified in consequence. No party rallies, no Youth Movements, no coloured shirts, no Jew-baiting or 'spontaneous' demonstrations. No Gestapo either, in all probability.[17]

There would be little disagreement with Orwell's idea that English civil society serves as a natural bastion against totalitarianism and we can take some pleasure in the relative ease with which it saw off the totalitarian era. On the other hand, Orwell's characterization and rejection of 'economic liberty' is much more controversial 60 years later. I shall argue that it is essentially right, not in assuming or suggesting that all profit involves exploitation, but in believing that a truly free sector of society must protect itself from both the state and the market. I shall also argue that the state and the market are much more similar and symbiotic forces than neo-liberal rhetoric ever allows.

The acknowledgement of the Englishness of amateurism does, however, pose a problem that runs throughout this book. Amateurism established what will be called a 'hegemony' over modern sport. Modern sport became established almost everywhere. Thus amateurism was embraced, to some degree, as a near-universal value through the writ of the Olympic movement and other global sporting organizations. But the sense of amateurism and the degree to which amateurism was accepted varied enormously from place to place. For example, in my own researches I have argued that South Africa did develop a genuine range of civil society organizations (in sport and otherwise) like the English, that Thailand developed them only at a narrow elite level, without a 'grass roots', while many of the crucial social concepts of modern sport were in the Soviet Union accorded only a kind of lip-service. It was in that respect like some tribe in the Dark Ages which signs on for Christianity without bothering to learn its tenets or build any churches. This is not a problem which can be solved, but one of which we must be constantly aware: when we talk about amateurism globally we are referring to different aspects of a cluster of ideas treated with different degrees of seriousness.[18]

Amateurism and Political Philosophy

Fortunately in the study of society and the humanities it is no longer necessary to aspire to be detached or objective. Neither condition is really logically possible: from the moment one begins an academic project it is filled with evaluation by one big decision – the object of study – and a hundred thousand little ones in the form of the vocabulary chosen. Instead of objectivity one can only offer honesty about the nature of one's preoccupations and prejudices, a determination to take alternative views as seriously as possible and an equal determination to expose the conceptual problems and complexities of the subject.

In other words, I believe in amateurism and want to examine it more as a theologian examines a religious ideal than as a scientist examines a theory. My belief is in amateurism in sport, but also in a broader conception of an amateur sector of society in which production and consumption are not distinguished and in which the state and market forces have only a minimal part to play. These beliefs are not universal in Englishmen of my generation, but they are still well represented now compared with at many other times and places. I have experienced amateur sport in school, at the university and in clubs, which all differ. I have been the chairman of an amenity society and of a cricket club. Perhaps it is just as important in the act of putting the heart on the sleeve, to state that I believe that no restaurant, however many stars or rosettes it has been awarded, can produce vegetables which taste as good as those you grow yourself. After some hesitation I decided to include a mini autobiography among the mini biographies in the second part of this book, partly to add to the variety (not least, by including a subject of considerably less talent than the others) but also to clarify some of the things I am saying by exposing my own background.

A belief in amateurism is not to be caricatured. The most determined and important amateur of the twentieth century was, arguably, Avery Brundage, President of the International Olympic Committee from 1952 to 1972. I have always found his opposition to professional sport and his attempts at the persecution of certain sportsmen tainted with professionalism to be repulsive in its fanaticism. It follows from my account of the nature of the concept that my revulsion would resemble that of a moderate Christian for a fundamentalist preacher or a pope, or of a moderate democrat for a extreme populist. Amateurism is not necessarily about an opposition to payment and certainly not about a total opposition to payment, though I shall have to argue that money is extremely important and nearly always changes the nature of social relations. It is perhaps most of all about preserving a voluntary sector in society and, in sport, about constraining and moderating professionalism and commercialism by ideas whose origin and nature is amateur. Sport must ultimately carry values which are not commercial, even where it is a commercial activity. Involvement in sport is not a mere taste or act of consumption, as pure commercial liberalism would suggest. There is something symbolic about the T-shirt misquotation from Albert Camus often seen in football grounds, 'All that I know most surely about morality and the obligations of man, I owe to football.'[19]

The grit in my oyster, so to speak, is that for all the importance that has been attributed to amateur values in the past, at the present they are no longer taken seriously. By the 1990s amateurism had come to seem outdated, inefficient and reactionary. It was thoroughly tainted by elitism and hypocrisy. Whereas earlier generations of sports journalists had largely admired or accepted amateurism, the generation in power in the 1990s seemed to accept its demise where they did not actually despise it: one broadsheet columnist, in his millennium piece categorized 'the amateur ideal' as 'the worst mistake of the century'. In this respect there is a considerable dissonance between the philosophies of practical men (as Lord Keynes put it) and the philosophies of philosophers. As will become clear, there is only a fringe of 'neo-liberalism' which is prepared to embrace an unrestrained commercialism as the basis for any social institution. Most forms of Marxism, liberalism and conservatism suggest hefty reservations about the 'commodification', 'alienation', 'coercion' or 'social breakdown' which commercialism induces.

The arguments about the value of amateurism in this book are based on a particular ethical and political philosophy the general name of which is utilitarianism. This is a philosophy with a well-known, if misattributed, definition: Francis Hutcheson's statement 'that action is best which procures the greatest happiness of the greatest number', but that statement is contradictory and inconclusive.[20]

I have suggested elsewhere that utilitarianism is a secular broad church, but the test of membership consists of three kinds of doctrine, all of which are necessary conditions and which together are sufficient:

> *consequentialism*: that action be judged according to the value of its consequences;
> *sensualist*: that the only consequences which count are *felt*; they are sensations or experiences; and
> *aggregative*: that policy can be justified only in terms of a population as a whole.[21]

Thus utilitarianism is an ethical and political philosophy which judges governments and social practices by the extent to which they make people feel good in the end. The form of utilitarianism which I will apply is 'liberal' in two senses. First, it insists that whenever in doubt we must err on the side of individual autonomy and choice. Secondly (which is, of course, connected), it favours John Stuart Mill's rejection of a single, calculable concept of 'pleasure' or 'happiness' in favour of an acceptance of the complexity of ideas of human well-being. Mill himself was keen to reject Bentham's assertion that, 'The quantity of pleasure being equal, pushpin is as good as poetry' with an account of pleasure which said that some pleasures were 'higher' than others.[22] Twentieth-century utilitarian philosophy tried many variations on this scheme, often specifically to avoid the accusation that utilitarians are committed to the view that they would favour a drug or machine which could leave people permanently 'happy'. Variously, it is 'meaning', 'flourishing', 'culture' and 'satisfaction'. There is no solution to this problem: we are in favour of happiness, but we do not know what it is and it may take forms which are so trivial as to be self-destructive. Perhaps it is best to say that utilitarians favour happiness in the most profound sense in which it can be defined and sought, which is generally from events and action which have meaning, framed with a culture which is likely to be complex.

Because utilitarianism is such an ill-defined doctrine it is as well to redefine it as what it is not. As a consequentialist doctrine, it is thereby not deontological where deontology is the ethical doctrine that goodness is adherence to the rules of duty. It is therefore not religious in the ethical sense that religion seeks ethical truth in the revealed word of God: indeed, the context of the development of utilitarian doctrine, the British Isles in the eighteenth century, can be seen as a society whose intelligentsia were insisting on the necessity of abandoning religion as the arbiter of ethical and political dispute. Because it is aggregative it is not individualist in the sense that no person can reserve a 'right' as a kind of moral trump to put against the imperatives of society as a whole, though it is individualist in its insistence that societies consist of separate persons. Because it is sensualist, it does not envisage the soul as having separate wants from the body. Above all, because it is a specifically ethical and political doctrine it rejects any covertness of judgement. As Samuel Brittan insists, the chief virtue of utilitarian is its '*reductionism*', an insistence on trying to think through and to debate what policy or practice means for actual people. Thus large parts of a utilitarian argument must always be empirical, depending on the evidence of how institutions work in practice. Therefore the balance of utilitarian politics has moved between (moderate) socialism and capitalism over time.[23] In this respect it must be contrasted with most academic writing about society, including that about sport by historians and sociologists.

Much of that writing is 'critical' in so far as it seems to contain some covert values with which actual practice is contrasted. Because it is covert one even has a sense of all the 'enlightenment' values, however incompatible, being cited simultaneously, including liberty, equality, human rights and several senses of justice, but without explicit premises or prescriptive conclusions. With utilitarianism at least the prescriptive direction of the argument is clear, which is why it has a unique status as a 'government house philosophy', as Robert Goodin puts it.[24] Governments must consider consequences and aggregates; they cannot pretend to hold to a single, absolute principle, let alone several incompatible ones.

Thus, in a sense, a debate about amateurism must be a debate between two forms of utilitarianism. On the one hand, there is a tradition of calculation, from Jeremy Bentham's 'felicific calculus' to its modern forms as public cost-benefit analysis and calculations of economic growth and the standard of living. This is the orthodoxy of modern politics, in the form of the utilitarianism applied by economists and treasuries. But there is also a much more intuitive approach to utilitarianism, likely to be critical of this orthodoxy. This says that our capacity for error about happiness is dangerously large and that it is possible that the more precise we make our calculations the more wrong they are likely to be: economic growth is not happiness and may, in some circumstances, reduce it. The tradition of calculation tends to emphasize production and commerce, that of intuition to be sceptical of them. The context in which such a relatively refined debate about the nature of happiness can exist takes us back to autobiography: it is a problem which moves up the agenda when you live in peace and prosperity, as those of us born since the Second World War have to an unprecedented degree.

In earlier books I have contrasted the two kinds of approach to happiness in terms of the environment.[25] Calculation builds us motorways, which move us around more quickly and get us to the viewpoint earlier. But it may fail to take sufficient cognizance of the way in which the achievement of getting there is undermined and the view itself devalued by over-population and over-development. The sporting analogy is that commerce gives us better performers to watch more easily and more exotic pastimes within reach, but it may also undermine the real sense of achievement and affiliation which existed under a partly pre-commercial regime.

It is highly ironic that John Stuart Mill should be invoked as a philosophical authority in this respect. Educated by his father, James Mill, and by Jeremy Bentham, Mill is said to have mastered classical languages earlier than any other child on record. He lived his life in a deeply intellectual atmosphere which offered little or no space for fun and games. In vulgar sportsmen's parlance, he was a swot's swot. Born in 1806, he was from the last generation, along with Marx, Gladstone and Disraeli, which knew and cared nothing about sports and games. Married, eventually, to Harriet Taylor he shared her view of a more intellectual, less masculine future. In debating high and low pleasures he unquestioningly inherited the assumption that a game – pushpin – exemplified the lower pleasures. Yet I think we can easily put aside the irony: those organized games which were developing rapidly on the periphery of Mill's society were about nothing if not about the higher pleasures of skill, of comradeship, of strategy and of honour in victory and defeat. That is, they were as the amateur elite conceived them, though not as one might conceive them as a circus-like performance in a purely commercial world.

Amateurism as Ideology

I suggested in the opening chapter that any set of ideas at any one time and place can either be taken seriously on their merits or treated as ideology, explained in terms of their function in respect of social status and power. Of course, we can do both at once, but there is a tendency for the one approach to undermine the other. If we construct sociological explanations of belief such that we are inclined to say, 'They would believe that, wouldn't they?' there is a tendency to consider the ideas as less important in themselves. Correspondingly, if we think that a body of ideas is logically compelling or ethically coherent, the explanations of why they may have been believed in a particular context seem less important. In understanding Isaac Newton's theological preoccupations it may be important to understand the social setting of late seventeenth- and early eighteenth-century England, but this is generally less true of his theory of gravity. Protestant theology in general presents a good example of this distinction. On the whole, in the twentieth century it has been widely discussed as ideology, but studied as doctrine only in narrow segments of society; many more people can tell you the difference between Marxist and Weberian accounts of the causal relation of Protestantism to individualism and capitalism than can tell you what Luther and Calvin actually believed.

Amateurism is like Protestantism in this respect: it is generally treated by scholars as the ideological covering for something else. As the historian Richard Holt remarks, 'Amateurism…has been widely but not directly discussed; it is usually seen in terms of something else, a dimension of "hegemony", or "Darwinism", "imperialism", "the Civilizing Process" or even a part of a revival of "chivalry".'[1] In seeking to develop the academic study of the politics of sport I and others have casually referred to the 'amateur-elite ethos' as if amateurism needed no distinction from elitism.[2] Thus the paucity of books which are overtly about amateurism. In short, we can distinguish two traditions of the scholarly analysis of amateurism. Amateurism as ideology has been widely researched and the subject of vigorous, even bitter, controversy which is now largely resolved in favour of one side: the resulting consensus will be summarized later. Amateurism as ethical philosophy or political theory has been barely treated seriously and it is one of the central objects of this book to begin to develop a coherent defence of amateurism.

An Outline History of Amateurism

Modern sport developed in England in the second half of the nineteenth century. It was developed as an organized, disciplined set of activities in the public schools, generally from disorganized and disreputable origins in the schools and villages, though with some influence from the study of the ancient world. There were two conflicting tendencies in the society of the time, one which saw the commercial possibilities of urban markets and new transport systems for mass sport and the other which abhorred those possibilities. On the whole, the 'amateur-elite ethos' was able to establish a hegemony. In some sports such as rowing and athletics it was able to ban professionalism altogether: the Amateur Athletic Association (founded 1880) and the Amateur Rowing Association (1882) were able to take almost complete control over their sports. Even in sports with a mass market such as Association Football, where professionalism was legalized in 1885, and cricket, where it always existed, amateurs were able to limit wages and profits and retain administrative control of the sports. In Rugby the sport split, but the amateur version (Rugby Union) remained the dominant form both nationally and globally.

The period of the establishment of amateur hegemony in British sport can be defined as 1863–95, from the institution of the Football Association to the schism in Rugby and the establishment of the modern Olympics. There is a curiously neat symmetry between this period and that of the disestablishment of amateur hegemony which can be taken as lasting from the abolition of the maximum wage in Association Football in 1961 to the full acceptance of professionalism by the International Rugby Board in 1995. In the period 1961–63 cricket not only abolished the category of amateur (or 'gentleman') but also introduced its first limited-over competition, the Gillette Cup, and football abolished the category of amateur player. Other important dates in this period include the 'opening' of the Wimbledon tennis championships in 1968 and the accessions of the 'pragmatist' Lord Killanin to the Presidency of the International Olympic Committee in 1972 and the 'flexible' Juan Samaranch to the same office in 1980.[3]

It is important to note the geographical extent of amateur hegemony. The orthodoxy is that in many respects its writ never ran much beyond areas in which the English middle and upper classes, with their 'gentlemanly' aspirations, were dominant. This meant, for example, that it was important among some colonial elites, but its impact on the United States was extremely limited. In most of the USA, beyond a narrow, anglophile, East Coast elite there soon developed a system of scholarship-based college sport which defied every rule of English amateurism. Ronald Smith notes eight ways in which college athletics flouted the idea of amateurism in the nineteenth century.[4] Predictably and paradoxically, some of the most virulent and theologically-pure amateurs have been drawn from this American elite. They include Caspar Whitney, who, in the nineteenth century, called professional sportsmen 'vermin'[5] and Avery Brundage, President of the International Olympic Committee (IOC) from 1951 to 1972, who frequently called them 'performing monkeys'.

There were pockets of society – in Bombay, Brisbane and Buenos Aires, for example – for whom amateur status was a serious and important issue. But there were also large areas in which lip-service to the global norm of amateurism was not accompanied by local enforcement or even much interest in the issue. In Rugby Union we can put New Zealand, South Africa, Wales and France in this category, and in Olympic athletics during the Cold War period it was true that the athletes of both the communist countries and the United States were completely 'shamateur' by Victorian standards. Indeed, it is widely held that if it were not for the institutional hypocrisy of the Olympic movement the amateur regime would have collapsed much earlier.

It must be noted that the establishment of amateur hegemony was never just about the absence of material reward or even social exclusion. There was invariably an important element of control over the nature and definition of sports and games, in favour of 'fair', 'manly' and athletic competition and against brutality, practised tricks and vulgar spectacle. Thus in athletics, for example, many traditional events were abolished by the AAA, such as the 'ten hops and a jump' and throwing the cricket ball. The Highland Games remained as the chief of those institutions which managed to continue practising athletics outside the control of the AAA.

Some Curiosities of Definition and Translation

The English word 'amateur' is from the French; it is used also in Spanish and several other languages. It is from the basic Latin root meaning 'to love', so an etymological definition of an amateur might be of one who does things for love or as ends-in-themselves, and of 'amateurism' as a tendency to do things for love or a belief in doing things for love. In the British press, at least, in the period of amateur hegemony the word would carry favourable connotations so that a man who transferred from Rugby Union to Rugby League, for example, would be said to have 'sold' or 'lost' his amateur status as if it were something of great value. Paradoxically, the adjective 'amateurish' has long been acknowledged by the *Oxford English Dictionary* as having a pejorative connotation. Equally paradoxically, the Italian word for an amateur – dilettante – with its origins in the verb meaning 'to take delight', is also used in English to mean somebody who dallies or trifles with a subject, though here again the adjective seems more pejorative than the noun. To add to the list of paradoxes the English word 'sportsman' has been in more frequent use in French and Italian than have 'amateur' and 'dilettante', denoting a man who has the time and inclination to take an interest in horses and the pursuit of game, but possibly also in professional football and boxing.[6]

Attempts to define amateurism can be divided into three groups:

Social Definitions

For many people in the nineteenth century 'amateur' was co-extensive with 'gentleman'. How you applied the word in practice then depended on how much moral or social content you could give to the idea of gentlemen. For some, there was such a person as a 'nature's gentleman'. For others, this was not possible and social criteria could not be waived to allow you entry to the virtuous circle. The Amateur Rowing Association implemented the Playford Report of 1878 in its procedures. This stipulated that an amateur must never have taken money,

> ...nor ever taught, pursued, or assisted in the pursuit
> of athletic exercises of any kind as a means of livelihood,
> nor have ever been employed in or about boats, or in
> manual labour; nor be a mechanic, artisan or labourer.[7]

Such a definition bans the lower orders *per se*: it famously led to the exclusion of the Olympic sculling champion J.H.B. Kelly (the father of Princess Grace of Monaco) from the 1921 Diamond Sculls at Henley on the grounds that he had laid bricks for a living. The particular context was that gentlemen ('called from office stools' in the words of the *Eton Boating Song*) could not, and could not expect to, compete with the full-time professional watermen of the Thames (who were happy to compete for money). But as a definition it was a great deal more popular in the London area, with its large population of old boys of public schools, than in the North where it was less easy to run a rowing club without mechanics, artisans or labourers.

Ethical Definitions

From an ethical position, the point about an amateur is that he or she competes for the pleasure of it and not for gain; a strong version of this might be expressed loosely in Kantian terms, that the activity is an end-in-itself rather than a means to an end. There are further implications of the idea of amateurism which do not follow logically from this but which might be said to be associated culturally or socio-psychologically. Andrew Strenk says that the term amateur is an ethical word, suggesting that a certain moral conduct is expected (fair play, honesty and a genuine respect for one's opponent).[8]

Of course, one might do something purely for pleasure but nevertheless cheat or treat one's opponent with contempt. Equally, many professional sportsmen demonstrate these amateur virtues: in golf they seem almost *de rigueur*, while in boxing they are relatively (if not absolutely) absent. Paradoxically, the more highly paid a sportsman is the more he may be concerned with his moral image and the more likely he is to be financially secure, both conditions which will encourage the amateur virtues. But in the period in which amateurism was defined, few people were prepared to see these contradictions and complexities. 'Gentlemen' neither took money nor cheated; 'cads' did both. To take an example almost at random, one of the two serialized stories in the principal public school magazine at the turn of the last century, *The Captain*, was 'Acton's Feud'.[9] Unusually, the story concerns Association Football: Acton is a brilliant young defender who saves the game by perpetrating a foul tackle (precisely what would now be known as a 'professional foul') in the closing minutes when the score was 2–2 between his school and the visiting Shannon's XI. The captain of the team, Bourne, continues to select him, but refuses to 'cap' him (a system which survives, a century later, in English 'first-class' cricket). A feud develops in which the school sides, to a man and boy, with Acton, but Bourne will not concede. Acton takes his revenge by introducing Bourne's younger brother to a sporting *demi-monde* of illicit betting and shooting and Negro boxing coaches. Eventually the matter is resolved not by fisticuffs (which do take place) but by Bourne's saving the life of Acton's mother in a matter of runaway horses. At which point Acton admits his error and expresses acceptance of Bourne's values.

The picture of what matters in sport to be found in stories like this is complex: in this case even public schoolboys do not fully understand or accept the pure version of amateur virtues. The main factor seducing them away from those virtues is their competitive instinct, their desire for the house and the school to succeed. But that (as Thomas Arnold reluctantly accepted) is an essential mechanism of the internalization of the values of sport in the first place. Yet, for all this complexity, the association of the true amateur with moral gentility remains absolute.

D. Stanley Eitzen offers a broad statement of the core of an ethical definition of amateurism:

1. The amateur derives pleasure from the contest.
2. The activity is freely chosen.
3. The process is every bit as important as the outcome.

4. The motivation to participate comes from the intrinsic rewards from the activity rather than the extrinsic rewards of money and fame.
5. Because there is a love of sport for its own sake, there is a climate of sportspersonship surrounding amateur sport.[10]

The reference to 'sportspersonship' in the fifth condition is either circular or relies on the reader's intuitive understanding and acceptance of the associated virtues of sport. Apart from that, and doubts about the coherence of 'intrinsic' in the fourth one, I accept it as a moderate and comprehensive stipulation of the central ethics of amateurism. It would not do, however, for most of the organizations which have enforced an amateur code: by their standards, it would be possible to be semi-professional and meet these conditions.

Finally, one could not claim to have given full consideration to ethical definitions of amateurism unless one considers the attitude to winning. First, a myth must be scotched, that the apostles of amateurism ever believed that it did not matter who won. The sentiment that 'The important thing in the Olympic Games is not winning but taking part' has often been attributed to de Coubertin, but there appears to be no evidence that he said it and it seems to have been actually said by the Bishop of Pennsylvania in a sermon associated with the opening of the Olympic Games in 1908.[11] The greatest poetic expression of this sentiment is Grantland Rice's: 'For when the One Great Scorer comes to mark against your name / He writes – not that you won or lost – but how you played the game.'[12]

It does not, of course, imply that winning does not matter, only that ethics matter more. The same point could be made about profit. In Christian ethics Luke's version of Jesus makes it clear that it is difficult for a rich man to enter the Kingdom of God, but not impossible, but this is normally interpreted to mean that wealth is permissible provided that it is acquired honestly and not prized above virtue.[13] So it is with amateurs winning: it may matter more when you meet the Great Scorer that one has not cheated, but given that one has not it is jolly nice to win. And that other great poetic expression of public school sport, Sir Henry Newbolt's *Vitaï Lampada* effectively stresses the virtues of winning: it is because we learn to win through in difficult circumstances that we are able to win on the imperial battlefield.[14] The amateur ethic on winning seems broadly clear: winning is fine, provided that it is not achieved by cheating and provided that it is seen in the proper moral perspective. It is, of course, also problematic, not least because 'cheating' is invariably a complex concept not simply defined by the laws of a particular game.

Bureaucratic and Financial Definitions

A commonplace definition of an amateur at any activity might be 'someone who doesn't get paid'. This apparently simple approach is the legacy of a century of effort, most notably by the Olympic authorities and the Rugby Union, to define and enforce a lack of reward for sporting participation. Both of these bodies may be said to have become increasingly fanatical about the enforcement of amateurism in this sense, the Rugby Union at least until the late 1980s and the International Olympic Committee until the end of the term of office of Avery Brundage in 1972. In the case of the Rugby Union I know personally of an England rugby coach in the mid 1980s who gave massively of his time and energy without thought of reward only to find himself billed for half of his hotel bill on the weekend of international games because his wife had stayed with him.

Yet in other fields the question of payment has no moral significance. An amateur actor who is paid for appearing as an 'extra' in a film is pleased to do so: nobody feels that he or she has thereby lost significant status. Indeed, such a person would be regarded as extremely pretentious if they called him or herself 'professional' for that reason. The same would be true of a good 'amateur' musician who managed the occasional paid performance. Even in other sports the issue is of little significance: every biography of cricket's first great star, W.G. Grace, has stressed that not only did he make a great deal of money out of the game, he made more than most professionals.[15] Yet in a game which permitted professionalism and in which 'amateur' was primarily connected to social status, 'the Doctor' was allowed to remain an amateur, frequently representing the 'Gentlemen' versus the 'Players'. Apologists for the French Rugby Union have always said that French Rugby was not bound to slavish acceptance of narrow 'Anglo-Saxon' definitions of amateurism and that French players were essentially amateur because they represented their local communities and maintained jobs and businesses: the French were banned from playing the four nations of the British Isles from 1932 to 1945 because of allegations of payment at club level.

Those who have attempted to enforce the principle of 'no material gain' have found its interpretation extremely complex. The 'International Congress of Amateurs' which met in 1894 (and which played an important part in the reinvention of the Olympic Games) considered such questions as:

> Can a professional in one sport be an amateur in another?
> What should be the limit on the value of medals and prizes?
> Does betting on himself disqualify an amateur?[16]

All have remained potent issues throughout the history of amateurism. The answer to the first question has almost invariably been negative: it is particularly important because of the campaign waged by Brundage against Jim Thorpe who beat him in the pentathlon in the 1912 Stockholm Olympics. Thorpe was a native American who had played some professional baseball and Brundage was successful in having him disqualified. Thorpe's place in the record books and his medals were restored in 1983 after both he and Brundage were dead.

Questions which were not discussed at the 1894 meeting included:

> Can an amateur charge for an interview?
> Can he or she be paid to appear on a television discussion or panel game?
> Can one compete as an amateur after receiving royalties from an autobiography? Does income from after-dinner speaking invalidate amateur status?
> What about salesmen and public relations experts whose ability to do their job is enhanced by their sporting fame?

All of these questions were incessantly debated in the last years of amateur rugby and athletics. In both cases the authorities tried to establish hard and clear boundaries but only succeeded in undermining their own authority by doing so.

These fundamental questions persistently rendered the implementation of amateurism difficult and tended to undermine its ethical credibility. But there were even more important factors involved in its delegitimation which were rarely discussed by committees and which forced even fanatical amateurs such as Brundage into acquiescence with shamateurism. Arguably, it will always be the case in a society which values sporting success that some sort of material gain will be available to sportsmen. Even in the heart of the homeland of the amateur ethos public school sportsmen became prefects and received preferential accommodation and other privileges as a reward for sporting prowess while oarsmen at Oxford were put on the 'rowing table' and given better food at no extra charge. But communist governments and American universities turned this sort of privilege into massive ramps, the former offering lifetime sinecures and superior accommodation to successful sportsmen while the latter offered a privileged and expensive education plus the wherewithal for subsistence. These forms of institutionalized shamateurism were simply too big to tackle, and even under the Brundage régime many an Olympic final consisted entirely of full-time athletes from the United States or the communist countries.

The one single fact which explains the demise of the 'no gain' principle is that it was never established in a clear and agreed form. Different sports formulated it in different ways and diverse cultures interpreted it diversely. Not only did this variety undermine the principle, it created an easy mechanism for its destruction. When Juan Samaranch became President of the IOC he was able to destroy Olympic amateurism by devolving responsibility for it to different sports and national Olympic committees.

Amateurism, Class and Culture

There is now a considerable consensus of historians, sociologists (and, in the case of the 'figurationalists', historical sociologists) about the working of the amateur ideology. What I aim to do here is not to challenge that consensus but to put it in my own terms, as a prolegomenon to developing an ethical theory of amateurism.

Seen as a class struggle, the imposition of amateurism was not primarily a contest between the working class and the middle and upper classes. Rather, it was a contest between two middle classes.[17] The struggle which led in 1895 to a full-blown schism in rugby can be typified as follows: in the south clubs were dominated by public-school-educated men mainly connected with the professions (the Church, the armed forces, the civil service, the City and the universities) while in the north the boom in rugby was in the hands of local elites educated locally at grammar schools and more often involved in manufacturing industry. It was *about* the working class (because it centred on 'broken time' payments for players training, playing and travelling as compensation for lost wages) but it did not directly involve the working class. The northerners faced problems not faced by the southerners. They lacked the positive belief in the virtues of amateurism. Moreover, they believed either more firmly or more overtly in competition, specifically in competition for prestige on the sports field between provincial towns. In these respects the struggle in rugby was the dramatic and explicit version of other struggles which were won more easily by the southern elite such as the protests of the Bolton and Ringley Rowing Club against the strictures of the ARA and the objections of northern and Scottish interests to the control of the AAA.[18]

An exactly parallel contest can be observed in the United States. In this case the commercial, provincial objection to the national elites came not from clubs but from colleges; for Huddersfield read Notre Dame. The USA between 1865 and 1900 was expanding and changing as no society on earth had ever expanded and changed and the context was favourable to a pure and overt commercialism. When Caspar Whitney claimed in 1894 that professional sport was dead in America and amateurism triumphant it was just dotty bravado: the reverse was the case.[19]

This historical struggle between amateurism and commercialism cannot be understood merely as a contingency of Anglophone societies in the nineteenth century; arguably it has its roots deep in European civilization. Alexis de Tocqueville remarked in the 1850s that the word *gentilhomme* in France, which had never been a precise translation for the English 'gentleman', was defunct, whereas in the English language to be a gentleman remained the aspiration of Englishmen and to be considered a gentleman was the right of free, white, respectable American males.[20] This observation was the linguistic tip of a cultural iceberg: in England the aristocracy have drawn in the commercial classes to their values and aspirations. In France the aristocracy of the *ancien régime* was notable only for its privileges: 'noblesse oblige' was a French phrase, but an English phenomenon. Thus the hatred, in France, of a class who were just like anybody else except that they did not have to pay taxes or pay tolls and who were allowed to hunt, fish and keep doves where nobody else was. He might have added that if you added up all forms of *noblesse* in France, including the *de la robe* variety, it came to something like 15 per cent of the population, whereas in the British aristocracy it was less than 1 per cent; thus the French Revolution and, in contrast, the survival of the British aristocracy.

For de Tocqueville the conventional French explanation of the difference between England and France in these respects – that the aristocracy in England were more worldly in economic and political terms and more open to outsiders – was a combination of falsehood and half-truth. They were actually less open to permeation from below than their French equivalents and, though they may have been in some respects a more modernizing force and more in tune with their times, their real triumph was in persuading the class below them to aspire to their values. The continuity of this aspiration has been stressed in more recent times by Martin Wiener's *English Culture and the Decline of the Industrial Spirit* which contrasts the record of the English industrial bourgeoisie in defecting to land and the professions with that of their American and continental equivalents who remained more faithful to their companies.[21] Wiener, as an American neo-liberal conservative, instinctively saw this as a British problem (though not to the degree that many of his interpreters and publicizers did) whereas to a politically dispossessed French aristocrat it was an admirable aspect of English culture.

The most effective mechanism for the transmission of aristocratic values to the bourgeoisie was, by all accounts, the public schools. In the eyes of such French conservatives as Hippolyte Taine, the Arnoldian model of the English public school, with its emphasis on physical development and morality as opposed to the purely intellectual activity of the French *lycée*, was much more capable of developing fully rounded human beings capable of leadership and of exercising freedom without abuse.[22] It was also capable of integrating classes, as petty snobberies were eradicated by a hierarchy of courage and achievement. (In *Acton's Feud* Acton's background is described as, 'Yorkshire people, I believe. Own half a town and no end of coin.' But his contemporaries are torn between the suspicion that he is a cad and the observation that 'he is a back out of a thousand').[23]

Pierre de Coubertin read Taine; he also read Tom Hughes's *Tom Brown's Schooldays* and regarded it as one of his favourite books. His own reports of visiting England and seeing *le régime arnoldien* for himself are positively ecstatic.[24] In a sense, the long tradition of French anglophilia – from Montesquieu to Voltaire and on to de Tocqueville, Taine and de Coubertin – has at its common theme the English ability to square circles, or at least to act as if they had been squared. Here, after all, was the most modern and commercial of societies, yet its elite (combining the aristocracy, the professions and parts of the bourgeoisie) continued to steep itself in the chivalrous values of the gentleman and the sportsman. The English public school provided an astonishing ray of hope in a world which seemed doomed to some combination of vulgar commercialism, mass democracy and avaricious socialism.

Forms of conservatism which are (almost) as opposed to unmitigated commercialism and the extremes of democracy as they are to socialism have been an important but under-publicized aspect of human thought in the age of World Wars and Cold War. In this general category fall a diversity of thinkers, some who are primarily religious (such as Alexander Solzhenitsyn and Pope John-Paul II) and many of whom would now be considered 'green' because of their emphasis on man's alienation from nature (ranging from J.R.R. Tolkien and Knut Hamsun to Jonathan Porritt).[25] The legacy of moral and theoretical reservation about commercialism – with different degrees of aristocratic flavour – is a long one. It is likely to become more prominent as the challenge of socialism fades into history. This is the context in which we must place the amateur objection to commercial forces in sport.

The Myth of Ancient Amateurism

Consider three propositions about the ancient Olympic Games:

> The games were strictly and purely amateur.
> The games were fully professional.
> It makes no sense to say that the games were amateur or professional because the concepts did not exist.

There is now a consensus which combines the last two propositions. However, from the constitution of the modern games in the 1890s until the 1980s there was an official orthodoxy which required the acceptance of the first. The new version is most emphatically expressed in the research of David C. Young who stresses that the Greeks had no notion of amateurism and received prizes, especially in the form of olive oil, which were extremely valuable.[26] The prize for winning the sprint over the standard stadium distance of 192 m is variously calculated at different times as worth $120,000, $67,000, ten years' wages for a free labourer and a substantial house. There is something spurious about the cash figures: even over half a century the bundle of goods available for consumption changes in such a way that it tends to be meaningless to compare costs and standards of living, so there is something slightly comical about extrapolating a figure back over two to three millennia. On the other hand, as Young is keen to point out, a house is a house and ten years' labour is ten years' labour in any human society.

A more moderate version of the same thesis is to be found in articles by the Dutch scholar H.W. Pleket published in the 1970s.[27] Neither Young nor Pleket allow any territory to the thesis of ancient amateurism: prizes were not a later corruption, but existed in all periods and they were always substantial. This was in complete contrast to the previous orthodoxy. Avery Brundage always asserted that, 'The ancient Olympic Games ... were strictly amateur ...'[28] His belief in the amateur principle became more rigorous, if anything, as his tenure of the office of President of the IOC continued. He came to be loathed wherever snow fell because naturally his position led him into conflict with the whole ethos of the Winter Olympics; in skiing, at least, virtually every serious competitor has, has had or will have connections with the skiing-equipment industry or the winter sports tourism industry and Brundage was against even indirect material gain from sporting status.

There was an apparent historical justification for the Brundage position based on British scholarship, especially the writings of the Anglo-Irishman John Mahaffy (who had actually attended the little known and all-Greek Athenian Olympic Games of 1875) and those of E.N. Gardiner.[29] In retrospect these writings seem massively and openly biased and full of 'outrageous error', as Young puts it,[30] ignoring most of the evidence in favour of an emphasis on laurel leaves, the odd remark by characters in the plays of Aristophanes and the anachronistic assertion that Greek athletes were aristocrats. That all this was nonsense is now officially admitted. John Lucas's account of the ancient games can be given an official status since it comes with a foreword by Juan Samaranch. It relativizes the two accounts of history, saying that:

> Historical exactitude is probably not achievable. Just how the ancient Greeks, for example, thought and then believed is difficult to determine. Historians of the late 18th and 19th centuries in Europe and North America, influenced by their Romantic Age, read the available literature on ancient Greece and made interpretations. So have late 20th-century experts on Hellenic culture and on the ancient Olympic Games, the other great Greek athletic festivals, and Hellenic physical training and competitions. But some of these later scholars, reading essentially the same body of factual data, come to different conclusions, finding earlier scholars' viewpoints unacceptable, unrealistic and almost Pollyannaish. Both groups sought truth, but both

visions are colored by the times and by the 'ether' that all must breathe.[31]

He is keen to accept and emphasize Young's devaluation of the issue, commenting that

> the restrictive concept of 'pure athletic amateurism' is infinitely less important than the possibility that Olympic athletes might not only break world records, they might contribute collectively to the uplifting of humanity and move us a little bit more in the direction of mutual trust, understanding and peace.[32]

This statement may be seen as part acknowledgement of a scholarly victory, part devaluation of the significance of that victory, but also an act of political revisionism connected with Samaranch's 'modernization' of the Olympics.

Two questions remain about the myth of ancient amateurism: how was such a poor piece of history allowed to stand as official doctrine for three-quarters of a century and why did it matter so much that the ancients were amateurs? The first is much easier to answer than the second. There were relatively few classical scholars and only a small minority of those were interested in the games. The field attracted men who were of a 'Corinthian' persuasion and their conclusions were readily welcomed among the wider audience who believed in the amateur ethos. They took to extremes the natural tendency to foist one's own issues on to a different historical period. For a long time no suitably qualified scholar was prepared to take them on.

The question of why it mattered is much more complex. De Coubertin was not a Hellenist, either by background or enthusiasm. Given his real enthusiasms – his commitment to physical education, to the revival of France and to learning the lessons of English success – it might have been more logical to found the Arnoldian Games. But he would have known immediately that this would not work. The virtues of one class in one country could not be transformed into a Great Universal Church of sport as a classical lineage could. The ancient Olympics were profoundly religious: one contemporary scholar has said that holding the games was 'not a commitment to athletics in a religious setting. It was a commitment to religion which had athletics as one of its most important modes of expression.'[33] This paganism could not be imported in its entirety given the Christianity of nearly all those with which he was dealing, though a hymn to Apollo was sung at early Olympic meetings. However, its universal values and nobility could be imported. These would have a much diminished appeal if they were seen as pagan and professional, given that the pre-Arnoldian professional sports in England – horse-racing, pugilism and even cricket – were regarded as irredeemably corrupt. It is often stressed by biographers that de Coubertin was not a particularly clear or original thinker; his genius lay in image-making and publicity. In these terms the appeal to an ancient, arguably universal, lineage has proved immensely successful, even if it was based on an historical myth which falls into the category of a Big Lie. Young points out that in some ancient games it was possible to win a slave girl as a prize, not something of which Dr Arnold would have approved …

Marxism and Amateurism

Consider Marx's differentiation of the nature of labour in capitalist societies from that in a future communist society:

> … the division of labour offers us the first example of how, as long as man remains in natural society – that is, as long as a cleavage exists between the particular and the common interest – as long, therefore, as activity is not voluntarily but naturally divided, man's own deed becomes an alien power opposed to him, which ensnares him instead of being controlled by him. For as soon as labour is distributed, each man has a particular, exclusive sphere of activity which is forced upon him and from which he cannot escape. He is a hunter, a fisherman, a shepherd, or a critical critic and must remain so if he does not want to lose his means of livelihood; while in communist society, where nobody has one exclusive sphere of activity but each can become accomplished in any branch he wishes, society regulates the general production and thus makes it possible for me to do one thing today and another tomorrow, to hunt in the morning, fish in the afternoon, rear cattle in the evening, criticize after dinner, just as I have a mind, without ever becoming hunter, fisherman, shepherd or critic.[34]

Future communism, in other words, will be a society of gentleman amateurs. Marx's complex analysis shares a common moral ground with E.N. Gardiner's simple observation that Scottish professional footballers playing for English clubs were mere 'mercenaries' or Brundage's view that if you did nothing but ski and that you did it for money you were dehumanized, a 'performing monkey'. This common moral ground serves as a starting point for what seems, superficially at least, to be an odd series of alliances between 'right' and 'left'. De Coubertin was classified as a 'progressive individual' by Soviet propaganda despite being also an 'incorrect thinker'. Brundage welcomed the Soviet Union into the Olympics and was an ally of Soviet interests on many occasions; the politician he himself most admired was Herbert Hoover. Samaranch, the former Francoist, proved a doughty ally of the Chinese communist government.[35]

There are at least two dimensions to the understanding of these strange bedfellows. In some respects the relationship between communism and amateurism was simply a political alliance based on mutual interest. When the Soviet Union, following the Second World War, abandoned both its original hostility to 'bourgeois' sport and its attempts to set up its own games and sporting institutions, the strategic calculation was that it would be good for the prestige of its system in the rest of the world and, perhaps even more importantly, in the semi-internal context of 14 non-Russian Soviet republics and six satellites. Apologists have argued that American policy in the Cold War left only sport (and, later, space) in which the USSR could express itself competitively.[36] The Olympics were the obvious target for this volte-face since those who made the decisions were well aware that it was going to be easier to top the Olympic medals table than (say) to win major international football competitions or produce a world heavyweight boxing champion. In any case, the universalism and anti-commercialism of the Olympics simply looked more respectable for a communist than simulating commercialized Western sport (and bearing all the consequences of Soviet stars competing with highly paid, Western professionals). The Olympic movement, for its part, gained a massive segment of the globe (about a third if you include eventual Chinese participation) and a corresponding enhancement of its claims to universalism as well as a further bulwark in the defence of amateurism.

Soviet policy was quite capable of alliances based on nothing but self-interest – witness the Molotov–Ribbentrop pact – so perhaps we need look no further for an explanation of their part of the alliance. For the otherwise conservative Western Olympians, however, there was clearly an ethical dimension. The Cold War was precisely the kind of circumstance which was in need of something which would 'move us a little bit more in the direction of mutual trust, understanding and peace'.[37] Nobody in the Olympic movement ever seems to have shared George Orwell's view that international sport would invariably lead to enmity and misunderstanding;[38] its opposite was an item of complete faith. This faith in the Olympics as a mechanism for peace was underpinned by a more general faith in the spiritual value of sport to enrich an otherwise materialistic life. But again, it is difficult to find much attempt in the Soviet Union and its satellites to develop an image of the communist sportsman as a fully rounded human being. Athletes were treated as mere mechanisms for the prestige of the state, conditioned, trained and drugged where necessary to that end.[39] Only in Cuba does there seem to have been any serious attempt to create a distinctively communist athlete, with sportsmen and women offered a thorough ideological education to accompany their training and taught to see themselves as unalienated and more free compared with their Western professional rivals.[40]

The philosophical relationship between Marxism and amateurism is genuine and complex. The strategic form of 'shamateurism' devised by the Soviet Union was simple and hypocritical. That there was *some* relationship between the two is obvious, not least that Marxism provided a legitimation of Soviet practice. But the precise nature of the relationship is difficult to resolve. Undoubtedly, though, communist support of amateurism strengthened it greatly. Communism and amateurism both experienced an accelerated decline in the 1980s. The reasons for the decline were predominantly independent of one another, but the demise of both together served to leave world sport fully open to commercial forces for the first time.[41]

3

Amateurism and the Forces of History

Western intellectual life in the late twentieth century seemed to be obsessed with ideas about epochs, periods and processes of history. Such ideas had played a much smaller part in the self-images of previous ages: the modest notions of an 'era of progress' or an 'era of reform' have little weight when compared with the supposed portentousness of ideas about 'modernity', 'post-modernity' and 'globalization'. Quite apart from the instinctive scepticism which terms of such breadth and ambiguity ought to stimulate there was also an immediate paradox between the prevailing discourse in some fields, which was still of 'modernization', the movement to modernity, and others in which the orthodox thought was that we were moving away from or beyond modernity. For example, in debates about sport and the British constitution (especially after the election of 'New Labour' to power in 1997) the assumption was of reform in the direction of modernity. We were moving away from the hereditary principle and the amateur legacy and towards democracy and the more efficient operation of the market principle. However, in many other fields, often discussed by more exclusive circles, the assumption was of a move away from modernity: these included architecture and planning, but also cultural theory, literary criticism (in so far as it ever had been 'modern' in any acceptable sense) and the social sciences, especially in their aspiration and relation to the idea of 'science'. It is, perhaps, tiresome of an author to remark on the overuse of these ideas and still insist of putting his own versions on the table, but I do think they can offer real insight into modern sport and can suggest interesting cross-fertilizations between a debate about sport and other contemporary debates. So, with apologies, some observations about modernity *et al.*

'Modern' society, I take it, is close to Adam Smith's conception of the 'commercial' as the final stage of social development. In a commercial society people are more free to produce and exchange than they have been in previous periods. More of their thought is 'rational' in the sense of being concerned with choices that produce beneficial consequences. There are fewer rules and taboos constraining the pursuit of rational self-interest. A modern society therefore exhibits progress largely through technological innovation; science and technology do not merely progress, but take over the spiritual and intellectual territory of other institutions, such as religion and nationality. The typical form of government in 'modern' conditions is democracy, since the belief structure offers no other source of legitimation: policy is made by expert bureaucrats, broadly directed by the people's will.

This vision of modernity, for most of its two centuries and more of life, has been under two shadows, one overestimated and one underestimated. The overestimated shadow was that of social class and, specifically, of a lower class which would destroy the property base of a successful commerce either by revolution or by electing a government which would pursue confiscatory policies in the name of equality. The vision was shared by Marx and Engels, who relished it, but was also the principal political concern of such writers as Lord Salisbury and Sir William Lecky.[1] It remained at the heart of British concerns about 'ungovernability' and 'the British disease' until the 1980s.[2] With the removal of socialism, in any serious sense, from the agenda almost everywhere by the end of the decade, that shadow lifted and, lacking its chief opponent, Adam Smith's version of history was again the front runner, most spectacularly popularized by Francis Fukuyama.[3] The major complication, which had been previously underestimated, was the persistence of ethnic and national identities and, therefore, quarrels.

The relationship between the modern and the post-modern is most easily defined and clarified in the field of architecture. In that context writers such as Le Corbusier were self-explicitly 'modernist': the creed involved a reduction of building to function and therefore the elimination of decoration, a universal geometry to supersede local vernaculars and the use of the materials which modern technology provided, principally glass, steel and concrete.[4] The modernist project was, in its way, totalitarian. At the very least it was preoccupied with totality, with reconstructing cities completely and as a whole and even in creating a world in which the only architecture would be modern. The post-modern in this context consists simply of the rejection of modernism or, at least, of the modernist project. Thus urban conservation and 'community architecture' can be placed under the heading of post-modernism, so can the 'hyper-modernisms' and 'second modernisms' which have to different degrees replaced or post-dated the modernist project.

In other fields the relationship between modernism and post-modernism is both parallel to this relative clarity, but also more laced with anomaly and ambiguity. At its broadest it has been described as 'a vast unmaking in the Western mind'.[5] As in architecture, it is most easily seen as rejection, partial or total, of totalities and universalities, of the human potential of science and technology and of the relevance to the human condition of logic and rationality. More subtly, it is a concern or re-emphasis on fractures and particulars rather than universals.

The concept of sport seems to fit that of modernity very well in many respects. We can quite clearly and relatively uncontroversially identify pre-modern sport.[6] It was predominantly rural, associated in its calendar with agricultural cycles and religious holidays and highly localized in style. It consisted of bull-running, cheese rolling, pancake racing and a hundred forms of football, among other activities. It lacked agreed rules, limits on participation, precise extents in time or space or any kind of institutional structure, and any authority other than tradition. As industrialization and urbanization proceeded in the first half of the nineteenth century it was in sharp decline. (That, at least, has been the orthodoxy for some time, though the extent of the decline has now been seriously challenged.)[7]

In that context, the evolution of organized games (as they were still called on the syllabus in my youth) in the public schools looks like a quite specific, even self-conscious, process of modernization. Games and sports were given precise limits in time and space, and formal rules and codes of discipline at least akin to the discipline required in industry and the professions. As they spread from the public schools to the universities, the professions, local communities and the Empire, they also acquired national and even international associations and became part of society and the economy. The game of Association Football on the field required no technology which was not available to the Romans. But the role it began to assume with the creation of the FA Cup in 1872 and, more particularly, the Football League in 1888, required new technology: the steam railway to transport players and spectators, the telegraph to transmit news, the hot-lead printing press to broadcast and record results. It all seems, rather neatly in Weberian terms, to be a transition from a 'traditional' set of practices to something that was either part of, or at least analogous to, a 'rational-legal' set of practices. The periods in which this transition took place can be defined fairly precisely: a first transitional phase from around 1830 to 1863 as organized games evolved in the public schools and spread to other institutions in society and a second one from 1863 to 1895 as those games became organized at national level, institutionalized in civil society and spread abroad. The 1830 date is approximate and relates primarily to the appointment of a new generation of educationalists. The year 1863 was the date of the foundation of the Football Association and much of the rest of the development of sport was in imitation of and reaction to this event. By 1895, with the organization of the Olympic Games and the schism in Rugby, most of the institutions of 'modern' sport were in place. Up to a point, the whole process seems to fit into the framework of either a functionalist or Marxist explanation of social change: the evolution of modern sport between 1863 and 1895 was the creation of a pattern of recreation and entertainment which fitted and served the purposes of an urban and industrial society.

But to explain them in this way and leave it at that would be to miss the whole point about modern sport. From one angle the period of modernization looks like a neat piece of functionalism, the creation of a set of well-defined and disciplined practices which complement the working of an industrious and ordered commercial society. From another angle it looks as if the meaning and style of modern sport were established in a way which was resolutely pre-modern and even anti-modern. Sport was established in the image of amateurism; it was about being a gentleman. The aspiration cries out from the rules and statements of policy, from the creed of the new genre of boys' stories about sport, from the sermons of the great educationalists and muscular Christians. Sport taught the virtues of war and chivalry, not those of commerce: Henry Newbolt's *Vitaï Lampada* is about how cricket prepares you for the blood-soaked square, not the commodities market.[8] 'School' stories were about how virtue could be achieved despite connections with trade, not about how those connections were virtuous in themselves. De Coubertin saw in the English public schools, not a set of disciplined recreations suitable for a commercial society, but a revival and modernization of ancient traditions. 'Sportsmanship' harked back to chivalry; it looked back, too, to a pseudo-classical tradition, the 'all-rounder' Greeks rather than the gladiatorial Romans, which was largely mythical. In short, sport was at least as much a reaction to the commercial and modern, and a refuge from them, as it was a part of them.

The presence of pre-modern and anti-modern values in modern sport puts a tension at the heart of its very nature. They are so much part of the concepts of sport, sportsmanship and sporting life that we can barely conceive it otherwise. Indeed, where we come across competition and games which lack these values, in the extreme gladiatorialism of ancient Rome or, sometimes, modern America, we would be inclined to include the values in the use of the concept and say, 'That's not sport.'

It is important to reiterate the qualification, perhaps to the point of tedium, that the 'we' used in this context is a difficult one. Modern sport is specifically an English creation, but its values spread to the Empire, informal as well as formal, Argentina as well as New Zealand. Through the Olympic movement they claimed sovereignty over the world of sport, but this was of little importance beyond the Empire, western Europe and the United States until 1945. Yet the United States remains a major exception; despite its games being predominantly of English origin, despite also its upper classes continuing to be Anglophile and English-influenced and despite its supremely successful participation in the Olympic Games, the USA was the one place which developed forms of predominantly commercial sport emancipated from English amateur values and (therefore) with institutional forms appropriate to a commercial activity.

The description of modern sport as being in part a refuge from and reaction to normal modernity suggests an important analogy. This is also the way in which we have treated the countryside and rural life. Just as John Ruskin, William Morris and Octavia Hill in a sense pleaded with society to preserve our rural heritage from commercial forces, so Thomas Arnold,

Pierre de Coubertin and Lord Kinnaird in different ways tried to preserve sport from those forces. In important respects both legacies have lasted into the twenty-first century and produced similar structures and tension. Most of the English countryside consists of privately-owned farms and estates which are subject to commercial considerations in the same fundamental ways as an industrial enterprise. Most of English sport consists of private clubs which are equally part of a commercial nexus. Yet in both cases we also consider the private property to be a form of public property and we express this consideration by designating, 'listing', aspects which are to be protected from commercial forces. In the countryside it is 'National Parks' and 'Areas of Outstanding Natural Beauty', a total of around a quarter of the surface of England and Wales, which are largely protected from development. In sport in Britain (and in Europe) there is a concept of the 'listed events', the 'crown jewels' which are to be enjoyed by the community and shown on free-to-air television. In my opinion, the concept is both more workable and more fully accepted in the case of the countryside than in the case of sport.

The argument that uncommercial, even anti-commercial virtues are part of the very concept of sport has serious commercial implications. Consider the case of track and field athletics. In the period of amateur hegemony there was no need to 'sell' athletics. It did not have the kind of regular following, the 'fandom' possessed by football or cricket. But it was able to appear on ceremonial occasions, so to speak, and be accepted as the oldest, simplest and noblest of sports. These occasions included the Olympic and the Commonwealth Games and the European Championships. Although the population as a whole spent only a tiny fraction of the time watching athletics than it did watching football or cricket, athletes were more successful icons. For example, they were more successful in winning the BBC Sports Personality of the Year award than footballers and cricketers combined. We can call this the 'Roger Bannister Syndrome': at its core is the image of the gentleman athlete, as amateur and as honest as the day is long, an educated man with an income from another profession, exhausting himself to run faster than anybody had run before, as Bannister did to become the first runner to complete the mile in under 4 minutes at Oxford in 1953. You did not have to 'sell' that any more than you had to sell religion.

But consider the fate of professional athletics. In the ten years which culminated in the bankruptcy of the British Athletics Federation in 1997 the total amount of money coming into the sport fell by over 70 per cent. Its image was tainted by drugs, corruption and money and by popular beliefs about the intrinsic superiority of black athletes. When I was asked by the athletics authorities of the United Kingdom, Germany and Sweden to comment on the future of the sport in 1998 it was all too easy to construct a 'nightmare scenario' in which it would never be possible to 'sell' deliberately, as a product, something which had previously sold well precisely because it was an 'other' to everyday pecuniary and commercial reality and thus did not have to be consciously sold at all. To make matters worse, it was not possible to redesign the sport as a commercial entity: it was effectively 'stuck' with the curious selection of events which had existed ever since the foundation of the Amateur Athletic Association in 1880. A forward-looking, commercial athletics would emphasize middle-distance running, the marathon and perhaps the decathlon. Throwing events excite little public interest, are the most subject to drug-induced improvement and are the most difficult to stage for an audience. Marketing reality was constrained by cultural history and sociology to a much greater degree than had been expected: the public were not so happy to watch and support a professional gladiator as they had been an amateur hero.[9] On the other hand, athletics administrators remained constrained by an uncommercial loyalty to the contingencies of their sport as they had become established: shot-putters and hammer-throwers were part of the 'constituency' and not to be discarded.

Three Periods in the History of Amateurism

In retrospect there were three periods in the history of amateurism which can be distinguished with unusual precision:

- the establishment of amateur hegemony, 1863–95
- the maintenance of amateur hegemony, 1895–1961
- the decline of amateurism, 1961–95.

The period of establishment starts with the formation of the Football Association in 1863. I have already suggested that what followed was either imitation of or reaction to this event: developments in rugby, such as the foundation of the Blackheath club in 1863 and the formation of the Rugby Union in 1871 were both. We can also identify the period with a second phase in the formation of modern sport and which followed a transitional phase in which the idea of organized games had spread throughout the middle classes without the concomitant development of 'modern' rational and quasi-legal institutions. But by 1895 the overwhelming majority of modern sporting institutions were in place in England: the 'league' and the 'cup' in football, the 'test' matches and the county championship in cricket, the international matches in Rugby, the Wimbledon Tennis and the Open Golf championship, and national associations to run athletics, rowing, swimming and boxing. The date 1895 is significant because it was the year of the split between the amateur 'Union' and what became the professional 'League' over 'broken time' payments in rugby, and also the year in which the arrangements for the first modern Olympics were put in place.

In different ways and to different extents all of these institutions were subject to an amateur hegemony. Precisely what is meant by 'hegemony' will be discussed in the next chapter, but in some important ways all of these sporting institutions were constrained by the assumption that the ideal of sport was that it should be something noble, unpaid and gentlemanly. Golf and cricket allowed professionals, but in subsidiary roles; the racket games allowed them as sparring partners and coaches but did not allow them to compete in major events; rugby split with them; athletics and rowing banished them to a tiny periphery. Even in football, where the commercial power of the game had become irresistible, a maximum wage and a limitation on dividends were put in place and a set of interests and institutions established such that football in England put up a stern resistance to the exploitation of its commercial potential in the 1950s and even in the 1960s. It is important to clarify the two aspects of this hegemony. First, in class terms, it is quite misleading to call it 'upper class' or 'middle class' or 'bourgeois' in origin. The important gulf of ideas was not between classes in this sense, but between two wholly different conceptions of the good life entertained by two different strands of the middle class. Elizabeth Gaskell's Mr Thornton or Charles Dickens's Mr Gradgrind would have had no conception of the aspirations of the amateur.[10] The 'practical man' looked upon the 'gentleman' as privileged, effete and outmoded. Such practical men tended to be found in manufacturing and trade; they were self-educated or educated in the grammar schools and more common and influential in the North than the South. Gentlemen were more common in finance and the professions; they were educated in the public schools and 'Southern' in style if not in geography. The clash of the two cultures was at its most simple and intense in the schism in rugby football. But in a sense that is an exception which seems to throw light upon the broader truth that, in so far as we can distinguish the culture of 'gentlemen' from that of 'practical men' in Victorian England, the whole idea of sport was central to the idea of the gentlemen, whereas to practical men it was in different degrees trivial, wasteful and immoral. The desires to foster civic pride and to unite the classes were sometimes part of a business world view and they helped to foster the formation of the Rugby League (and, in some part, the Football League) but they were not shared by a majority of the business class.

It is also important to note that the thrust of the amateur hegemony was much more fully directed against commercialism than against professionalism. Admittedly in athletics, rowing and Rugby Union there did exist, from time too time, a tendency to purge the sport of anyone who had ever received payment for playing, and in rowing this extended to the exclusion of anyone who had ever been paid for manual labour. But in most sport in Britain and the Empire amateurs to some degree competed with professionals and amateur institutions were symbiotic with professional practices. The supposed odium attaching to the professional coach in athletics had no resonance in golf or racket games; amateurs competed in small numbers with professionals in football and in large numbers in cricket. It was perfectly normal for amateurs to compete with professionals and reserve their own competitions: Corinthian Casuals FC played against professional teams for many years and the practice of Oxford and Cambridge University teams of playing against professional clubs and receiving coaching advice from them lasted throughout the twentieth century. In mainstream British sport, professional as well as amateur, resistance to the full logic of commercialism was much stronger than to the practice of paying professionals.

The working of the system of amateur hegemony and the reasons for its decline and collapse will be examined in the next chapter. The single greatest cause of collapse was a technological development, television, and each stage of its development – colour, satellite, cable, digital – enhanced the commercial potential of major sport. But the development of television was accompanied by a growing acceptance and extension of the commercial principle as socialism collapsed. (For the purposes of my argument I assume that any serious elite support for further, or even existing, restrictions upon the working of the commercial principle collapsed in Britain in 1976–79 and that the collapse of communist regimes in 1989–91 marks the end of a coherent anti-commercialism on a global scale.) To a degree the hyper-commercialism which followed the demise of amateurism (and of socialism) naturally had an American flavour. During most of the period of amateur hegemony in America sport had been the archetypal example of American exceptionalism, reported on by the minority of citizens of Europe and the British Empire who ever saw it as a strange world of vast excess and 'razzmatazz' (a word which emanates from American popular music in the inter-war period but came to be extended to all the frippery and self-promotion that was part of American politics and American sport).

In short, American sport, chiefly in the forms of professional baseball and college football, went its own way for three-quarters of a century without having much of an influence on the world outside. The potential for influence really began with satellite television and was transmitted into those countries which played rugby (either code) and cricket through Australia. The structure of media control in Australia was much more easily reoriented to see the commercial potential of televised sport, the culture was much more receptive to American ideas and the amateur establishment was determined to defend the status quo. It was American sport which first accepted that television could be the principal source of income, which first suggested the possibility of the massively rich professional sportsman and which first began to 'sell' individual sports competitively and aggressively. That the formally Bradford Northern Rugby League Club is now the

'Bradford Bulls' and that the Lancashire and the Surrey Cricket Clubs have to call themselves, for some purposes, the 'Lightning' and the 'Lions' can therefore be traced partially to the fall of Singapore in 1942 and the consequent reorientation of Australia towards a new 'great and powerful friend'.

It would be hard to exaggerate the changes in career-pattern which hyper-commercialism or hyper-modernization have wrought in sporting careers. I have written elsewhere about John Connelly, one of the most successful of post-war English footballers who won champions' medals with both Burnley and Manchester United, played successfully in European competitions with both of those clubs and was in the England squad which won the World Cup in 1966. Connelly was lucky in the sense that the maximum wage (then £20 per week) for footballers was abolished when he was 21 years old in 1961. Yet it was the extent of his ambition, when he retired in 1973, to own and run his own fish and chip shop ('Connelly's Plaice' in Brierfield), which he has continued to do for more than a quarter of a century. His career is in sharp contrast to the cosmopolitan, 'made for life' modern English footballers who, at the highest level, can earn £50,000 or more per week and enter a glamorous international world of big money, second and third homes, artists and musicians. Connelly does have the compensations which money cannot buy, however, of remaining a well-liked and well-respected member of a community. Connelly's story is the late and successful version of the place of the professional sportsman in the period of amateur hegemony and it represents a way of life quite different from that of the professional in a fully commercial society.[11]

Post-modern, Post-Industrial and Post-Urban Sport

The collapse of the old amateur hegemony into hyper-commercialism took place at the same time as the development of something which might be called post-modern sport, but also post-industrial sport or perhaps post-urban sport. Consider the historical process, a century earlier, of the modernization of sport. Games and sports came to be clearly defined in time and space: no longer the terrain between two villages, but the 2-acre rectangle and 90 minutes on the watch. They had a legalistic order and quickly came to develop formal institutions on a national and international scale. Teamwork, hierarchy and the division of labour were central features of the most popular sports and especially of football. From the start there was something of an obsession with records and statistics. The complementary fit between sport in this form and the modern factory is so good and so obvious that we ought to be suspicious. The two complemented each other in creating new civic loyalties and identities in an industrial

society. Though sport did add dimensions to an industrial life including, as
Fred Inglis points out, dimensions as simple and obvious as colour: the
green grass and brightly coloured clothing of the footballers contrasting with
the grey walls and stones of an industrial town.[12] Many social historians have
argued that the educational system and sport served to impose the new
industrial values (and especially the obsession with precise timekeeping)
even on to rural and seafaring communities where they did not have the
same functional relevance and where they initially seemed to be absurd and
fanatical.

So it is not surprising that a period in which industry has declined in
those countries in which it first developed has also seen the development of
hyper-commercialism in sport, but at the same time a steady and significant
development of something quite different and alternative. There has been a
massive movement in most Western societies to (sometimes back to) forms
of sport which are not well-defined in time and space, are not regulated in
the quasi-legal manner of modern sports and which do not generate precise
records and statistics. It became apparent, for example, after the election of
'New' Labour in Britain in 1997 and the opening of a rigorous debate about
fox-hunting that, although the sport was clearly unpopular among the
majority, participation had actually trebled over the previous 20 years. But
this is a minor example compared with the global movement since about
1960 towards a kind of sporting engagement with nature.[13]

According to the General Household Survey all such activities in the
United Kingdom were on the increase in the 1970s with field sports, sub-
aqua, water-skiing and surfing all more than doubling.[14] Walking, swimming
and cycling also more than doubled in participation in the 1980s.[15]
According to some estimates the number of people rock climbing in the
United States increased sixfold in the five-year period between 1989 and
1994. Even the most conservative estimates have participation trebling in
under a decade.[16]

The massive increase in the extent to which people all over the developed
world wish to engage with slope, surf and snow demands conceptual
clarification as well as explanation. In the world of commercial and modern
sport, the definition of what counts as sport – of what goes on the 'sports
pages' – is relatively easy. But in a traditional or postmodern context it
becomes extremely difficult and the marginal cases begin to outweigh the
clear examples. Just going for a walk or a swim or slaughtering an animal
for food is not sport. But once there is a challenge, a 'narrative of risk and
achievement', there is a sport. Setting out to complete a marathon or walk
further than you have walked before or swim across a bay when you are not
certain to get to the other side, or if any of these activities are done to a time
or against somebody else or as an attempt at a 'personal best' they surely
become sporting activities and only the most blinkered modernist

preoccupation with organized games could reject this essential perception. Such activities are also challenges to, and competitors with, the more established modern sports.

Two explanations of this phenomenon suggest themselves immediately. The first is simply that greater prosperity and mobility free people to pursue 'traditional' and 'natural' activities in a way that the industrial workforce was not free to do. Certainly the most pronounced rejection of the limitations of industrial society is the rejection of its constraints on space. Post-industrial sport is most clearly a reclaiming of the whole landscape, the 'wilderness' in the United States and the 'countryside' in Britain. This creates complex political conflicts not only between 'sport' in various senses and 'conservation' (also in various senses), but also between sports: canoeists and fishermen become rivals, so do walkers and mountain bikers, even hang-gliding exponents and aeroplane modellers.

The second explanation is that post-urban sport in this sense is a reaction to or against hyper-modern sport. It is certainly seen in this way by many sporting sub-cultures in the United States: many surfers and mountaineers (but not many skiers) see themselves as part of a counter-culture, rejecting the consumerism of major sport.[17] In English terms this generates an even more complex perception. One could argue that to support a 'Premiership' football team, which plays in an all-seater, modern stadium and which is seen regularly on television is simply to be a normal, modern consumer. However, lower down the hierarchy in a world of terraced stadiums and dubious pubs and pies and small fan communities who engage in vigorous rivalries, the activity of being a 'fan' is more participatory and has a greater urge towards counter-culture. I sense something in common between surfers and second-division football fans: both tend to decry the mainstream. But, of course, one must acknowledge that modern and post-modern sport are not logical alternatives, even though the one might be a reaction to the other. It is possible to have sub-aqua, skiing *and* Manchester United: in a broad sense all of these things were part of the 'yuppie' style which developed in the 1980s.

Thus there are important developments in modern sport which can quite precisely be described as 'post-industrial' in so far as they embody movements away from the kind of sport which evolved in industrial society, the structures of which were parallel to the typical institutions of industrial society. They may usefully be described as post-urban, because arguably the most important point about them is that by their nature they break free of the constraints of urban life and they use the larger environment. But is it accurate or useful to describe them as post-modern?

It is easiest to answer this question with reference to the concept of post-modernism as it has been used in the fields of art, architecture and (derivatively) planning. This is because there were in those fields modernists who explicitly stated their position, the most notable, perhaps, being Le Corbusier, as I suggested earlier: for him, to be a modernist was also to be a 'functionalist' (rejecting spurious decoration), a 'purist' (using the simplest and most symmetrical shapes available), an 'internationalist' (rejecting local tradition) and – a term added later – a 'brutalist' in so far as one aggressively uses the most technologically advanced materials, especially steel, glass and concrete, and welcomes the full development of the motor car. Post-modernism in this context becomes a rejection of, or retreat from, not modernism as such, but the modernist project of reconstructing all urban forms along modernist lines. The analogy works reasonably well for sport since the retreat to the surf and the mountains or to knurr and spell and 'fun-running' involves a rejection of the total domination of competitive organized games rather than a rejection of those games as such.

Naturally, when we move to the broader senses of post-modernism, particularly in relation to structuralism as it is famously treated by Jean-François Lyotard, the issues become more murky as well as more interesting.[18] Post-modernism is variously a rejection of totality, universality, rationality, science, the enlightenment or perhaps only of the intellectual hegemony of these concepts. However, in respect of the idea that the Western mind has been vastly unmade, I am induced to borrow a phrase from the first Duke of Wellington and to say that if you believe that that has happened then you will believe anything. It is about diversity, fragmentation, the rejection of necessary futures and right. In this latter sense, I am inclined to accept that the tendencies in sport I have been describing are 'post-modern' in ways which are not captured merely by their post-industrialism and post-urbanism. There is also a tendency, as with some forms of popular music, to absorb the post-modern back into modern structures, to get the surfers' get-together organized, competitive and on television. In the 1990s Kelly Slater emerged as surfing's first millionaire. But so long as that tendency is resisted and marginalized post-modern sport represents an important maintenance of amateurism and a means for its revival which must be discussed later.

Globalization

Another contemporary theory of the epoch which is highly relevant to sport is 'globalization', though the term is fraught with ambiguities. It may be broadly defined as either a process whereby all kinds of human relations (including social, political and economic) come to exist at the level of the planet as a whole rather than within states or empires, or a period in within which this tends to happen. It is sometimes seen as the breakdown of the 'Westphalian system', a reference to the treaty that brought the Thirty Years

War to an end in 1648, an event which is assumed to have accelerated a process of the strengthening of individual states and to have redefined the world as a system, or at least a set, of states. Similarly, there is some use of the term 'new medievalism' to indicate the current development of a world in which a wide variety of claims to authority, over different and overlapping territories, replace the monopoly predominance of the state as an institution. Globalization is likely to be confused with internationalization (where states become more involved with and dependant on each other while remaining the sole sources of authority) and with regionalization in which relations move on to a level higher than the state but lower than the globe: in contemporary Britain 'globalization' and 'Europeanization' are confused with each other and are rivals with distinct bodies of support both descriptively and prescriptively.

There are many dimensions of globalization: the extent to which economies are dependant on trade and the extent of the trade, the nature of capital formation and its control, and the extent to which labour moves between state economies are the essential economic variables. But there are also political and social dimensions: the extent to which organizations can exercise authority over all or most of the globe and the development or not of elements of global culture. Loosely, there may be some systematic tendency for these to correlate and thus for 'globalization' to exist as such, but the evidence suggests that these factors, considered as variables, have a fair amount of independence. The level of trade, expressed as a percentage of the aggregate of all countries' gross national product, for example, did not get back to its 1914 level until the 1970s. The level of global labour mobility has never returned to the pre-1914 conditions of massive movement within the British Empire and to the United States. It probably never will: outside the European Union, states control immigration at least as much as they ever did. Although a form of global culture seems to be developing and is often identified with Americanization (*Coca-colonisation* as Jean-Jacques Servan-Schreiber described it in the 1950s) it may be very superficial and it certainly has to co-exist with such diverse exceptions and reactions as nationalist movements, language revivals and the resurgence of Islam. It seems indisputable that the period 1850–1914 was marked by considerable 'globalization', an 'opening up' (to use a phrase of the time) of continents by the telegraph, the steam train and the steamboat. One could roam most of the world in this time in relative safety and without a passport. In some respects sport was globalized almost as soon as it was modernized: in rugby and cricket games between sides from Britain and the southern hemisphere were established by the end of the nineteenth century and they still continue to thrive in the current wave of globalization. Lord Tennyson, whose career will be discussed later, played his cricket on five continents (Hollywood as well as the Caribbean in the Americas). But that observation may be misleading: most British sports authorities were under no real constraints in their administration from forces outside their boundaries and the Football Association showed disdain for contact outside the British Isles except when pressed by the Foreign Office, ignoring invitations to the first World Cups in 1930, 1934 and 1938.[19]

The strong thesis of globalization talks of a 'borderless world', but even this thesis portrays economic globalization as far in advance of any concomitant political processes.[20] The world without borders may be one in which transnational and multinational companies and major sources of capital are able to operate over a wide range without being subject to much democratic control or regulation. Conversely, the sceptical thesis questions whether there is anything very new in the process and emphasizes the uneven development of parts of globalization in relation to the whole.[21] It also suggests that the reference to globalization may serve for many governments as an ideological strategy or trick of statecraft. Surely it is easier to govern a country if it is generally accepted that employment, for example, is subject to global forces and thus out of your control as a government? A sceptical approach might suggest, for example, that the level of autonomy which a British government might choose to exert in the early twenty-first century if it had the will to do so would actually be greater than that which Ramsay MacDonald had when facing the New York bankers in the financial crisis of 1931. 'Globaloney' and 'glocalization' are theses which must be put on the table along with globalization.

There is no space here to investigate the ambiguities and complexities which surround the concept of globalization even though they are interesting and important. What must be remarked is the relatively simple and dramatic application of the idea of globalization to sport. Quite simply, many of the constraints on the process do not apply to some important sports. The global market for television images is generally constrained by language, ideology and culture. But none of these applies to football: even in the 1960s I remember discussing Sir Bobby Charlton (as he now is) in a *Bedou* tent and 'Match of the Day' is seen even in culturally isolated countries such as Myanmar. It is this global market for televised football, especially in Asia, which has transformed the game from an industry in which hundreds can gain a modest living by being watched by thousands to one in which dozens can become mega-rich by being watched by billions. It is like the move from repertory theatre to cinema in the dramatic arts. Since the end of the Cold War and aided by decisions of the European Court of Justice the labour market in some parts of sport has become truly global. In football, as opposed to the arts, you do not need language or qualifications to work: in 1998–99 for the first time the majority of players in the Premier League in England were non-English. In English cricket there is a much larger, but lower paid, phenomenon with some estimates suggesting ten thousand overseas players in English club cricket.[22]

But it is also true that global governance is well developed in sport, in that world bodies exist which wield genuine authority in relation to states. Consider how the world's largest state, which also happens to be one of the prickliest in its protection of its own sovereignty, reacts to attempted influence from global organizations. China gives short shrift to Amnesty International or Friends of the Earth, but the International Olympic Committee and the Federation of International Football Associations (to give it its English title) are accorded a long and courteous hearing. So are representatives of Newscorp, Star Sports Asia and other parts of the Murdoch empire. This is because they have genuine control over things which the Chinese value such as broadcasting rights and the allocation of major games, whereas in most other fields the aspiring institutions of global governance lack such assets.[23]

Consider this power also from the point of view of states, specifically the British state. A certain kind of nationalist might argue that throughout the 1990s the control of 'our' games and sports has ebbed steadily away in the direction of global sports associations and global media corporations. They have determined the rules of 'our' competitions, the timing of 'our' events, even the laws of 'our' games. An English sports fan who had been in a coma for 20 years, revived at the beginning of the twenty-first century, might find it difficult to believe how un-English many of our practices have become. Ministers for Sport of both major parties have shown extreme reluctance to interfere with any of these processes, barring rather feeble attempts to 'list' sporting events which should remain on 'free to air' television (attempts required, in any case, by Directorate General VIII of the European Union). One could imagine the political response as having been very different, of a Minister for Sport putting up a stern defence of existing English practices, justifying himself or herself on grounds of democracy, accountability and the defence of public goods.

Instead, such ministers chose to ignore the big struggle and to declare their own little agendas of restructuring the Sports Council system, creating 'academies' to produce top sportsmen, and so on, while playing a largely 'dignified' role of ceremonial openings and appearances at major events and on television. This may well have been as rational a piece of statecraft as the government's opting out of responsibility for the level of unemployment and for similar reasons. In any case, the hypothetical minister prepared to engage in the big struggle would have been unlikely to find sufficient support either among the political elite or among sports fans generally, so immersed were both groups in hyper-commercial values. But their choices were also self-fulfilling: we will never know whether global power could have been challenged at this stage.

The lack of popular will to resist globalization suggests that we must talk about nationalism at two different and contradictory levels. On the one hand the commercial basis of the power of those who control international sporting organizations depends entirely on a crude kind of nationalism. Australian television companies, the Chinese Communist Party and the one-third of British women who watch the World Cup even though they ignore domestic football are all attracted by the desire to identify with national success. Yet this desire is at odds with nationalism in another, and arguably more important, sense, the desire to exert a national democratic control on sporting practices and institutions.

In short, even those who are sceptical about the current phase of globalization must see that it has had a huge effect in sport and has served to accelerate the process of hyper-modernization and hyper-globalization by creating global markets and genuinely powerful global institutions. At the same time, sport has also developed in post-modern directions which may be to some degree a cultural reaction to globalization.

Finally, an illustration. In 1995 I was walking down a street in Thailand with my youngest son Stephen, who was wearing the livery of Nottingham Forest Football Club. An old Chinese man, grinning broadly, with hand outstretched, stopped us. 'Nottingham Forest', he said, 'Jason Lee, pineapple on head.' (The peculiar way in which Lee tied up his dreadlocks had inspired a song, 'He's got a pineapple on his head' sung to the tune of 'He's got the whole world in his hands' and this had moved from the stands to national and international television.) As we laughed together I was aware that we were not laughing at Lee himself but at the process of globalization which had led the old man to know about his hair. Perhaps there was even a little post-modern irony in our laughter.

4

Amateur Hegemony and Decline

On 27 August 1995, almost exactly a century after the schism between (amateur) Rugby Union and what became (professional) Rugby League, the International Rugby Board voted to allow professional players in Rugby Union. Only slightly fancifully, perhaps, this might be compared to the fall of Byzantium in 1453: in both cases the event had been predicted for a long time, but still seemed unexpected when it finally happened; in both cases powerful commercial forces were released or redirected. The world, in each case, was neither to be nor to seem to be the same again. Less fancifully, we can see that what fell in each case was a last bastion: Byzantium itself was all that remained of the Eastern Roman Empire while Rugby Union was following athletics, tennis and the Olympic movement down the road to professionalism. In making their decision the International Rugby Board were conceding the demise of the ideological hegemony of amateurism in sport which had lasted for a century, but had been in decline for the last third of that century.

It is important to clarify the concept of 'hegemony'. In its contemporary, revived form its use and popularity descends from the analysis of capitalism in Antonio Gramsci's *Prison Notebooks*.[1] Gramsci sought to develop a concept of power within the Marxist tradition which could explain some of the diversity and subtlety of power structures in a world of capitalism which had survived and developed in the half century since Marx's death. To do so he distinguished 'hegemony' from 'domination', the former referring to the cultural constraints and assumptions within which power operated within a given national society and the latter being closer to coercion, the power of A *over* B. Many non-Marxists have found Gramsci's conceptual framework useful and interesting and it is a moot point, of no importance here, as to whether it is a development of Marxism or a departure from it or something of both.

But it fits the bill quite neatly in respect of the working of amateurism – at its peak sport was run as if amateurism were the 'ideal' condition; it was run by amateurs and large areas within its space, so to speak, were cleared for the use of amateurs only. Yet professionalism and commercialism were not eradicated, nor always treated with hostility. Instead they were bounded and subordinated for the most part. The professional knew his place. This was as important within predominantly professional sports as within those which were mainly amateur. In football in England, for example, it was not just a question of limiting wages and dividends. There were also those who saw the potential power of television as entirely malevolent. Bob Lord, for example, the Chairman of Burnley Football Club (Champions of England in 1960) and a member of the League Management Committee, wrote in his autobiography in 1963:

> Television is not for professional football. It will damage and undermine attendances ... if football were to surrender and allow regular live TV showings the menace would increase, because commentators would gain experience and give much more expert service than the mere descriptive, on-the-surface stuff by non-players which we mostly get today. If TV is ever allowed to give live shows we shall have expert players and talkers like Danny Blanchflower at the mike and we'll get no spectators at all! The present ban must be maintained: is that not obvious when we have to end Football League matches before Cup Final Day because of the national stay-at-home to watch the Wembley pageant on TV?[2]

Lord's objections went beyond opposition to a televised Cup Final and extended to the compromise of showing 'highlights' which was introduced in the form of BBC's 'Match of the Day' the following year. Lord unilaterally banned the cameras from Turf Moor, Burnley's ground, and did not allow them in for another five years.

But there is something strange about Lord's worldview. In image, he was the bluff Lancashire butcher, a caricature of a northern businessman from an 'industrial' novel. His argument, though, is rather inconsistent since he seems to believe simultaneously that televised football is both unwatchable and irresistible. The truth was that, for all his humble origins and 'businessman' image, he was an extreme version of his times, much more conservative than commercial. His place in the world, shaking hands with generals and royalty, and Burnley's place in the world, as the smallest town to be represented by a club which reached the pinnacle of the game, were far better served by the amateur hegemony in sport than by the unrestricted commercialism which has made Manchester United a global name and a financial institution worth more than a billion pounds.

All this throws an interesting light on Gramsci's concept of hegemony. It works well to explain the hegemony of the amateur-elite ethos over professional-commercial. This is quite different from its Marxist use to explain the hegemonic control of the *bourgeoisie* over the proletariat through nationally-specific cultural controls such as 'Fordism' in America and Catholic social theory in Italy. In the case I am concerned with here the 'hegemony' is of 'blazerati' over 'businessmen' *within* the bourgeoisie.

And, of course, this means the hegemony of the blazerato over the businessman inside a single soul.

However, the introduction of the term 'blazerato' and its plural must be accompanied by a certain amount of conceptual and political caution. The 'blazerati' are, literally, those who wear blazers, more generally, officials of broadly based sports associations. It is natural to associate them with the amateur ethos: they are, for the most part, unpaid and part of their role is normally to represent the interest of their sport as a whole against the interests of commerce. But it would be quite wrong to allow the assumption that the blazerato thereby represents the interests of amateurism in any morally significant sense. A model derived from public choice theory which suggests that men in blazers will be mainly interested in their own status and self-preservation seems to work all too well. It is the corruption of the blazerati which has done more to denigrate the image of the Olympics than anything else. It is also true that they can become something like an expenditure class in themselves, even where they are hostile to or partly rivals to the interest of business. In India, for example, it was pointed out at the beginning of the twenty-first century that the Board of Control for the country's major sport, cricket, technically a non-profit charity and was spending less than 2 per cent of its revenues on coaching. The vast majority was spent on 'administration' which turned out to include, travel, clothes, whisky and cigarettes for officials as well as the maintenance of subsidized social clubs. Sometimes honest commercialism is preferable to corrupt officialdom.[3]

Clubs

The public school is generally agreed to have been the most important institution in the development of modern sport, followed by the university. But even by 1961 only about 8 per cent of the population had attended either of these institutions in Britain, and 3 per cent both. At any one time only a tiny fraction of the population were at either. The form of organization through which most people were introduced to amateur sport was the club.

Sports clubs come in all shapes and sizes and it is impossible to do justice to their variety in a general account, except to insist that it was enormous. Some were free-standing institutions concerned with a single sport, others were attached to a larger institution such as a school (as in 'old boy' or 'former pupil' clubs, many of which were 'open' to anybody to join). There has always been a great regional variation in the dominant forms. In Warwickshire, for example, including Birmingham and Coventry, the most important clubs were often based on the official 'sports and social' facilities provided by companies, the area being one of late industrialization, from 1880 onwards, with 'paternalist' tendencies on the part of the employers. In some parts of Lancashire, where industry was established much earlier, the Sunday school often became the institutional focus of the development of modern sport. Paradoxically, the Sunday School Cricket League of Nelson and Colne in north-east Lancashire now consists almost entirely of players of Pakistani (and therefore Islamic) origin.[4]

In the Home Counties perhaps the most typical and important clubs were the relatively exclusive institutions, based on individual sports, especially golf and tennis whose atmosphere is so well captured in John Betjeman's verse and which had an important role in matchmaking. Some clubs had immensely complex constitutions which required a company lawyer to interpret them, while others had almost nothing in the way of formality. The Warwick University Staff and Graduate Cricket Club, which I have chaired from 1987, has no constitution at all and no defined relationship with its 'parent' body, the University. So far as I can tell, there would be no law or rule against the club's selecting an entirely non-university side, no formal requirement for the University to provide facilities and nothing (legal) to prevent the treasurer from absconding with the funds. Equally, some clubs owned valuable real estate while others operated without a clubhouse, using municipally-provided facilities. Perhaps this variety is not surprising when one considers the number of clubs involved: the Chester Report shows just under 31,000 football clubs registered with county associations in 1967 in England alone and the number of football clubs in the United Kingdom has probably topped 40,000 at its peak, with 7,000 cricket clubs.[5] The number of sport clubs altogether has almost certainly been more than 100,000 at any one time; the figure must be elusive and ambiguous, because many clubs which have a real existence have not been registered with any higher body.

But all of these clubs had some things in common: they all had budgets, committees and chairmen (or women) and they were nearly all run primarily by volunteers. They also had an innately high degree of political and legal independence, a phenomenon which will be explored below. This was particularly true of those free-standing clubs which owned their own grounds. One of the tiny handful which have been thoroughly researched is Stanmore Golf Club in Middlesex (or north-west London), the subject of an archival study by the distinguished sports historian Richard Holt.[6] The overwhelming impression of Stanmore is of the club itself being a place apart: physically and culturally it was an oasis in the growing urban sprawl. Its class system – the relationship between the full members, the lady members, the 'artisan' members (who worked on the course and paid a tiny fee to play at unfashionable times), the caddies, the professional and the green-keepers – was almost a society apart, one which you did not join unless you accepted its ways. Only in its own time did Stanmore catch up with the ways of the world. For example, W.H. Parrack, the club captain, pushed through a resolution in 1950 that 'a candidate shall not be refused election merely because of his Race [*sic*]', though such opposition as there was apparently concentrated on the size of the cars owned by Jews in relation to the limited car parking facilities.[7] A general image of political incorrectness about Home Counties golf clubs has now become established in popular culture, but one condition of this has been their high degree of independence, of their being a world unto themselves.

Even in team games such as hockey, Rugby Union and cricket the free-standing club was largely a law unto itself. Rugby clubs played games which were simply called 'fixtures' or 'matches': that they were 'friendlies' was only significant once competitions were created. Rugby Union in England did not have a national 'knock-out' cup until 1972 or a 'pyramid' league structure until 1987. The role of the fixtures secretary was vital, and securing a pair of fixtures against a club formerly regarded as being of higher status was looked on with the kind of satisfaction that promotion gives in a league system. This was as true of schools as of clubs. Whereas this system was universal in Rugby Union, the picture in cricket was more complex; some of its implications will be described later, but it is generally true that the North organized cricket from the start in leagues as it did football.

There were many kinds of internal political issue within free-standing sports clubs: how to break even was a principle source of controversy and often had many aspects, including that of the level of subscriptions to charge and to whom and how many paid staff should be employed. (Even Stanmore Golf Club – a 'well-heeled' organization, as it would be commonly assumed to be – was never quite financially stable because golf is a labour-intensive business.) Intertwined with these immediately financial issues would be the collective management of real estate: some clubs, especially in the London area in the 1980s which had the kind of constitution in which current members are, in effect, equal shareholders, faced the dilemma of immediate personal profit or the survival of the club because of the premium paid for building land under the planning system. There were (almost) always personality clashes tangled with the issues of finance and real estate. But these were the issues of highly autonomous institutions, places of retreat from the commercial world which could run their affairs as they wished and answered to no one.

Consider the fictional Nicetown Rugby Club, *circa* 1960. The club is not of the first rank, but does have a few fixtures against clubs which are considered 'first-class' and whose games are reported in the national press. At least as important as these are the two games against Old Nicetownians, especially the game on Boxing Day when both teams are strengthened by players back from the university or from working in London. There are no trophies, in the modern sense, in the clubhouse, but there are the shirts of players who have played for the county and the single player who went on to play for England. There are also innumerable team photographs, pride of place being given to the unbeaten team of 1934–35, though, by common consent, the fixture list was much weaker in those days.

The most divisive issue in recent years has been the dropping of the pair of fixtures with the (equally imaginary) Grimtown RUFC, despite Nicetown's recent poor record against Grimtown. The problem was that Grimtown had been actively recruiting players from other clubs; their behaviour on the field was also thought to leave something to be desired. But there are no serious financial issues: the club is lucky enough to own its own ground, a ten-acre field snapped up in the agricultural depression: its bar takings are excellent, especially if the Christmas holiday weather is good enough to allow the Boxing Day fixture to be played. Players are not paid and receive no expenses, but it is known by everybody that the best four players in the first XV are all employed by members of the committee.

Cast your mind forward to the end of the century. The Nicetown club is now part of the national pyramid, bottom of the league called 'Midlands East Two' and about to descend into 'Midlands East Three'. There is no longer a game against Old Nicetownians, who sold their ground to a supermarket and were allowed to build a new one in the Green Belt. They play in 'Midlands One', with a full-time coach-manager and they pay win bonuses to the players. Their new clubhouse meets the aims of its business plan and has joyously exceeded them in the revenues from conferences and weddings. Four talented young players who learned their Rugby in Nicetown's mini-Rugby system have recently defected to Old Nicetownians.

The committee are struggling with an horrendous financial situation. When the game went professional in 1996 they felt obliged to pay the players, at least nominally, in order to retain them. But there are no 'gate' takings and bar revenues continue to slide: these days everybody arrives by car and can never manage to consume more than a 'quick one'. Payment to players has now been abandoned; the club's only real hope is a new clubhouse with facilities which will make money and attract new players. This hope is turned in the direction of the National Lottery and the committee are scratching their heads to produce a business plan which can be subsumed within the aims and objectives of the Rugby Union's 'corporate strategy' to serve the community and foster sporting excellence. None of this is easy; other members of the committee sometimes wonder how the club got itself into the position in which it has to fill forms in correctly to please bureaucrats in order to survive.

The Decline of Club Autonomy

There are really two sources of the erosion of the autonomy of the sports club. The first might be described as 'footballization', in which other sports have come to imitate the structures which football set up in the nineteenth century and which they, for the most part, originally eschewed: these include leagues, cups and pyramids. It is difficult to attribute responsibility for this change: it is norms which have changed and television has surely played an important part in their changing. The loss of autonomy is from the club to the larger organization within the sport: when the cricket club of which I was chairman and captain finally entered a league in 1995 I was well aware that we were losing control over whom we played (and perhaps even over such minor decisions as which company's ball we used) in return for the chore of the organizing of fixtures being done for us. We were losing the old incentive of a 'good season' in exchange for the chance to 'win something'. In fact we had little choice, because there were, by then, few clubs left to play on a Saturday who were not part of a league. The great fixtures fair which the Midland Clubs Cricket Conference had held at Edgbaston every October, in which club fixture secretaries made the arrangements to fill blank dates for the following season, an event which was still lively and exciting in the mid 1980s, had died out by the 1990s.

The second reason for the loss of autonomy of clubs is, in a liberal perspective, more sinister. It is the growing control by the state of the sport. The steady growth of control can be traced back at least to the publication of the Birmingham University report *Britain in the World of Sport* in 1956 and the subsequent establishment of Sir John Wolfenden's Committee of Inquiry into British Sport which reported to the Central Council for Physical Recreation in 1960.[8] Milestones include Harold Wilson's appointment of Dennis Howell as Minister for Sport in 1964 and the establishment of the Sports Council in 1971. The Council, in its various forms, was one of the mysterious British 'semi-state institutions' or quangos (quasi-autonomous non-governmental organizations) which transformed itself, unseen, from a 'ginger group' pressing the interests of sport in government to an agency used by government to control sport. The objectives of this control varied wildly from the 'targeting' of 'excluded' groups (as they came to be called) such as Asian women and inner-city inhabitants, to 'Sport for All', to remedial doses of sport for the urban underclass following the riots of 1981, to an emphasis on 'excellence' in the 1990s.[9] But the consistent pattern was of government seeing sport as a political resource in ways which would have been unthinkable to the Attlee governments of 1945–51 and of the organization itself increasingly dancing to the tune of its paymasters. The effect at the grass roots of sport was a loss of autonomy from the club to the national association and a parallel loss of autonomy from the sport to the state. This was often much more pronounced in minor sports, some of which became effectively 'nationalized' with 70 per cent or more of their revenue coming from the state, than with major sports, although it was real in all sport. The creation of a National Lottery in 1994 added an immediate £200 million to state funding for sport and its later extension to revenue as well as to capital grants further increased state control. These are important events which must later be put into a more theoretical setting.

Amateur Careers

Of course, there is a sense in which to be an amateur was precisely not to have a career in sport. But amateur sport was (and still is) a career in all kinds of ways. The amateur career might run alongside the 'day-job' or complement it or set it up or transcend it. In some cases it could do all of these things. Consider four ideal types of amateur, defined by the extent to which sport was their career and helped to mould their careers.

The Golden Youth

For many upper-middle- and middle-class participants at the height of amateurism sport was a 'childish thing' to be put aside after school and university, leaving a warm memory of a golden youth. There were great runners whose only participation by the age of 30 was an anonymous jog in an old sweater. As recently as the 1988 Olympics one gold medal winner in the Great Britain hockey team told me that the Olympic final (effectively a world championship in field hockey) was the last game he would ever play. 'Forty years hence this weather/ Will call us from office stools' sang the Etonians: the prediction could be interpreted either as an intention never to give up or of a single instance of nostalgia. In editing the *Wisden* obituaries on cricketers Benny Green pointed out the plethora of 'gentlemen of the cloth, most of whose first-class careers were confined to their days at Oxford or Cambridge, after which they succumbed happily enough to the rusticities of some sleepy rectory'.[10] Perhaps their pastoral duties allowed for the occasional game for the village.

The Missionary

Eric Liddell, gold-medallist in the 1924 Olympics, was a real missionary, who died in a Japanese prison camp, after a career attempting to convert the Chinese to Christianity. But he falls into my category of 'golden youth'. Here I am referring to sporting missionaries, those amateur sportsmen who, with or without a specifically Christian motive, tried to convert the world to the values of sport. They rarely included clergymen, except those of a pedagogic persuasion, but they certainly included tens of thousands of schoolteachers, in Britain, the Empire and the world, and a considerable number of factory owners and managers. My own experience of global cricket includes a college team of Californians created by an Australian physical education lecturer and a factory team from Lima, Peru, created by Lancastrian management. One of the most famous missionaries in this sense was Cecil Tyndale-Biscoe whose forceful introduction of organized games into Kashmir left some part of Indian culture changed forever.[11] Sudan (sometimes the whole of Africa) became, in Imperial legend, a continent of 'Blacks ruled by Blues'. But the general category is of men who proselytized sport and, in doing so, transcended the distinction between jobs and hobbies.

The Club Man

The grass-roots history of amateur sport is an extraordinary story of the devotion of individuals to clubs and, to a lesser extent, to representative bodies and governing bodies. Holt's account of Stanmore Golf Club shows that members of the Gordon family have supported the club for most of a century and Holt's own father-in-law, George Glass, was club captain in 1964 and again in 1993. Perhaps many clubs, apart from their presidents and chairmen, have someone who occupies the role of 'Oldest Member' as it is played in many of the stories of P.G. Woodhouse. But this is much less of a class phenomenon than are the 'golden youth' and the 'missionary'. Walk into any village cricket club in England and look at the photographs: you will see the same players, balding and greying over four or five decades, reappearing as president, chairman or groundsman. Family connections are often all-important: it is more common than not at this level of cricket that at least two players with the same name from the same family will appear in a team. One club team in Warwickshire throughout the late 1990s could open the bowling with a junior county player, replace him with his father and then replace *him* with *his* father. The grandfather (almost) invariably returned the best figures. Sport in this context becomes a unique civic institution and a bond between the generations.

The Covert Pro

But there were also amateurs whose sporting distinction formed the foundation for a career. Just as in the United States, many of the overwhelming majority of college athletes who do not make it into the formally professional ranks could find jobs in sales and management which used their sporting reputations, and in the Soviet Union sportsmen could develop a career in the armed forces and the security services on a sporting base, so, in Britain, there were always jobs in 'promotions', sales, finance and publicity for sportsmen of the upper second rank. Indeed, amateurs may often have been better off than professionals in this respect. There seems to have been relatively little opportunity for former professional cricketers and footballers in these fields and breweries, for example, have usually preferred to employ a minor county cricketer or a one-cap international rugby player to a former professional footballer. There is one slightly sinister aspect of the sportsman's career: in all countries there are aspects of security which mainly employ former sportsmen. This is particularly true in former communist countries where Bulgaria may be the extreme case of a network of bodyguards and security services based on the former communist sports machine.[12]

Cricket: The Texture of Decline

In the early 1980s during the overlaps between the cricket and the football season (principally in April and September) I was often playing football on Sunday mornings and cricket on Sunday afternoons. Each game was largely typical of the grass roots of its sport: in Warwickshire they were still utterly different, with norms so precise that it almost felt as if you could touch them. The football games were league games, part of a formal structure; the cricket games were 'friendlies' which lasted approximately six hours altogether and which were assumed to be drawn unless the side batting second was either bowled out or exceeded the total of the side batting first, in which case the game ended.

In the football games cheating was normal and the 'professional foul' common. Players constantly shouted abuse at opponents, team-mates and the referee and 'bad' language was more common than 'good' language. There was no social life after the football, at least no social intercourse between the two teams, though each team might retire to its own pub, or even to opposite ends of the same pub.

The cricket was entirely different. Incoming batsmen were clapped in to bat by their opponents and complimented on good shots. Batsmen often 'walked': that is, they declared themselves to be out irrespective of the umpire's decision. The two teams took tea together and, when the game was over, retired to the pub together. Invariably, the two captains bought each other a drink and assessed the days play together. It was normal to apologize for any weakness in one's own team, or for inappropriate strength or any bad behaviour. The long day ended with handshakes, best wishes and anticipation of the next fixture between the two teams.

Cricket's norms are drawn from a long amateur tradition developed in the public school, the country house and the rural village. Those of football were drawn from the professional game, then familiar to everybody through television. It should be noted that the superficial popular explanation of the difference – social class – simply does not work: a large number of the cricket teams were working-class Coventry factory teams and even then some of the football teams represented organizations (such as computer companies) whose entire workforce was reasonably well educated. In some cases, the same players were involved and behaved completely differently in the two contexts. The difference can also be remarked as existing in the English literature of sport in so far as the fiction of cricket is dominated by such grass-roots contests as Charles Dickens's All Muggleton vs. Dingley Dell in *The Pickwick Papers,* L.P. Hartley's big house vs. the village in *The Go-Between,* P.G. Wodehouse's tale of the Sedleigh XI in *The Lost Lambs* (republished as *Mike and Psmith*) Dorothy Sayers's tale of the game between the Pym's and Brotherhood's advertising agencies in *Murder Must Advertise* and A.G. McDonnell's classic account of the village against the intellectual tourists in *England, Their England.* The literature of football, by contrast, is much less distinguished and overwhelmingly concerned with the professional game.

Every ground force in society seemed to be pushing cricket to become more like football. Even in 1970 Lord Constantine (Learie Constantine, a West Indian professional cricketer for Nelson in the Lancashire League which had been founded in 1892 and always was like football) commented that 'the spirit [of league cricket] is spreading to the south'.[13]

In 1996–97, with the help of the National Cricket Association, I sent surveys to 68 long-established figures in the amateur game throughout the United Kingdom. The survey was open-ended, asking respondents to comment on and evaluate changes in the game.[14] Thirty-six responses were received, a healthy rate of 53 per cent; the average length of time that the respondents had been involved in club cricket was 35 years, the variation was from 16 to 50. Three-quarters of all participants mentioned an increase in competitiveness, referring both to the form of cricket played and the spirit in which it was played. Some thought this was a good thing, some a bad thing; most thought it had good and bad aspects. (In terms of skills there was near unanimity that this had improved the standard of fielding, but also a prevailing view that bowling was less skilled and imaginative because most of the competitive formats used rewarded the negative bowler, who could stop batsmen scoring, rather than the imaginative or experimental one who could trick the batsman out or 'buy' his wicket.) Fifteen respondents (43 per cent) volunteered comments on a decline in 'discipline', 'etiquette', or 'behaviour'. Six bemoaned the decline of social life and ten discussed the effects on English cricket of the recruitment of overseas players (which has been an issue even at fairly low levels of the game: one respondent estimated that there were more than 10,000 recruited overseas players in British club cricket).

As a player who had been involved throughout this period, the responses mirrored my own experiences: my own club had played in a mid-week league from 1977 but did not join a weekend league until 1995. However, one must add the reminder that social change is never simple or absolute. During the writing of this chapter I played in two successive Sunday games. The first took place as if it had been a quarter of a century earlier: not only were all the old rituals maintained, but the game contained an incident in which we looked in vain at the elderly umpire to give out a talented batsman whom we thought had very finely 'edged' the ball to the wicket-keeper, only to realize that the batsman was already walking back to the pavilion. One young player, brought up on league cricket, told me that it was the first time he had ever seen such an incident. The second game was played in the hard, unfriendly manner of much league cricket, dominated by negative bowling, its crucial incidents being disputes over umpiring decisions.

The felt pressures to be more 'competitive' have come from several sources. Football has enhanced its cultural domination, especially in the 1990s. In cricket itself, highly competitive foreign teams have generally got the better of England in international competition, suggesting that we should change our ways. Television has established a hegemony of the professional game over the amateur, reversing the previous situation; this is particularly true of the coverage of cricket by the transnational Murdoch empire. When the Warwick Centre for the Study of Sport held a conference on the future of English cricket in 1997 a number of officials attended who were involved in administering the game at the very highest level. Their commitment, intelligence, open-mindedness and concern for the game were heart-warming. But in neither formal nor informal discussions did any of them ever acknowledge that grass-roots cricket existed for fun, as an end-in-itself, as part of a national culture. To them, it was part of a 'pyramid', a structure which must help to guarantee the future of the game by producing a successful England team, the necessary condition of cricket's commercial success.

Amateur Institutions and Civil Society

'Civil society' refers broadly to a level of social organization which is more extensive and diverse than the traditional structures of family and clan yet independent of the state. The term had a considerable revival in the 1990s, being taken out of 'its coffin in the crypt of the great church of political theory'.[15] Much of this revival had to do with the collapse of communism. For Marxists (and a variety of non-Marxists arguing in a broadly similar tradition) the problem was to rethink theory in a world which seemed less explicable by a determinist form of Marxism than it once had. The concept of civil society, as John Urry put it, offered a way out of the 'dichotomy between reductionism/functionalism and autonomism'.[16] For liberals the job was often to analyse and influence the extent to which former communist societies might develop the kinds of structure which would allow political stability and economic growth. In that context Ernest Gellner defined civil society as

> that set of diverse non-governmental institutions, which is strong enough to counterbalance the state, and while not preventing the state from fulfilling its role as keeper of the peace and arbitrator between major interests, can nevertheless prevent the state from dominating and atomising the rest of society.[17]

It became a kind of official doctrine of the Soros Foundation that the key task of post-communist reconstruction was to nurture civil society in former communist countries (and Gellner became a Soros employee). Somewhere between the two kinds of definition was the more neutral concept of political science defining civil society as 'the organised society over which the state rules'.[18]

There is a tendency to see civil society as a good thing and as being functional in respect of other good things such as democracy. Diamond lists the roles that the institutions which form civil society perform in a democracy: they check government power, develop participatory skills and democratic values, recruit and train leaders, disseminate information and provide channels for the expression of interests. In specific contexts they can also legitimize the state by engaging with it, mitigate class conflicts and help to create consensus.[19] The relevance of sport to civil society is that sporting organizations can be an important part of civil society, though they do not necessarily play this role. Nobody has ever doubted that the fifteen hundred or so 'amenity societies' in England (which are local organizations largely concerned with urban conservation and the quality of town life) have civil society functions, but it would also be difficult to exclude approximately 40,000 football clubs and 7,000 cricket clubs. In all of these people learn to act as secretaries and treasurers and to make collective decisions; in certain circumstances they may also learn to engage with government (most probably through a federal body), to influence it and accept its decisions. Arguably, the sporting elements of civil society have their own particular contribution to make to the broader idea (just as women's or arts organizations do): the Arnoldian values of accepting competition while retaining respect for opponents, the ability to express and suppress individual talents within a team and the idea that there are higher values – the good of the game – beyond immediate institutional interests are all sporting values which are also special and functional in respect of civil society as a whole.

Yet sport is not necessarily part of civil society, nor does it necessarily have a positive impact on civil society as a whole when it is. Studies of soccer in Australia in the 1980s show how ethnically-based clubs may simultaneously have created and preserved communities of immigrants; but they also fostered bitter and often violent rivalries between ethnic groups (especially those teams from the Balkans) and created barriers between these groups and the broader Australian society.[20] On the one hand we have to be careful not to impose our own values as a test of which groups contribute to civil society: we must not arbitrarily exclude groups such as bikers' and peasants' organizations which may behave uncivilly, but which do provide bulwarks against excessive state power while still legitimizing the state. On the other hand, we must apply some values and most commentators would be reluctant to accept Mafia organizations as part of civil society, despite the apparently productive co-operation between Sicilian Mafia leaders and allied forces in the Second World War.

My own research on three varied examples shows that the relationship between sport and civil society differs in reality about as much as one could possibly imagine.[21] In the Republic of Georgia, for example, in the mid 1990s I was interviewing to find out whether and how state-sponsored sporting organizations were being maintained or replaced on a voluntary basis. Many of the people I talked to simply did not understand my original question: of course, sport had declined, they said, and it would revive when capitalist investors moved in and replaced the financing of coaches and facilities which had previously been provided by the state. The idea that even in conditions of extreme political instability and economic collapse one only needed a ball to set up a children's football club was not part of the outlook of my interviewees. There was no conception of the kind of motives for action upon which civil society is based, let alone a civil society. It was reminiscent for me of talking to an African student, a former professional boxer, who simply could not understand the idea of amateurism: there was no way he would have learned to box, he said, without the prospect of being paid for it. After all, the work was hard and painful, considered as work. The idea of choosing to box as an amateur caused him to double up with laughter. In this context the voluntary principle must be seen as at the heart of both amateurism and civil society.

In Thailand a judgement on the overall 'strength' of civil society proved more complex. The country is run by a Bangkok-based elite of about a quarter of a million people. The personnel of the elite are found in the extended royal family, the upper echelons of the army, the major capitalist organizations, the universities and the political parties. In their sporting manifestations they appear as a 'blazerati' of national sports organizations combining all these elements. In some respects the state is weak and unstable: 17 military *coups d'état* between 1932 and 1992. Yet the monarchy has thrived and survived as a symbol of national continuity. Democratic party competition often recycles the generals who have dominated military government and, anyway, on almost all occasions has been increasingly loathed for its corruption as time has passed since its re-establishment. In some respects the elite do act as a kind of civil society (capable of running, among other things, sport and capitalism) of precisely the sort that is absent from Georgia. But a quarter of a million people is a small fraction of 40 million, though sporting organizations, at least, naturally extend their tentacles down into society (through recruitment and 'white elephant' sporting scholarships, for example) to a greater extent than do many others.

South Africa can in many respects be quoted as a 'strong' civil society with its sporting element as, arguably, the strongest in the world. The country has an impressive range of organizations from national associations set up by 'whites' to the local 'civics' which aided black-community self-help under the apartheid regime. National sporting associations played a huge part in changing the regime: crucial incidents include the direct attack on petty apartheid by the cricket authorities in the 1970s and the 'Safari in Harare' when the South African Rugby Union negotiated direct with the African National Congress in 1988. Both of these initiatives were responses to sanctions from outside, but they arguably demonstrate how a strong civil society was able to respond more flexibly to the need for change and thus allow South Africa to institute a revolutionary change without a revolution. Conversely, it allowed the ANC to adopt a strategy of 'putting out feelers into civil society, in order to understand it and to know with whom it was dealing before formal talks began with the government'.[22] The Dutch Reformed Church also, in the end, played an important part in the change of regime. One dimension of the truth about South Africa is that it has had a civil society strong enough to allow the entire basis of the state to be changed. But another dimension is that civil society does not penetrate a huge underclass whose criminal responses make the country one of the most violent on earth. Perhaps only in the long term will the relative importance of these dimensions be comparable.

Civil society in Britain is, in most respects, extremely well developed. To visitors from more *étatiste* societies it is sometimes quite difficult to explain that such functions as providing lifeboats (the Royal National Lifeboat Institution), lighthouses (Trinity House) or paramedical services at sporting events (the St. John Ambulance Brigade) are provided by private organizations, or that some of the road signs are erected privately by the National Trust and the Automobile Association. The cliché that England (in particular) is a 'land of pubs and clubs' is an important truth. In general, the strength of civil society in England can be explained by the two factors which seem to explain almost everything about England: the lack of a political revolution and the early industrialization. In combination they created a national approach in which society responded to problems when the state and the powers of the state were relatively undefined and unclear.

British sporting institutions grew up before and without the state and, for a long time, treated the state as an irrelevance. Thus it came quite naturally to all the national sporting organizations (except the tiny minority with military connections) to defy the then Prime Minister Margaret Thatcher and send competitors to the Olympic Games in Moscow in 1980. By contrast, there was a complete observance of Ronald Reagan's boycott in the United States. But it should be noted that the state's penetration of sport in America has been far greater generally than is the case in Britain. Professional sports clubs mostly exist in a corporatist relation with city authorities which own their stadiums, effectively subsidize them and look to them for 'major league' prestige. American sporting careers are overwhelmingly developed through a public education system which means, for example, that the state's expanding conception of its role in protecting individual rights intrudes constantly upon the organization of the sport.

'Political correctness' and civil society do not fit easily together in this context. 'Title IX', part of an Act of Congress passed in 1972, requires all educational institutions in receipt of federal funds to provide equally for males and females. In effect this means private universities as well as state. By contrast, the Race Relations Acts of 1968 and 1976 and the Sex Discrimination Act of 1975 in Britain (all passed by Labour governments) specifically exempt private clubs, which are the backbone of British sport.

In this regard it is important to understand that as amateurism has declined in Britain, particularly since 1980, so also has civil society. The relationship between this and the Thatcherite 'rolling back the state' is important and complex. In effect, civil society has lost ground to both the commercial principle and the state. There was, for example, a revolutionary change in the organization of charitable bodies in the 1980s. They paid higher salaries, employed more independent consultants, looked for executives with MBA qualifications and decentralized more activities for self-funding. Academic comments on this process referred to 'major changes in organizational philosophy, ideology and culture' which were 'largely irreversible'[23] and claimed that, 'Questions of competitive performance, strategic change and professional management seem to be the keynote themes of individual charitable organizations ...'[24]

The development of charities furnishes a good and important example of disjointed incrementalism. Imagine a bright young person with an (American) MBA approaching a British charity at a certain stage in its history. He or she says,

> I don't think that you are anywhere near fulfilling your potential in terms of raising revenue. You could take a lot of the money now going to other charities if you presented yourselves better and got your message to a wider variety of people. There is also the question of the

large amounts of public money which are now being effectively administered through charities: you haven't achieved your potential in this field, either. I have the techniques and contacts to help you do this and I am sure I could double your income within three years. Naturally, I would expect to be rewarded as the expert business manager that I am.

If that charity adapts this strategy, others must follow suit, in what becomes an increasingly competitive field. The net effect, which seems to be generally agreed in the research, is to change and undermine the whole nature of charity. In part, this is because of a blurring of the altruistic motive and a weakening of its capacity to provide an autonomous incentive for action. The classic example of this effect is in the giving of blood where it has been long observed that (in complete contradiction of pure market theory) systems which do not pay donors get more and better blood than those which do.[25] It is not just that the desire to give can be stronger than the desire to earn a fee, it is also that the desire to give can be undermined by the fee. Thus both givers and traditional voluntary workers felt undermined by the efficiency and high salaries of the new system. Between 1993 and 1997 the total amount of charitable giving in Britain fell by almost a third, over a billion pounds.[26] Charity had simultaneously become a more commercial and more state-dominated activity. State interference was increased by both direct funding and by a perceived need for much more vigilant control by the Charity Commission. It is odd to read that, 'Over recent years, there has been a greater degree of centralized government funding',[27] given that the comment was made by an academic expert on charity at the end of a decade in which government had supposedly been 'rolling back the state'.

In some respects the development of sport in the 1980s has been broadly similar, but it is also true that there has been a long-term trend for greater interference by the state in the running of sport which can be dated back to the report of the Wolfenden Committee in 1960 and to the Birmingham University research project that preceded and inspired it. (The bodies which produced the reports shared several key personnel.) The ideological direction of government has shifted about from 'Sport for All' to 'Raising the Game', from sport as a palliative for problems of national health and urban decay to an emphasis on emulating governments (especially the Australian) with successful sports policies, winning things and accruing the resulting prestige. But the intrusion of the state has been constant. When the Sports Council was established in 1971 its primary role was seen as parallel to that of the many other 'semi-state' institutions such as the (then) University Grants Commission in representing its sector in government. By the end of the century it was perceived to be primarily a government agency for running sport; from the 1980s, for example, it had increasingly required development plans from individual sports which would contribute to the creation of more efficient structures and, ultimately, to national sporting success. These corporate plans trickled down to form the constraining context for individual clubs. By the 1990s all sports had to conform to a set of items on a government agenda, including both performance and catering for 'socially-excluded groups'. As with charity, the creation of a National Lottery has introduced funds on a relatively huge scale (initially £200 million for sport as compared with less than the £50 million being distributed by the Sports Council at the time). From 1997 revenue funding from the lottery for sport required plans which would be oriented to producing 'world-class performance'. Nicetown Rugby Club was once able to live in a world of its own, relatively free from both the constraints of market forces and interference by the state. By the end of the century it was running itself into a more coercive and constrained environment in which it was increasingly constrained by both commercial forces and government.

There are some important and polemical propositions in political theory which emerge from these observations. The 'neo-liberal' view that commercialism, private property and civil society go naturally together is unconvincing in this context. At the very core of the problem of reconstruction in former communist countries is the truth that it is easier to have an electoral democracy and to remove dependence on the state (which disappears very quickly once the state is incapable of providing anything) than it is to construct a civil society. It is at least plausible that Hann is right to say that civil society was stronger in Hungary under communist rule than it is now;[28] a similar argument could be put about the strength of the Catholic Church and the Solidarity movement in Poland under communism and their subsequent respectability and decline. The Thatcher governments may have reduced the state role in the management of industry, but they increased the role of the state in sport, creating a structure of corporatist power which constrained and coerced sporting institutions. Understandably, perhaps, in view of the working of communism, both Thatcherism and neo-liberalism equated commercialism with a weaker state and a stronger civil society. But in reality the commercial principle and the state can advance together at the expense of civil society. It would seem highly unlikely that British sport could in a future instance show the kind of independence from government which it had demonstrated in 1980 by choosing to support the Moscow Olympics rather than Margaret Thatcher. From this perspective, amateurism in its classic form can be seen as a genuine 'third way' which protected sporting organizations, among others, from the power of both the state and the market.

Amateurism and the Law

The process of sport moving from non-commercial to commercial space within society raises interesting legal issues. What follows is a political theorist's account of these, which makes no claim to legal expertise.

In a delightful paradox, English courts acknowledged that amateur status had a monetary value. This was particularly apparent in the case of *Tolley* v. *J.S. Fry & Sons Ltd* which went to the House of Lords in 1931.[29] Cyril Tolley was a stockbroker who had won the English amateur golf championships in 1920 and 1928. An advertisement for Fry's chocolate showed a cartoon of Tolley playing golf with a packet of their chocolate protruding from his pocket; his name was used in an accompanying verse. Tolley sued on the grounds that members of the public would infer 'that he was seeking notoriety and gain by the means aforesaid; and that he had been guilty of conduct unworthy of his status as an amateur golfer'.[30] Thus he had been held up to ridicule and contempt and his credit and reputation injured.

The Lords upheld a judgment in which Tolley had been awarded £1,000. Dissenting from this judgment Lord Blanesburgh said,

> The caricature is a piece of offensive vulgarity – so vulgar indeed, and this is to my mind the fatal obstacle to the appellant's success in these proceedings – that it is almost beyond reason that anyone knowing anything of the appellant, as he and his record were disclosed at the trial, could for a moment have supposed or even suspected that he had anything whatever to do with its publication. That publication was, surely, only another instance of the toll levied on distinction for the delectation of vulgarity.[31]

The argument against Blanesburgh was, in effect, that reputation also mattered as the opinion of those who were less sophisticated than his 'anyone'. It was crucial that correspondence had been produced in which the advertising agency (who were not the defendant and were not named) had baulked at using the tennis players Miss Helen Wills and Miss Betty Nuthall on the grounds that they were amateurs and instead had used Mlle Suzanne Lenglen, who was by then a professional.

A thousand pounds in 1931 was the sort of annual salary to which men aspired, but few attained. It was ten times the wages of an agricultural labourer and five times that of a worker at Ford's new factory in Dagenham; it would have bought a large detached house. Tolley was awarded this sum in compensation for the defamatory implication that he might have accepted a lesser sum for agreeing to advertise chocolate. What is so striking about the Lord's discussion of the case, read 70 years on, is the assumption that one was demeaned or tainted by associations with vulgar commerce. It must be remembered here that Tolley was not a landed aristocrat, nor a bishop, but a stockbroker.

As sport becomes a business its latitude for self-government becomes threatened by two doctrines in common law: natural justice and restraint of trade. They are closely associated, as was illustrated in a Court of Appeal decision on the case of *Currie* v. *Barton and Another* in 1988.[32] Ian Currie was an Essex county tennis player who also earned his living as a tennis professional. In 1982 he quarrelled with the Essex County Lawn Tennis Association as a result of being asked to play as the county team's number five and was consequently banned from playing for them for three years with the possibility of the ban being lifted after two years. The procedures of this decision did not meet the canons of natural justice in so far as he was not informed about them and neither represented nor allowed to speak. The court ruled against him, considering that the ECTLA was acting as a 'domestic tribunal': they 'would only interfere with the decisions of such a body when the person affected was in a contractual relationship with it or when the decision resulted in an unreasonable restraint on that person's capacity to earn a living.' They were not impressed by Currie's argument that his ability to make a living through coaching and sponsorship would be adversely affected by his absence from the Essex (amateur) team. Lord Justice Nicholls said that he 'did not think the rules of natural justice could apply to a position where a monopoly power over a sporting activity made decisions about team selection, provided the decision did not affect a person's ability to earn a living.'

Restraint of trade was defined by Lord MacNaughton in 1894 as follows: 'all interference with individual liberty of action in trading and all restraints of trade themselves, if there is nothing more, are contrary to public policy and therefore void'.[33] A reasonable interference is one which protects the interests of the parties involved without being injurious to the public interest. That sport is a trade was established by *Eastham* v. *Newcastle United* in 1963 when Judge Wilberforce declared that an employee could bring an action for restraint of trade not only against an employer but also against an 'association of employers whose rules and regulations place an unjustifiable restraint on his liberty of employment'.[34]

The important case in this context is *Greig* v. *Insole* in 1978.[35] The case arose out of the efforts of the Australian media entrepreneur Kerry Packer to control the television rights to cricket in Australia. His overtures had been rejected by the state-owned Australian Broadcasting Corporation, despite his offering six times as much money. As a result in 1977 he established World Series Cricket Pty Ltd to contract players direct to play 'supertests' and other competitive games. The International Cricket Conference retrospectively banned the 34 players who had signed contracts with Packer and the Test and County Cricket Board banned the three English county players from playing first-class cricket. Led by Tony Greig, they contested this ban in the courts, giving rise to two cases heard together. Judge Slade ruled that, despite the lack of contractual relationship between the players and the TCCB (whose chairman was Doug Insole), the ruling was in restraint of trade, though he indicated that had the ban not been retrospective and had it affected only (international) test matches and not the county cricket from which players derived their basic livelihood it might not have been considered as an unjustifiable restraint. He rejected arguments that the ICC and the TCCB had acted in the best interests of cricket in favour of the view that it was in those interests that the public should be able to watch the best players.

The 'Packer affair' ended in compromise 18 months after it started; its minor legacy is the continuation of a 'World Series' competition as part of the Australian season, its major legacy a more-or-less free market in the global television rights for cricket.[36] In a sense the cricket authorities were forced into change earlier than those of other sports and were able to get off relatively lightly. A set of organizations still operating on predominantly amateur assumptions fell into conflict with an entrepreneur who wanted to exploit the global commercial possibilities of the sport. As a result, the structure was created which succeeded in making cricket financially viable while preserving many of its traditions. (Estimates of the global viewing figures for the 1999 World Cup ranged from 500 million to 2 billion.)[37] The path to global commercialization was much smoother for cricket than for Rugby or athletics.

Some of the legal issues involved in these cases seem horrendously complex. In what respects and to what extent is the governing body of a sport an 'association of employees'? What is the legal status of a system of 'retaining and transferring' professional players? Fortunately, they are not my concern. The issues in sociological and political theory are relatively clear and dramatic. In Ferdinand Tonnies's terms sport has moved from the realm of *Gemeinschaft* to that of *Gesellschaft*, from civil society to the sphere of regulated commerce.[38] If you are running an amateur sporting community it is your right to say to a participant you do not like, 'You cannot be a member; you must go and start your own club, association or sport.' But if the sport becomes a business you must meet the canons of natural justice and free trade, which are a major limitation on your autonomy. Legal developments, perhaps more clearly than any other phenomena, have illustrated the contradictions which lie at the heart of sports and their governing bodies, the difficulties of running an activity which is a pastime to some and a means of livelihood to others.

Conclusions

The objective of this chapter has been to analyse the working of amateurism both at its height and in the period of its decline, much as historians simultaneously discuss the *ancien régime* and the causes and processes of its deterioration and collapse. There remains an insistent ambiguity about where it is, geographically and socially, one is describing when one deals with the amateur system and its decline. The core of the territory is one part of the English middle class, but the territory itself can never be well defined. In some respects, not in others, it stretches over the whole of the British Isles. In a sense, through Olympic sport, it was sovereign throughout the globe. But it is more realistic to understand it as predominant in a 'pale' of territory where the ideals of the English public school, university and club were influential. Amateurism has been important in Buenos Aires, but not in Tblisi. It was more important in Philadelphia and Boston than it was in Chicago, but, for that matter, it was more important in London than it was in Manchester.

There was always a tension between amateurism and commercialism. They were not themselves social systems, but they have always shown systematic tendencies, so that commercialism could undermine and reject features of amateurism and vice versa. In some incidents they seem wholly incompatible; in others they develop a compatibility, even a symbiosis, which is capable of great persistence. Perhaps the appropriate analogy here might be democracy and monarchy which, though incompatible principles, have shown a remarkable capacity for cohabitation. One of the features of this cohabitation is that not only may the monarchical characteristics in the political culture or the legal system be difficult to eradicate when that system becomes democratic, they may also be necessary to support democracy. Thus the 'legacy' of amateurism, of committees of 'old farts' running sports and legions of volunteers coaching skills may not be something which commercialism can modernize or eradicate so easily as some modernizers might imagine. There are questions of political theory which must be addressed more fully when the future of amateurism is considered.

Some Preliminary Arguments for Amateurism

One aspect of the story so far, of amateurism as an ideology justifying a range of social practices and institutions, serves as kind of indictment. Amateurism was 'classist' in that it distinguished between social classes in favour of those already dominant. It was also 'racist' in that within the British Empire and the United States it favoured 'white' elites over other races. Just as in English cricket it was the universal practice for about a hundred years until around 1960 that first-class teams had to be captained by an amateur, in the West Indies it became the practice that a 'white' man had to be captain. In most accounts of amateurism it stands accused of institutionalized hypocrisy: all over the history of 'amateur' sport – in Olympic athletics, Rugby Union in France, Wales and the southern hemisphere, American college sport, even football in Northumbria – the amateur principle seems more honoured in the breach, a case of who cheats wins.

There is an important threefold distinction to be made before we accept the story of amateurism as an indictment, between three kinds of property of an 'ism', a social practice which consists of both beliefs and institutions:

- those activities and beliefs normal among practitioners
- those activities and beliefs which are essential to the practice
- the necessary implications of the core principles which justify the practice.

'Sexism', for example, was almost universal among those who established amateurism: they considered women inferior in several important respects and thought most sport was an unsuitable activity for women. But these beliefs were purely contingent: not only does an amateur principle apply to women in exactly the same way as it does to men, women's sport, because of its lesser commercial potential, has tended to remain more purely and devoutly amateur than has men's sport. There are also complex judgements to be made about the extent to which a 'vice' which is part of an institution follows necessarily from the principles of that institution. Even the most militant atheist would have to concede that witch hunts, child-molesting priests and the Spanish Inquisition were not part of the essence of Christianity in the same way that the Holocaust was to the essence of Nazism. (As it happens, this is a distinction which de Coubertin was always keen to make in this context, declaring that, 'Clericalism is no more synonymous with religion than imperialism is with patriotism.'[1] He was from a traditional Catholic and legitimist background, but he was something of a rebel against this background and many of his statements seem radical and socialist. He was not very consistent, however, and, in the Dreyfus case, he sided with the 'right' in declaring Dreyfus guilty.)[2] On the other hand, Christianity cannot be declared entirely innocent of all charges simply because a belief in a theistic and revealed religion offers justifications for authoritarianism which could never be generated by (say) the liberalism of a John Stuart Mill or a Bertrand Russell. A truly liberal society would give no one the spiritual authority of the inquisitor or the child-molesting priest.

It is the same with amateurism. The snobbery cannot be considered mere contingency, like the sexism. A doctrine that says that certain activities must always be unpaid even though they would generate wages through a market undoubtedly favours the rich over the poor and, with only slightly less certainty, the salaried over the hourly-waged. But these essential biases are logically separate from the pure principle which may be sociologically connected to snobbery but does not require it. The fictional character Alf Tupper was resolutely amateur and stereotypically working class. Before running he ate only fish and chips and often had to work all night as a welder to save his small business employer from bankruptcy.[3] Still he beat the 'toffs' against whom he had to race the next day. They lived in special colleges where they were able to concentrate on training for athletics. In other words, Alf was a much 'purer' amateur than his middle-class rivals. Being a Thames Waterman may be too good a preparation for rowing, but welding is surely of negative value in relation to middle-distance running. As a real life case one thinks of Don Thompson, who won a gold medal in the 1960 Olympics in Rome: he practised by walking on the spot in an over-heated bathroom in order to be prepared for the Italian summer.

There are important differences between the kinds of critical thinking which sociologists and historians apply to subjects like amateurism and a philosophical treatment of the subject. Typically, the sociologist sees a body of doctrine in its context as serving the interest of a group, as being structured into practice in a certain way. Of a society, for example, in which men are dominant over women, sociology shows how this structure works and how it serves male interests. This generates a 'critical' account of doctrines by portraying them as ideologies, functioning in the interests of some people and against the interests of others. Thus of a doctrine of male supremacy, the sociological account typically says that its claim to 'natural' status is merely a cover to the artificiality of the structures within which males are superior. By this method, philosophical questions, those in philosophy and political theory, are avoided almost entirely. Sociological accounts of doctrines do not make overt moral judgement about the doctrines and therefore do not have to clarify the ethical standpoint from which those judgements are made. Neither do they have to examine the viability of alternatives. In other words, their 'critical' accounts proceed without a clarification of the ethical standpoint from which criticism flows or any requirement that the institutions subjected to critical thinking are compared with alternatives. The really interesting question for political and ethical philosophers is surely, 'Do societies in which males are sharply differentiated from and dominant over females work better or worse (judged by one or several ethical standpoints) than societies in which this is not the case?' This is not a possible question for sociology, which seems to judge the bias implicit in existing social practices from the understated standard of some absolute and equitable set of arrangements, presumably derived from the 'enlightenment' values of liberty, equality, human right and happiness – as if these were compatible.

In politics there are both sociological and philosophical accounts of institutions: limited forms of democracy are shown to be limited by sociological accounts, but also defended as sustainable or compatible with other political values by political theorists. In the study of sport, however, the sociological method has been dominant. Therefore, in a philosophical sense, amateurism has not been taken seriously. Take, for example, one of the more bizarre manifestations of amateurism, the tradition of having amateur and professional players in the same English county cricket team, while naming the players differently (professionals just surnames, amateurs with initials) and, sometimes, requiring them to change in separate dressing rooms. The distinction was abolished in 1962, having been in existence for half a century. Until the 1950s it was almost invariably the case that only amateurs could become captain, a role which is far more important in cricket than in other team sports. The institution of amateurism – and particularly the amateur captain – in cricket must be understood in the setting of the English class system and, in particular, the notion of the 'officer class' which it contained. Such an understanding portrays the institution as antiquated and by implication unfair and restrictive of equality of opportunity. 'Ronnie' Burnet, for example, the last amateur captain of Yorkshire (in 1959) was allowed to select himself for the team despite a batting average of 11 (30 in professional cricket is the basic par, 40 a success). He was necessarily leaving out of the team some poor professional who was a better batsman. But who thinks the issue should be decided on grounds of fairness or equality of opportunity? Burnet's leadership won the county championship for Yorkshire and he was widely credited with having welded a highly fractious group of men into an effective, collective force.[4] Judged by consequences, in the world as it is, there is a case for an officer class, just as there is a case for empires which can treat local enmities as a *deus ex machina* from outside and above. A particular example of this argument will be presented *en passant* in the profile of Lionel Tennyson later in this book.

In the opening chapter I stated that the philosophical basis on which I would attempt to erect a defence of amateurism was utilitarian (in the philosophical sense). The appropriate form of utilitarianism is 'broad' and 'liberal', eschewing precise calculation in favour of a search for the most profound possible idea of happiness and a debate over its nature. Where would one look in academic writing from the last 50 years to find such a debate? The answer is not in ethical philosophy, where utilitarianism has been unfashionable since the 1960s, and such debate as there was has been preoccupied with traditional problems about the apparently counterintuitive consequences of the philosophy for our ideas of virtue and punishment. Nor is there much help from orthodox economics where concepts of benefit and advantages based on preference theory offer precise formulae at the cost of philosophical oversimplification. The most rewarding source is to be found in the words of a set of distinguished, though unorthodox, economists who philosophize about well-being rather than merely calculating it. I have called these 'the affluent society' economists and the principal figures are J.K. Galbraith, E.J. Mishan, Tibor Scitovsky and Fred Hirsch.[5]

The name that I have given them comes, in one respect, from the title of Galbraith's book but in another it comes from the period in which their ideas developed. This lasted from the period of high growth rates throughout the 'developed' world in the 1950s to the economic crisis created by OPEC's tripling of the price of oil in 1973. During this period it seemed as if traditional economic problems had been banished by Keynesian solutions; there was full employment and constant growth. The 'affluent society' concern was twofold: did these solutions actually produce the benefits that we might expect? And what did they cost in terms of such goods as landscape, community, culture and family structure? In all cases they are unafraid to write with great rigour: Galbraith's description of a prosperous working-class family setting out from the city in a brand new automobile to discover a polluted and littered landscape of advertising hoardings and electricity pylons to which they have little access is a return of economics to the level of literary achievement at which Adam Smith originally placed it.

Scitovsky argues that our problem is an intellectual one: we have forgotten how to debate happiness properly. In the eighteenth century such writers as Hutcheson, Hume and even Bentham tackled sophisticated problems about the nature and forms of happiness, whereas we tend to simplify it into the precise forms of economic growth and cost-benefit analysis. His own principal distinction is between 'comfort' and 'culture'. Comfort is a primarily negative goal, the removal of irritations such as excessive heat and cold, the need to exert oneself or having to deal with boring or embarrassing people. Culture, on the other hand, consists of those goals which give meaning and a sense of achievement, which often establish relationships between us and people or places. The 'joyless economy' (meaning the economic achievement and direction of the United States) is very good at providing comfort, but poor at, even obstructive of, culture. It is interesting to note that despite Scitovsky's enormous distinction – he is, among other achievements, a Nobel Laureate – this aspect of his work is almost ignored in departments of economics. It is hardly surprising though, since in some respects it undermines the entire foundations of the subject.

Although Scitovsky is not interested in the sporting applications of this approach, they seemed obvious to me when I read the book. It is comfortable to watch football from an executive box, avoiding the smells, dangers and offensive language of the terraces. But to support your team on the terraces (this was the 1970s) creates a greater sense of being part of a collective and even of having lived. It is comfortable to confine one's interest in cricket to a good quality television and, perhaps, a collection of videos. But you might have a much greater sense of achievement if you are prepared to put some effort into keeping your local cricket club in being.

The following table illustrates the different destinations made by the four economists:

	Affluence increases	**Affluence fails to increase**
Galbraith:	private goods (motor cars, consumer desirables)	public and free goods ('unspoiled' landscape, clean air, secure urban environment)
Scitovsky:	comfort (air-conditioning, fast food, drive-ins, all of which remove irritations and wastage of time)	culture (creative skills, sense of community, successful family life, all of which give meaning and a sense of belonging)
Mishan:	maximization of 'internal' revenues and minimization of 'internal' costs ('exchangeable' and 'material' goods)	maximization of 'external' benefits and minimization of 'internal" costs (silence, 'unspoiled' landscapes and townscapes)
Hirsch:	material goods (travel, computers, cars, restaurants)	positional goods (places worth travelling to, cars and houses which carry status, university degrees which carry kudos)

Because of diminishing returns it is the case that as affluence increases the scarcer types of goods become more important in relation to happiness. Thus there are clear limits to the human benefits of successful commercialization which become more obvious and more important in an 'affluent' society. Scitovsky's distinction, expressed in terms of sport, for example, suggests a society in which we could watch the highest level of sport in comfort on excellent televisions virtually 24 hours a day, but in which the 'atmosphere' of stadiums and the number of participating and communal activities (like village cricket) was in decline. A society in which the supply of *all* of the typical affluence goods was continuing to increase and all of the others to diminish suggests some kind of grand composite of twentieth-century literary and artistic nightmares of commercialism: a lonely, drug-ridden, air-conditioned megalopolis.

All these economic arguments suggest that we should be sceptical about national income accounting – about any attempts to measure economic growth and prosperity – and should accept that it is a consequence of the law of diminishing marginal utility that the relationship between prosperity and happiness decreases as prosperity increases. The relevance to amateurism becomes readily apparent if we consider an argument from 'classical' economics, in this case taken from the most successful economics textbook in history. Kenneth Boulding's explication of 'The Principle of Comparative Advantage' is, in an important respect, the equal and opposite of Marx's considerations on work under capitalism and communism which I quoted previously. Boulding demonstrates how a doctor whose labour is worth $5 an hour will create greater wealth by extra doctoring and by employing a gardener to tend to his garden, whose labour is worth 30c an hour, even though the doctor is the better gardener:

> By working at his profession, however, for eleven minutes, he will have earned enough to pay for three hours of the hired man's time. Consequently he can do his gardening in eleven minutes by staying in his office, as against the hour it would take him if he were out in the garden itself! In this particular case the situation may be complicated by the fact that the doctor may like gardening for its own sake. But this complication does not affect the general principle. If the doctor is fond of gardening he may prefer an hour of direct gardening to eleven minutes of indirect gardening, but it remains true that for him medical practice may be an indirect form of horticulture.[6]

Boulding avoids saying that it is 'better' for the doctor not to garden. But it is clear that the logic of a society which follows the principles of specialization and exchange suggests that the aggregate of income increases if the doctor stays out of the garden and that all our measurements of 'growth' and 'prosperity' register higher if he does so. Hirsch applies a sceptical analysis of our preoccupation with growth and his own conception of the 'duality in the growth potential';[7] his argument also suggests that the doctor's gains may be largely part of a 'zero-sum game' in so far as his gains in status and scarce resources – the possession of 'positional goods' – may be effectively at the cost of somebody else not gaining such goods. For Scitovsky the gardening may be a 'cultural' activity which gives joy and meaning to the doctor's life and bonds him to his own Earth. For Mishan, Boulding's argument fails to take account of external benefits to the economy, such as the effect of the doctor's own health and the visual quality of the garden (since he is a better gardener in any case). This might be paralleled by Galbraith's concern for 'public' and 'free' goods though, it is only fair to point out, contemporary economic theories and calculations take much more account of 'externalities' of cost and benefit than was the case when Boulding was writing.

I guess that when faced with the lifestyles suggested (though, in neither case, prescribed) by classical economics and the early Marx, most of us would favour Marx. But since Marx can offer us nothing by way of a remedy except a radical transformation of society which involves the abandoning of all the advantages of the market most of us lose any enthusiasm for him. Hirsch, on the other hand, offers a critique which is potentially more practical of what he calls 'the commercialisation bias'.[8]

Commodity Fetishism

All our concepts of prosperity and many of our attributions of status suggest that when Saturday comes the accountant should put aside thoughts of cricket and do some more accountancy in order to be able to accrue more wealth and own more prestigious goods. On the other hand, in terms of 'culture' in Scitovsky's sense (and therefore 'utility' in its broadest sense) batting number eight for the village cricket team may be the one meaningful thing that he does.

Manic Instrumentality

Fred Hirsch, sadly, did not live to see the expression 'quality time' become part of the English language, but its existence could be predicted from his analysis. Increasingly, from the 1980s, people in Western society have lived more functional, instrumental lives, pursuing activities which are means-to-an-end rather than ends-in-themselves, leaving only a little residue for 'quality time'. As I have demonstrated elsewhere, the 'leisure age' has never arrived, even though a substantial proportion of the population holiday much more than in the past and we are much less bound by domestic chores.[9] The ends–means distinction must not be conceived as equivalent to a distinction between production and consumption. It is important to Hirsch's argument that much consumption is partly, even largely, instrumental: we have to go on holiday to meet a norm. He draws on the work of Staffan Linder to show that the leisured class are under much more pressure to use their leisure efficiently in terms of status when compared with the idle rich in previous ages.[10]

There may, of course, be a supremely ironical aspect to modern instrumentality which is that in one transcending dimension – that of health – it might be better to avoid instrumentality – and certainly manic instrumentality – wherever possible in favour of doing what comes naturally: eating, drinking, making love and taking the sheer joy which is available from the eternal business of looking after one's own children. Scitovsky resorts to the idea of a 'puritan ghost' in American culture to explain the 'joyless' instrumentality of many aspects of American life. It is certainly true that the lists of best-selling books in the United States seem to contain many more books about how to achieve than books about how to live well.

Excessive Self-interest

A self-consciousness about pleasure is often said to diminish the possibility of pleasure. (As John Stuart Mill put it, 'Ask yourself if you are truly happy and you cease to be so.')[11] It is equally true (even in the formal context of game theory) that it can be counterproductive to pursue one's own interests too relentlessly. Good societies contain large amounts of trust, mutuality and reciprocity which amount to systems of altruism or communities. Perhaps this can be best illustrated, as Hirsch suggests, by talking about sex.

The Significance of Amateur Sex

There is a general agreement that sex is an important aspect of human happiness and that it ought not to be subjected to full commercialism and professionalization.[12] However, the traditional ideal of love and marriage is ludicrously inefficient by commercial standards. As Hirsch says, 'It requires the double coincidence of pure barter in which the buyer has to find a seller who not only has what he wants, but also wants what he has ...'[13] Faithful, loving marriage is a lousy system commercially while prostitution could be organized efficiently (and properly accounted as part of the gross domestic product).

What is it about sex that makes this suggestion risible and equates it with Jonathan Swift's 'modest proposal' that Irish babies should be sold as meat? It is essentially that the mere gratification of a physical desire seems to be the trivial dimension of sex. What makes it 'ethereal', as Hirsch puts it, removing it from a (very) low pleasure to a (very) high one in Mill's terms, is *romance*. In economic terms, romance blurs the distinction between supply and demand, between the self and the other and between means and ends. The distinctions thus blurred, we can enter a realm of meaning and excitement which is closed to the mere consumer: one must cease to be a consumer in order to attain a higher form of consumption. (The structure of this argument is recognizably Buddhist and paralleled in some respects to E.F. Schumacher's call for a 'Buddhist economics.')[14]

Although in Western societies we do retain the romantic idea of loving marriage, we have also (as Hirsch is keen to point out) tended to 'commodify' sex and to subject it to a relentlessly consumerist appraisal. How much have you had and how good was it? *The Good Sex Guide* lies alongside *The Good Food Guide* on the coffee table. Hirsch noted (even in the 1970s) the preoccupation of women's magazines with the physical sensation of orgasm – mysteriously treated by society as a much more important and respectable subject than the male orgasm – and commented, 'Orgasm as a consumer's right rather rules it out as an ethereal experience.'[15]

The Romance of Sport

It is often assumed that romance in this sense is a dimension only of sexual relations. Popular versions of neo-liberalism generally say that sport is a mere 'taste' among others, an activity which must stand or fall by commercial criteria, but this argument is not normally extended to a defence of prostitution. Whereas sport can be consumed, as a product, it clearly has, for many people, a kind of meaning quite different from that of mere acts of consumption. Consider four cases of involvement with sport:

1. *The football fan as consumer.* He or she watches the highest quality football and admires the skills and drama of the game. The season ticket at a top division club is a source of status and conversation, parallel to skiing holidays and meals in prestigious restaurants. If the quality declines or is seen to be below the highest standards the attraction of these other goods increases at the expense of football.[16]
2. *The football fan as romantic.* He or she watches the same team for a lifetime irrespective of the level or quality of the football. Only rarely is being a fan a source of pleasure (in any obvious sense) or status; often it is a source of pain and humiliation. Support is involuntary, an imperative rather than a taste. But it gives an extra dimension of meaning to life, arising out of a sense of being part of a community and of involvement in a story which began before the fan's birth and, it is hoped, will never end.
3. *The village cricketer as consumer.* Village cricket is a good with a 'rural' status like four-wheel drive vehicles, shooting jackets and thatched cottages. The consumer wears all these badges of rurality and, having paid his club subscription, expects a fair share of participation, such as a place in the first seven of the batting order and a few overs with the ball. He is likely to become disillusioned with cricket quite quickly if not offered a sufficient share of the action.

4. *The village cricketer as romantic.* For a certain kind of cricketer the purpose of cricket is *membership* of the team, the club and of the wider cricketing community. There is sensuous pleasure in everything that is symbolic of cricket: the sound of bat on ball, the smell of a newly-mown field, even in the sight of a distant game seen from the motorway. Achievement within the game is not a source of status but a necessary condition of continued membership and the survival of the institution.

The contrast in these cases is not between professional and amateur, but between two forms of what is, in the ordinary sense, amateur, but one of which is far more amateur in the etymological and philosophical sense than the other. The contrast is with commercialism rather than professionalism. It is important to note that romanticism in this sense overlaps with communalism and creates a sense of property rights which exist separately from, and in contradistinction to, the system of ownership which underlies a system of commercial relations. We perceive the communal rights in landscape: though the countryside is overwhelmingly privately owned, we feel ourselves to have a legitimate interest in it which is represented by such institutions as rights of way and the nationalization of development rights. Thus the Forests of Pendle and Bowland are in some sense 'mine' even though I do not own so much as a bramble bush in them. But this sense of property is also the origin of objections to the 'privatization' of sports television, the removal of a 'free to air' status which everybody could share provided that they could see a set. Both landscape and sport are communal in these respects because they are romantic goods rather than mere consumer goods; the analogy seems quite precise when governments talk of 'listing' the 'crown jewels' of sport.

Alienated Gardening

Consider the following attitudes to gardening: gardener *A* lives in England and loves his small kitchen garden. He is intensely proud of the herbs, flowers and salads he produces in it. It is a great pleasure to sit in it when it is well ordered and he boasts that he will take the taste of the first picking of asparagus, steamed within seconds of being cut, with him to his grave and die with a smile on his face. His produce is worth many times its market value to him. Every morning he goes into his garden when he first wakes up and notes that each day it is slightly different. The garden is there to add to pleasure when things are going well and to console when they are going badly.

Gardener *B* lives in the former Soviet Union. He looks at his hands, grimy from working his mother-in-law's hectare of land on what was a collective farm and says, 'My God, I hate soil.' He explains that he hates it because it represents what has happened to his life: his academic salary is now about worthless since the Soviet system collapsed and in order to be sure that he, his wife and their children have food he has to grow it himself using primitive technology. He knows gardener *A* and regards his attitude to gardening as sentimental; what gardener *A* has which is valuable is a salary in hard currency and access to a supermarket.

Gardener *C* maintains the grounds around the headquarters of a transnational company. He would not admit to actually liking the work, but he certainly prefers it to his previous employment in a car factory. He does not much like his employers, who, as an institution, have a tendency to rediscover their grounds from time to time and come up with new and urgent policies with respect to them.

Gardener *D* is not a gardener at all, but a consumer of his own garden. He is a busy and prosperous Californian who employs a firm of Japanese specialists to keep his grounds in order: he himself swims in the pool, sits and reads sometimes, holds parties and barbecues and occasionally picks a lemon from the tree to put in drinks. He, too, knows gardener *A* who joshes him in respect of the Japanese specialist gardeners by asking him what is the ethnic background of the firm that he employs to make love to his wife.

Marx's concept of alienation is both too simple and too complex in respect of the relation to work of these four gardeners. It is too complex because of the Hegelian philosophical baggage which it brings with it and too simple because it fails to comprehend the range of different factors which account for the extent to which we can identify with the object of our labours and get satisfaction from production. Gardener *B* ought to be the least 'alienated' because he is working to provide necessities for his family on land which he controls in conditions which are due to anarchy. Yet he loathes both the work and the land and yearns with bitter nostalgia for the division of labour, the right to specialize, which kept his hands clean. Gardener *D* has accepted the full benefits of capitalist comparative advantage: he likes his garden, but merely as a consumer. He is in some respects alienated from it, but is quite happy about the psychological distance. Gardener *C* is relatively but not absolutely alienated from his labour in psychological terms. But it is gardener *A*, the amateur, who has a rapport with his land and for whom it is a hobby. He has achieved, at least in a small corner, the 'labour of love', where production is also a form of consumption which is the predominant feature of the English vision of future communism portrayed in William Morris's *News from Nowhere*;[17] a society in which everyone pursues hobbies and thereby produces enough for subsistence while leading fully satisfying lives.

In utilitarian terms the suggested prescription which I draw from the tale of the four gardeners is of a commercial society which is not obsessed with maximizing production and which urges constraint on individual ambition, which leaves us relatively free from structures of authority but also from market forces which appear to give us no choice – whether it is providing material necessities, like Gardener *D* or status consumption like the Hirsch-Linder harried leisure class.

Alienated Play

In considering the direct implications for sport I must, in honesty, report an example which may be at one of the roots of the motivation for writing this book. In 1968, after a dozen seasons playing rugby at boarding school and university, I joined a reasonably successful local football club and found myself in a team most of whom had been attached to professional football clubs before being 'released' in their late teens. It was a sad and illuminating experience. In a very real sense the players hated football (though they may also have loved it as well). It was a constant source of irritation and frustration for them: they cheated, whinged, quarrelled and postured their way through games. What they hated was *not* being professionals, not playing with better players and in front of a crowd, not being able to train properly. The problem was that they could not enjoy football because it was their principal source of self-esteem. We had been taught the Arnoldian virtues of discipline, loyalty and knowing one's place. These had made rugby very important, but without emphasizing either individual or collective success. Paradoxically, at both school and university we had, in important ways, been far more professional than the footballers because we were able to train throughout the season, during the day and work out our tactics and set plays.

This set up a suspicion that professional team sports are not the dreamworld that most of us believed them to be in our youth. How can you have a team, a real team, when a player's loyalty must ultimately be not to the club or the old school, but to his career? Is it not like the old joke about the young Member of Parliament who refers to the Opposition as the 'enemy' only to be told by an older Member that the Opposition are merely the opposition: your own party are invariably the real enemy because they are your rivals for favours and advancement? Is it not the case that professional players, however highly paid, are mere rival instruments, of little interest to their employer when they are injured or rejected? The aftermath of the 'big bang' transition of Rugby Union from amateurism to professionalism has produced many people who will answer these questions in the affirmative. Arthur Holmes, the Chairman of Bristol Rugby Club, commented, when his club was on the verge of bankruptcy in 1998,

> I'm sickened by professionalism. What you have now is a load of mercenaries. They have no loyalty to any club and they are getting far too much. They are bored out of their tiny minds by full-time training and they'd be far better off as part-time professionals.[18]

A similar view was expressed by Austin Healey of Leicester and England,

> When I was at college and the weekend came round it was a case of 'brilliant, we've got a match'. Now it's more like, 'Oh right, yeah, we've got another game.' [My girlfriend Louise] reckons since I became a professional Rugby player our sex-life has decreased by about 100 per cent.[19]

Of course, this is only one view, a dimension of experience which has to be put against the often-expressed sentiment by professional players that, 'It's wonderful to be paid to do the thing you love.' But there can be no doubt that there is a systematic bias in all forms of expression – autobiographies and interviews in different media – from professional sportsmen in favour of the favourable side of the experience simply because it is the successful and those on form who are heard. Only recently and in a tiny proportion has the 'journeyman' been heard and the failures are still silent and likely to remain so. Simon Barnes, reviewing Gary Nelson's *Left Foot in the Grave*, one of the first books by an 'ordinary' professional footballer, comments that, 'Fear is Nelson's companion, fear lit with occasional shafts of relief. And that is what sport is about.'[20]

Fear, not joy. The suggestion is that professional sport is a good hobby spoiled, that the utilitarian theory of alienation applied to gardening applies at least as well to sport. It is a theory which must be put against a range of detailed experiences of professional and amateur sport.

PART II

'The Lived Experience'

1

Introduction

The purpose of this section of the book is to compare the ideas about amateurism gained from the library, so to speak, with the personal testimony of people who had in some way or another operated in the borderlands of amateurism and professionalism or on both sides of the border at different times. Martin Roderick was keen to suggest that this testimony might add something different, not suspecting at the time of his suggestion that he would be one of the people whom I would seek to interview. The most obvious sources were Rugby Union and track and field athletics, both of which had made the transition as a whole, but cricket and golf have had their own distinctive ways of interpreting the relationship between professionalism and amateurism, and Association Football and American sport both proved richer sources than I would have imagined.

The decision to interview raises the questions of 'methodology' as they are urgently discussed in graduate schools and research seminars across the globe. Of course, one can learn from talking to people, but unless one does a full sample survey of 1,200 people answering the same questions then there is no guarantee that what you learn will be typical of anything. Mercifully, this technique is now fairly unfashionable in academic study because, although its statistical reliability has been refined, it has been at the cost of recognizing that sample surveys can give the truth only about superficial, well-defined opinions: they can find out how many people would vote for Party X tomorrow, if they voted, but not whether they would really vote nor why.

So one must interview in greater depth, sacrificing any pretensions that answers are necessarily typical or even classifiable. There is no guarantee, of course, that answers will be honest or, if honest, realistic. A question and answer session with the interviewer writing the answers down and using a tape recorder might be the worst possible source of information on (say) a person's ambitions or sexual desires. Should one merely fit interview material alongside other sources of information into the argument or should it be presented separately?

'Ethnographic' sociologists (to whom the expression 'lived experience' is a mildly ironic reference) tend to produce a narrative of anonymous individuals. I see no advantage *per se* in anonymity and I am also concerned that it gives an unfortunate impression of a claim to typicality ('Rugby coach, England', 'Sports official, United States'). Anonymity may be necessary, however, in order to be able to quote people as saying things which are important testimony, but which they would not want to be on record as having said.

My own intuitive response to these methodological questions was that I wanted to use the testimony of real, named individuals who would speak only for themselves and not be portrayed as typical of anything. I wanted to put their experiences and ideas in a form that they would sign for, so to speak. The interviews should be conducted around some broad themes, but never structured to the degree that the survey of cricket officials which I had earlier conducted was structured. The themes should concern what it felt like to be an amateur and a professional, what the transition felt like and the extent to which money changed perceptions and relationships. In short, I wanted to use the methods of serious journalism with a high degree of integrity and regarded my subjects as individuals, interesting in themselves. Fortunately, they all proved to be honest and clear-minded individuals, though this was not entirely providential because most of them were selected in advance, on the grounds that I knew they had these qualities.

If these 'research design' choices were fairly straightforward so far as I was concerned, there was one methodological issue which raised many more doubts. This was the already familiar question of cultural geography: where was one talking about when one talked about amateurism? In one sense it was England (in that the concept arose out of specifically English conditions) and in another sense the world (since much of the world acknowledged the formal hegemony of amateurism for most sport through the Olympic movement). But between the cultural importance of amateurism in the history of the English middle classes and its formal, often reluctant, acceptance in most of the world lay a plethora of meanings, values and practices. I could to some extent escape the question by saying that I was mainly interested in English conceptions in any case, that I was not claiming that my subjects were typical of anything and that most of them operated on a global stage. But the question still troubled me: with my established contacts in the former Soviet Union, should I not include 'amateur' athletes developed in that system?

In the end, I rejected that possibility. My previous experience of interviewing in Georgia suggested that my questions would not be fully understood. I had, with what turned out to be naïve optimism, asked people involved in Georgian sport whether there was a development of the voluntary principle and a sporting civil society to replace the near-collapse of the state. The inference I drew from the consequent misunderstandings was that Soviet athletes were essentially 'hungry fighters' operating within an authoritarian system. That system selected and honed intensely ambitious athletes within a framework of an equally intense, collective purpose. No system of sport was more purely gladiatorial and less amateur than the Soviet system. One of its most famous products, the gymnast Olga Korbut, has spoken of how the *joie de vivre* which Western journalists remarked in her performance in the 1972 Olympic Games was an act deliberately created to mask a system which starved and sexually abused her and was prepared to risk maiming her. More than a quarter of a century later, Ms Korbut still has no conception that sport might be a lighter, secondary side to life. She talks approvingly of the Spartan regime to which she was subjected and rejects the idea that gymnastics can be anything other than a total commitment: 'But you must have a goal. Every day, you must think only of your ambition. Otherwise, you will soon find you have fallen behind.' Of her own current life she says, 'I don't have time to enjoy myself. I have no friends. I must work and take care of my family.' She was not even an amateur in the most narrow negative sense, being paid DM900 per gold medal, money which was spent on 'a ring, a gold watch and a fur coat'.[1]

This may not be entirely the whole story. Although most academic writing about Soviet sport stresses the gladiatorial intensity encouraged by the system[2] there are hints of a more complex conception of sport in Jim Riordan's account of the life of Nikolai Starostin, one of four talented sporting brothers born in the early part of the twentieth century.[3] The Starostins played football and ice hockey at the highest levels for Spartak teams, but Nikolai fell foul of Laventi Beria, head of the security forces and honorary president of the Dinamo club. As a result, he spent ten years in Siberian camps. One interpretation of Starostin's career is that the Spartak clubs had absorbed some independent sporting values, whereas for Dinamo victory and prestige (even achieved by corrupt and coercive methods) were everything. Certainly, Nikolai Starostin, who survived into the post-Soviet period, was keen to stress that he had always believed in football as part of the all-round development of the personality, but that late Soviet commercialism encouraged an even narrower speculation than did the Soviet system. He commented in his autobiography that, 'It always astonishes me that today's players seem to have no interest beyond video and rock cassettes. I believe wholeheartedly that you cannot separate culture from soccer; a soccer cognoscente [*sic*] must be an art cognoscente at the same time.'[4] There are some suggestions that the official Cuban view of sport is much closer to Starostin's conception than was the Soviet system.[5]

The Japanese case is more complicated and in many respects more interesting. The Japanese Amateur Athletics Association regulated all amateur sports from its inception in 1911 until what was effectively a military takeover in 1941. A successor organization, the Japanese Amateur Sports Association was established by the occupying forces in 1948. The JAAA in two major respects took over the English conception of amateurism: it banned payment and encouraged social exclusivity. Having said that, the concept worked very differently in a Japanese setting. For one thing, no clear Japanese meaning of 'amateur' became established, but a range of concepts were used to distinguish amateur sport from professional, including 'sport', 'general sport', 'honourable poverty', 'uprightness' and 'unscathed integrity'. Moreover, according to Japanese scholarship, the English conceptions of 'pleasure', 'recreation', 'leisure' and 'amusement', which all featured in early English definitions of amateurism, were replaced by conceptions drawing on the Japanese tradition of *bushido*, the 'code' of the Samurai. Thus, according to Murao, the concept of 'play' is absent from Japanese conceptions of sport and is replaced by the concept of a preparedness for death.[6] The *do* in *bushido* means 'way' or 'path'; as in judo and kendo the assumption is not of a diversion or amusement, but of a way of life, a route to transcendental self-improvement.

On the one hand we might remark that there could be no contrast more sharp than that between *bushido* and the studious frivolity of Lionel Tennyson, a profile of whom appears below. On the other hand, the contrast may not be as sharp as all that: is there not an analogue to *bushido* in the sporting attitudes of public school literature and muscular Christianity? Might not Lord Tennyson have been closer to *bushido* than his determined frivolity would ever allow us to know? Amateurism remains a complex concept interpreted in a wide variety of cultures. In this sense, it resembles 'democracy', which also achieved a formal global intellectual hegemony after 1945, but which meant many different things in different cultures.

Amateurism in Japanese rugby is essentially a tale of two institutions, the university and the company. The first rugby was played at the end of the nineteenth century at Keio University, an exclusive and wealthy institution which was soon to find itself in a dispute with poorer institutions over the 'impurity' of taking gate money at matches. But the principal development of the game in the second half of the twentieth century has been in company teams, creating an intensely competitive contest where the player's career is very much bound up with his performance on the field. In these respects Japanese rugby looks to be 'shamateur' in the way that northern English rugby before the schism of 1895 was accused of 'shamateurism' and Welsh and French rugby have allegedly been shamateur for most of the twentieth century. On the other hand, Hiroyuki Ishii's interviews with contemporary Japanese rugby players reveal an enthusiasm for the game and a sense that it is something extra which can add meaning to life; it is this real sense of amateurism and a love of the game which contrasts sharply with *bushido* or the fanatical devotions of an Olga Korbut. At the same time, a New Zealand international player with experience in Japanese rugby was keen to suggest that it was in many ways amateur and amateurish compared with Japanese soccer or New Zealand rugby.

It is important to register the breadth, diversity and complexity of the experience of amateurism before focusing more narrowly on the experience of a selection of anglophone sportsmen and women for whom amateurism has been an issue. What follows is eight profiles, six of individuals, one of a family and one of an institution. Six of the profiles consist principally of interviews, the other two do not (unless I am allowed 'interview' in a bizarre and extended sense). The concentration is on a generation of English people with wide international experiences and who lived through the decline of amateurism, though there is one foray into the past and one across the Atlantic.

There are a number of issues which I would like to have covered, but have not. One is the apparent symbiosis which exists between amateurs and professionals as separate categories in some sports, especially golf. Another is the issue of 'amateur' referees in professional football, unpaid or relatively lowly paid officials, who make split-second decisions which can cost others millions. Much writing on corruption in police forces might suggest that they should be reasonably rewarded to protect them from bribery. Conversely, public choice theory might be taken to imply that the last referee you would want is someone who is making a career out of the activity, who will behave fearfully and slavishly to the latest directive and the whim of the powerful individual. One might infer that referees, like British spies before 1939, should be unpaid, since one would not want the sort of person making important decisions who would need or want to be paid. But this issue, interesting though it is, is really a side-issue in comparison to the main themes which follow.

2

His Lordship: Scrapes and Japes

Lionel Hallam Tennyson, third Baron Tennyson, was born in 1889. He first played competitive cricket for a junior side at Melbourne Grammar School when his father was the first Governor-General of the Australian Federation. He went on to play for Eton, the army, Hampshire, the Marylebone Cricket Club (MCC) and England. He captained Hampshire from 1919 to 1933. Perhaps his most famous feats were achieved in a hopeless rearguard action against Australia in 1921. His resistance was the fiercest from what was regarded as the weakest England team to that point. He scored 74 not out in the second test, but ran out of partners, and, as captain, he scored 63 and 36 in the third test despite acute pain from a hand injury which left him batting one-handed much of the time. He had originally been primarily a bowler, but for most of his cricket career he was a hard-hitting batsman, scoring 16,828 runs at an average of 23.63.

Lionel Tennyson was an aristocrat, albeit an unusual one from a recently ennobled family, his grandfather Alfred being perhaps the only man to achieve both fortune and the highest rank as a poet. The title came into existence in 1884 and Lionel succeeded to it in 1928. He was brought up in two country houses, Farringford in the Isle of Wight and Aldworth in Surrey. His father devoted most of his life to the memory and achievements of his own father.[1]

Tennyson's only profession was as a soldier, starting in the Coldstream Guards in 1911, but transferring after a year to the Rifle Brigade in which he served for the whole of the First World War, being wounded three times and mentioned in despatches twice. He was colonel of the 51st (London) Anti-Aircraft Brigade Territorial Artillery and in the Second World War was re-employed with the Royal Naval Air Arm. This account of his career and beliefs is based on the standard sources plus the memoir that he published a year before his death in 1951, Sticky Wickets.[2]

To use the terminology of his time, Lionel Tennyson's life was a saga of japes and scrapes. On the jape side he infuriated his father by dressing up his grandfather's bust and putting a cigarette in the mouth; he pushed Winston Churchill in full morning dress into the Thames (finding the fully dressed MP, fresh from Parliament, an irresistible target – Churchill appears to have taken it in good part) and he held a very lively Christmas party in the Tower of London while supposedly guarding it in 1909. Scrapes included being held at pistol point by a manically jealous husband in Chicago, finding himself part of a lynch mob of 8,000 people in San Jose, California, being rushed by a panic-stricken crowd in India while playing cricket as the pavilion collapsed in an earthquake and being more likely to die than not as a V1 'doodlebug' fell from the sky in London in the later stages of the Second World War.

There were also serious financial problems. Indeed, Tennyson seems to have had little grasp of elementary financial management. *Sticky Wickets* was written because he was 'broke' and in that condition partly because of the Labour government and partly because of 'an unjustified optimism in the probabilities that racehorses will do what is expected of them'.[3] But 30 years earlier he had agreed with his father on a transfer to the Rifle Brigade because he had just lost £12,000 in a week at the races, leaving him £7,000 in debt.

The scrapes and japes are described in detail. However, Tennyson's lip remains stiff on the question of his war record and on his divorce from his first wife (the Hon. Clarissa Tennant) in 1928 and his remarriage to Mrs J.W. Donner (an American) in 1934; such incidents would surely have been the centrepieces of a contemporary autobiography.

Tennyson's social and political views were conservative, with both a large and a small 'c'. He seems to have assumed the essential rightness and naturalness of global arrangements as they existed in late Victorian times. However, this conservatism, as often in England, was combined with a liberalism in several senses. In 1899, *en route* with his family to Australia, seeing slaves being taken from Africa to Arabia (and invoking the family poetic tradition) he had urges to write an 'Ode to Liberty'. Prohibition caused him to reflect on the futility of governments' attempts to control people's lives and his experiences of the Second World War led him to reflect on the untapped potential of women and their essential equality with men. He was also a rebel, rather than an 'establishment' man, a peer who never spoke in the House of Lords and a noble captain of England who was never on the committee of the MCC.

Under these circumstances we might expect Tennyson to be the classic exponent of the amateur-elite outlook, or at least the particular version of it existing in cricket, whereby amateurs and professionals took the field together. Undoubtedly, he assumed the propriety of an amateur–professional distinction, treating it as a 'given' of caste, as it were. He specifically argues in favour of the practice of the England captain being an amateur, one that only just outlived him.[4] In so far as he advances an argument for this position, it is that when it comes to dealing with the inevitable frustrations and rivalries in a cricket touring party (and the corresponding wives),[5] it is better to be an outsider, an officer and a gentleman, rather than one of the career professionals.

It is important to explain to those unfamiliar with cricket that the position of the captain is unique in team sport. He must decide who bats or bowls in any particular circumstance and where people field. Therefore he must have considerable say about who is in the team. His role naturally and necessarily pre-empts that of a manager or coach: this is true even now, when managers and coaches do exist. Thus there is a strong case, as an application of what would now be called 'public choice' theory, for the independence of the occupant of the role, as with the theories of officer classes, imperial stability or management consultancy. As recently as the early 1980s the England team was captained by Mike Brearley. Some would that say he was the finest of England captains and he succeeded in such diverse feats as winning the 'Ashes' against Australia in 1981 and taking England to the second World Cup Final in 1979. He was not an amateur, since they no longer existed in first-class cricket, but he has nearly all the features of the traditional amateur captain, being brought into professional cricket from an academic career and playing for England even though most people thought he would not merit selection merely as a player.

Tennyson often expressed liking and respect for his team-mates who were professionals. He was proud that he was the first captain to lead professionals and amateurs out at Lords through the same gate, commenting to the MCC President who objected, that 'if they were good enough to play on the same ground as me, they were certainly good enough to come out through the same gate.'[6] He welcomed the change in practice whereby the two categories shared the same dressing-room. He appears to have been well liked by professional players and would hardly have lasted 14 years as a county captain if he had not. In these respects he was far, naturally, from the Olympian assumptions of an Avery Brundage that professionalism was unacceptable, as any first-class amateur cricketer must be. He had few scruples about trying to cash his status as a cricketer: for example, he wrote a set of verses to celebrate the success of Percy Chapman's XI in Australia in 1929. They end,

> And how, defying even fate
> They fought and turned the game again
> Therefore from those who watch and wait,
> A health to Chapman and his men.

In negotiation with the representative of the editor of a 'well-known national newspaper', Tennyson demanded £100 for his verses.

> 'A hundred pounds!', exclaimed my friend. 'A hundred pounds. My dear Lionel, that's more than your respected grandfather ever got; more than Mr Rudyard Kipling gets; and incidentally 20 times as much as

the poet Milton got for writing the whole of Paradise Lost.' 'That may be so', said I, 'but none of them ever captained England at cricket, and when did one captain of an England eleven ever before write a poem in honour of another captain of an England eleven? My dear fellow, these verses are unique in English literature.'[7]

In fact, the editor offered Tennyson £50 which he proudly refused; he should have employed an agent. But it does not seem to have occurred to him that the business of trying to cash one's sporting status, a big issue for protagonists of pure amateurism in the Olympic movement and the Rugby Union, was really an issue at all.

But what about the true spirit of amateurism rather than the technical issue of payment? Tennyson quotes with approval Bernard Darwin's remark that 'the best way of playing cricket was not necessarily the best way of winning Test Matches'.[8] He claims that 'Cricket, however, has more in it than mere efficiency. There is something called the spirit of cricket, which cannot be defined',[9] and that 'There also is an outlook which is peculiar to cricket...Many other countries have taken up English games and reached to, or even above, the English standard of efficiency, without learning and practising the English outlook.'[10] This sounds as if he leaned towards the Bishop of Pennsylvania rather than Vince Lombardi on the question of the importance of winning.

But the matter is much more complicated than that. Tennyson was a great defender of Jardine, Voce and Larwood. Cricket followers will be almost excessively familiar with this particular story, but I shall offer a brief explanation for those not versed in the game.[11] Douglas Jardine was the (amateur) captain of the England tour to Australia in 1932–33 and Bill Voce and Harold Larwood were his leading (Nottinghamshire professional) fast bowlers. Jardine devised a tactic of 'body-line' bowling in which the two fast bowlers would direct the ball on the 'leg' side of the stumps, at the upper part of the batsmen's body, concentrating fielders on the area where the ball must go when he defended himself. The tactic was designed to counteract some brilliant Australian batsmen, particularly Donald Bradman. It necessarily resulted (in almost everybody's view except Jardine's) in the batsman being hit regularly on the upper part of the body. The resulting ill-feeling between the two countries reached governmental level and perhaps ranks only below the Honduras–El Salvador 'soccer war' of 1969 as an example of sport creating enmity between two countries. In 1934 the MCC effectively conceded the rightness of the Australian case, ruling against 'the type of bowling regarded as a direct attack by the bowler upon the batsman and therefore unfair'.[12] The three main protagonists lost favour with the selectors.

Jardine always had his passionate supporters and Tennyson was one of them. That the 'jovial' Governor-General's son, who usually acted and spoke as if he believed that when it came to cricket – and particularly to cricket tours – there were many considerations at least as important as winning, should be such an ardent supporter of the 'body-line' trio and a fervent opponent of the MCC for not backing them, is a surprise. Correspondingly he found Norman Yardley (who captained the unsuccessful England effort against Australia in 1948) 'too nice'.[13]

Is there a resolution of the apparent contradiction between the noble amateur who talks, as one would expect him to, about the spirit of the game, but wholeheartedly supports its supposedly most famous exponent of the ethos of winning at any cost? Perhaps Tennyson's views were just an incoherent mixture of his natural conservatism and the normal tension between the value code of a game (especially of cricket) and the desire to win.[14] A strong desire to win is naturally corrosive of the code because it can be countered only by a version of itself: Yardley was specifically 'too nice' to deal with the 'ruthless' Bradman. Many a cricket captain (as well as leaders in other fields) has put the code of values on hold because he believes the opposition are too bad, morally, to be allowed to triumph. In any case, Tennyson probably had a special feeling about contests with Australia, given his position as the Governor-General's son and his education at Melbourne Grammar School.

In other words, Tennyson seems in many respects to be far from the classic amateur: he tried to cash his sporting status, he helped to emancipate professionals in cricket and he favoured the 'ruthless' over the 'nice' when it came to hard cases. He would have failed tests set differently for 'gentlemen' and 'amateurs' by Thomas Arnold, Pierre de Coubertin or Avery Brundage. What is more, when faced with American sport he soon became an enthusiast, not for baseball, but for football, which he watched while wintering in California on several occasions in the 1930s. At this period, of course, it was college football and particularly the 'Big Game' between Stanford and UC Berkeley:

> It was not their partisanship, however, that took hold of me so much as their battle-cries, their songs, their flag-waving, their wisecracks, their professed intolerance of the opposition, their gospel of 'win at any price', the mad gamble they made of it...I stand unashamed as an American football fan.[15]

Nevertheless, in an important sense I think that it can be argued that Tennyson was the classic amateur. There is an enormous sense of fun that comes through *Sticky Wickets* and no sense of career or ambition. Tennyson was on for any sport: hunting foxes (he managed to kill his host's expensive horse), jackals, panthers (he managed to shoot the goat being used as bait) and pretty much anything that moved. He would play tennis and golf whenever possible and broke a valuable mirror playing 'billiard fives'. He was also an enthusiastic photographer (bare-breasted, 'native' girls a speciality) and occasionally continued the family tradition of poetry. There was no distinction in his life between 'work' and 'pleasure': income divided into that which was his birthright and that which came from spotting an opportunity. In any case, there was never enough of it. In the classic sociological categorization of Edward Banfield, the financially feckless Tennyson was as much a member of the 'lower class' (time horizon ending almost immediately) as of the 'upper class' (time horizon stretching to future generations).[16] 'Jovial' and 'frivolous' were the adjectives most used about him. He was very much at home in the 'yobs and snobs' atmosphere of the English racecourse.

Tennyson detested Bradman who, in any case, snubbed him in a much-publicized incident in 1948: Tennyson, who in his own view had gone out of his way to help Bradman break a record at an earlier stage of his career, paid what he regarded as a routine courtesy visit to the Australian dressing-room before the Lord's test. The Australian captain was 'too busy' to see him.[17] Tennyson gives Bradman full credit for the excellence of his play, but commented that Denis Compton was a greater player because he had the 'right outlook': he was courteous and fun-loving. Tennyson pointed out that Bradman was an amateur while Compton was a professional. I think we may rest assured that, had he lived, Tennyson would have preferred David Gower to Geoffrey Boycott.

For Tennyson there was only one imperative which overrode fun and courtesy: patriotic duty. It should not be forgotten that he spent a quarter of his adult life at war and his financial fecklessness – apart from its spectacular early stages – was that of a survivor of the Western Front. Looking back on his life half a century after his death, in a society which seems to more fully resemble the 'commercial' model of Adam Smith, perhaps we ought to bear in mind Smith's concern that a purely commercial society would be endangered by its lack of 'military virtue'. Fifty years on, almost everybody in developed societies seems to lead more instrumental lives than Lionel, Lord Tennyson, lacking both his sense of fun and his sense of duty.

3

Local Hero

Dave Moorcroft was born in Coventry in 1953. At school he showed much more enthusiasm for sport than for academic work and left after failing all his 'O' levels. He chose to continue his education at Tile Hill College, however, rather than to take an industrial apprenticeship and succeeded in passing both 'O' and 'A' levels and entered Loughborough College in 1972, eventually graduating as a Bachelor of Education (Hons) in Physical Education.

His early athletics coaching came from his father Bob Moorcroft, from his school and from Coventry Godiva Harriers. He showed ability at all distances from 800 m up to 5,000 m, first running for a junior British team against West Germany and Sweden in 1971. In 1976 he reached the final of the Olympic 1,500 m in Montreal. In 1978 he won a gold medal in the 1,500 m in the Commonwealth Games in Edmonton and a bronze medal in the same event at the European Athletics Championships in Prague, being the only British athlete to win medals at both of the major meetings. In 1982 he achieved similar success at a longer distance, winning the gold medal in the Commonwealth 5,000 m in Brisbane and the bronze in that event at the European Championship in Athens.

Moorcroft competed in three Olympic Games, though illness and injury sent him home disappointed from Moscow in 1980 and Los Angeles in 1984. Perhaps his most famous achievement was to take 6 seconds off the world record for the 5,000 m by running the distance 0.41 seconds over 13 minutes in the Bislett Stadium in Oslo on 7 July 1982. He last represented Britain in 1989 at the age of 36. In 1993 he ran the fastest mile ever run by a man of 40 years and over outdoors, the time being 2 seconds over 4 minutes; the record still stands at time of writing.

Moorcroft has commentated on athletics for BBC Television since 1983. From 1981 to 1997 he was involved in a charity, latterly called Centre AT7, which organized sport for young people in inner city Coventry. In 1997 he took over the British Athletics Federation for two weeks as it was wound up, bankrupt. He then headed the interim body which took over, UK Athletics '98 and subsequently UK Athletics as a new governing body. He was awarded an OBE in 1999. Dave has been married to his wife Linda since 1975 and they have two children; he still lives in Coventry.[1]

L.A.:   To what extent were you paid as an athlete?

D.M.:   I remember receiving £5 at Gateshead for 'expenses' when I was quite young. Otherwise the first substantial payment I remember was $150 for racing in a meeting in Zurich a couple of weeks after I'd reached the Olympic final in 1976. It worried me, and I actually lost sleep over whether I'd done something wrong and would lose my amateur status. Until 1981 everything was expenses. I had a contract for £1,000 pounds a year with Adidas in 1981 as a 'consultant'. I was also able to winter in New Zealand on a Kraft scholarship and I ran in a rather well organized series of races there. But I had to teach when I was there, as did Linda, my wife, and we lived in the school. In 1982 they invented trust funds, which allowed athletes to put away money into an account which they could draw on to meet their 'needs'. This was interpreted pretty liberally by the athletics authorities though not by the Inland Revenue, so there were two completely different definitions of income in operation and you had to be very careful. There was no such thing as actual prize money during my career and even though I held a world record I never made the kind of money that would set you up for life.

L.A.:   So the sport did change its nature during your career?

D.M.:   Definitely. If you compare the three Olympics I ran in, 1976 was still the era in which we were a bunch of amateurs there for the time of our lives and expecting to go home and get on with serious careers. I actually shared a room with Frank Clement and we ran against each other in the 1,500 m! Six of us shared a bathroom and I spent half the time sneaking off to see my wife. By 1984 in Los Angeles the atmosphere was much more one of older, dedicated athletes who were professional in all but name.

L.A.:   At the end of your autobiography published in 1984 you favour more open payment and are concerned that 'criminalizing' payment and drugs in the same way actually encourages drug use. At the same time, you can see the argument that professionalism might simply encourage people to take drugs to win. What are your current reflections on these issues and on how much difference money makes?[2]

D.M.:   I don't think money was ever an important motivation for me and my guess is that it wasn't for many athletes. The desire to win was much more fundamental than anything else; I don't think I'm a particularly competitive or aggressive person generally, but I was on the track. I wanted to win and I didn't in the least bit mind that somebody was going to be miserable because they'd lost, even if I knew and liked them. In the period before I broke the world record this aspect of my personality took over. I was focused, moody, difficult to live with. I was 29 years old, I'd had a lot of problems with illness and injury and it seemed like now or never. I trained aggressively and masochistically. I believed that I *might* just have what it takes to be the world's best and my injury problems *might* just have been solved. You put all your eggs in one basket, psychologically, and it's not surprising that you're difficult to live with. You are completely focused, 'in the zone' as they say now, but it is all about performing to your limits. Money means very little. The relation between drugs and money isn't a simple one. I believe there were probably more athletes doping in the 1970s, when nobody was being caught and we didn't know what we now know about the side-effects, than there have been in the 1990s. We had to compete with people from communist countries who were made to take drugs. But the Western athletes in the 1970s had no serious financial incentive. A professional athlete risks his income, though, of course, the drugs are still ahead of the testing procedures. The most obvious sorts of drug use have been in the power events where there's never any serious money. In middle-distance events in my day the issue was blood-doping in different forms. I didn't do it and I honestly believe that none of the other well-known British middle-distance runners did it, but I wouldn't say the same of some of our European rivals. I think athletes are basically pretty sound on the drugs issue. You don't train like serious athletes have to train unless you honestly want to do your best and you don't want somebody to come along and beat you because of chemical assistance: of course, you face a nasty dilemma if this does happen. I think the whole culture and education have improved in athletics.

L.A.: Professionalism has been a disaster for athletes, hasn't it? What went wrong?

D.M.: I think that in my heart I would like it to be an amateur sport, but that isn't really possible. Just think of what it was like to be an athlete at a big meeting in my day. The TV people were on good money, the journalists were on good money, even the ice-cream man was making good money, but the athletes, the centre of the whole thing, were not, until the late 1980s. You have to remember that the biggest TV contract for athletics came in the mid 1980s when the sport was still semi-amateur so, for a time, it was a very profitable business. But then athletes started moving towards the meetings which offered the most money, rather than those with tradition and status, so it became much less easy to make a profit. I think it's very difficult to say how much damage money did to the image of the sport. My opinion is that the public are very tolerant of sportsmen making money, but they are only interested in genuine competition which really means something and far too little athletics passes this test. You also have to remember that when athletics was at its peak in the 1980s football had a very shabby image and when football revived it had to have an effect on the whole context of athletics. I think in some respects we are just like rugby: we drifted into professionalism without any clear idea of the level of professionalism we could afford and how we would define the sphere of professionalism. Athletics is a very difficult sport to finance in terms of its market and structure and a bunch of athletes with agents upping their demands and chasing a diminishing public interest was a recipe for disaster.

L.A.:   I wonder to what degree you can mix amateurism and professionalism as systems. Your father Bob coached for years and was even down at Godiva coaching young athletes at the exact moment you broke the world record. Is there a problem about introducing money and professionalism into a predominantly voluntary system?

D.M.:   Yes, there is a problem. After all, we have more than 120,000 unpaid workers helping to run athletics and one estimate has valued their services at around £13 million per year. We could run the sport without professionals, but we couldn't run it without amateurs. There can be tension between paid and unpaid people, but I think the unpaid are probably more tolerant than you might assume. I think the big problem in that respect is the 40-year-old ex-athlete who should go into coaching, but he or she looks at the prospect of dealing with difficult teenagers on wet evenings for no reward and thinks, 'I don't need this.' But that might have as much to do with changes in society as a whole as with the coming of professionalism into athletics. It might actually be more difficult to work for nothing in a sport where you've earned money, I don't know.

L.A.:   Have you returned to being an amateur sportsman since you were a top athlete and, if so, what does it feel like?

D.M.:   Not really. In many ways I would like to. I remember seeing the New York marathon in 1981 when we were travelling round the States: I found it was inspiring, all these people expressing themselves through running, measuring themselves against purely personal goals. It was the same at the London marathon in 1984: it is moving to see merchant bankers in tears of joy because they finished the race in under 4 hours. It reminds you that athletics is really about fulfilling your own potential and coming to terms with your own limitations. Linda has run a marathon, which is more than I've ever done, and she finished in under 4½ hours which meant a lot to both of us. But it's very difficult to be a real amateur runner after taking it seriously for 20 years. I still enjoy running, but not against the clock. Sadly, veterans' athletics is about getting worse every year but fighting a losing battle against it. I couldn't run the Coventry Fun Run, for instance, because everyone would notice me and they might feel sorry for me. I like to play other sports, especially tennis, when I've got time. I'm pleased to say that my son Paul has got a healthy attitude to sport: he dabbles in all sorts of things and has been a devoted QPR fan since he was their mascot when he was four. I don't know of any international athletes who have produced children of the same standard, so there hasn't been any pressure on him. I don't think I'd want him to be too serious; in a way I believe that sport wasn't meant to be professional.

Historic Compromise

Brian Ashton was born in 1946 in Leigh, Lancashire; his father had played Rugby League for Wigan in the 1938–39 season before the war ended his rugby career. He played Rugby League as a child, then Rugby Union for Lancaster Royal Grammar School, where he was a boarder, and Leigh Grammar School. He represented Lancashire schools at Rugby Union. All his rugby was played as a scrum half.

His first club rugby was for Tyldesley; he played for Fylde from 1966 to 1972 and Orrell from 1972 to 1975. He moved to AS Montferrand in France for the 1975–76 season, played for Roma in 1976–77 and was player coach at Milano 1977–79. His club rugby career ended at Preston Grasshoppers where he both played and coached. In representative rugby he played for Lancashire from 1966 to 1975, during which time they won the County Championship three times. He also played for the Barbarians and for the North of England, including the highly controversial game against South Africa in 1971. He played for the England touring team in Australia in 1975 and was just about to receive a full cap when he returned to England because his wife Monica had suffered a miscarriage.

His coaching career began in 1969 when he began to teach and was captain of Fylde, both positions requiring an element of coaching. He had qualified as a senior coach in 1981. His real coaching experience began in Italy and he went on to coach Lancashire Colts in 1979–80 and England Colts from 1981 to 1985, acting as assistant coach to the senior England team in 1985–86, with responsibilities for the backs. He was a coach at the Bath club from 1989 until 1996, as assistant to Jack Rowell until 1994 and then as Head Coach. During those seven years Bath won the Courage League Championship five times and also the Pilkington Cup five times.

In the summer of 1996 when English rugby became fully professional Brian Ashton resigned his job as a teacher at King's School, Bruton in Somerset to become a full-time rugby coach at Bath. He resigned that post six months later. From January 1997 until January 1998 he was coach to the Irish national team. Since May 1998 he has been full-time coaching adviser to the Rugby Union.

In 1996 Brian was instrumental in initiating a pair of games, at Twickenham and at Maine Road, Manchester, between Bath and Wigan Rugby League Club, one game played in each code. The games were the first ever between Union and League clubs since the schism of 1895 and were given enormous publicity, partly because each club was completely dominant within its own sphere. The games have not been repeated since.

L.A.:   Why did you go to play on the Continent and how did it work?

B.A.:   When I came back from Australia we both wanted a break. We'd wanted to live and work abroad at some stage and this seemed as good a time as any. Actually, the job I thought I'd signed up for in Clermont-Ferrand didn't really exist. I thought I was going to teach physical education and English – for the club, not a school, which is a peculiarity of the French educational system – but they didn't really require me to do anything. They were only able to get me a 'red card' so I was only allowed to play in friendlies. All in all, it was enjoyable and a good experience, but pretty frustrating. The club attracted crowds of from ten to fifteen thousand and they had four internationals in the back division. When I did play the outside half was Jean-Pierre Romeu. The players were paid at the office door on a Monday morning: not a fortune, but considerably more than the average wage in France at the time. It was slightly different in Rome where they put money in your account and gave you a flat and a car. The crowds were much smaller – perhaps, five hundred to two thousand – but the club had backers and, curiously, money distributed through the Italian Olympic Committee, even though rugby isn't an Olympic sport. In Milan I was player-coach and succeeded in getting the club promoted.

L.A.:   You were coaching at the leading club in England during the last days of amateurism and the first days of professionalism. What was that like?

B.A.:   It wasn't really [such] an issue as you would imagine. We didn't pay players or coaches at Bath; it wasn't an issue which preoccupied people. Many of the established players had what I would describe as rugby-friendly jobs, which gave them opportunities to train and tour and let them use their rugby reputations even when they'd finished playing. It was a very exciting time. I enjoyed working with Jack Rowell, who was a good friend, and we had developed a style of rugby and a group of players that made us almost unbeatable. Money didn't come into it much.[1]

L.A.:   What were your own feelings about working for nothing?

B.A.:   I had been offered good terms by Salford Rugby League Club in 1971. At the time they were recruiting heavily from Union – David Watkins, Mike Coulman and Keith Fielding all signed for them. It was a serious dilemma, but I was just getting established in Union and felt I'd be missing a lot. I discussed it at length with my father and he advised me to stay in Rugby Union. I often said to Monica that it was ironic, to put it politely, that I'd found myself coaching at the top level in the one remaining sport where I was never going to make a penny. I was four years at Bath before I even asked for travelling expenses and it's a 60-miles round trip from Bruton to Bath. It could be annoying to think that the journalists who interviewed you and maybe criticized you were well paid for it while you weren't paid at all, but I didn't think about it that much.

L.A.:   What are your views on the transition from amateurism to professionalism?

B.A.:   First of all, it was a big surprise. I thought that the game would eventually become professional in some form, but not when it did nor as completely as it did. I and most people I know heard about the IRB's decision through the television and the newspapers without an inkling it was going to happen. There were plenty of people who did know, I suppose, especially in the southern hemisphere. Like a lot of people, I thought it was very sensible of the Rugby Union to establish a moratorium, so that the game would not be professional until the start of the 1996–97 season and we would have a year to adapt. But that year wasn't used, except by entrepreneurs like Sir John Hall at Newcastle and Ashley Levett at Richmond who moved into clubs and contracted players. What should have happened is that the home unions should have put players on contracts as they do in the southern hemisphere. It is beginning to happen now, at last, especially with the Scots and the Irish. I am in favour of professionalism in principle, in that sort of form. But some of the things that actually happened were staggering in their ineptitude. I couldn't see how some of the supposedly top clubs could pay 40 professional players, even the lesser ones, £20,000 a year or more each, given the sort of income the club had. Even small clubs, watched by two men and a dog, were offering win bonuses of fifty or even a hundred pounds. The result is pretty predictable: after three years contracts ended and everybody released players. Some of those players should never have been encouraged to think of themselves as professional sportsmen: they were just not at that sort of level. Many clubs have continued to organize themselves in a very amateurish way; there's not enough development of players, not enough work on individual skills and far too much reliance on importing established foreign players. Paying players does not make them better players in itself. I am totally mystified by what some of the businessmen who moved into the game thought they were playing at. Apparently they weren't doing it altruistically or for the status, but these supposedly hard-headed and experienced financial minds really thought they could make money out of club rugby. It's very noticeable that Ashley Levett and Sir John Hall got out of the game even before the first batch of three-year contracts was up.

L.A.:   So, like athletics, Rugby Union went professional at the wrong level and to the wrong degree?

B.A.:   Yes. The game can only support the payment of a handful of the very best players. As in nearly every other sport, it would be a tiny minority, but they should be given their chance to be full-time professionals at the activity they're best at, just like people in other walks of life. If we don't imitate the southern hemisphere by contracting representative squads then one could imagine a workable system with joint contracts between club and country covering four to six clubs who would play in European competition.

L.A.:   There must be a lot of tension when you introduce professionalism into an amateur system. You yourself only lasted six months in charge of a professional club and John Allen, the Leicester secretary, resigned immediately. What were the problems?[2]

B.A.:   In my case, the main problem was not directly connected with professionalism. I was 'Head Coach' and John Hall was 'Director of Rugby' and we both thought we were running the team. But this was in the context of a club with a wage bill that had gone up from zero to probably over a million pounds and having to answer to business interests who were profoundly ignorant about the game. You have to remember that Bath, like Leicester, was always an elite club, running only three senior teams and an under-19 side. It was very different for some of those London clubs who ran a dozen teams ranging from top level to pretty coarse rugby. I could easily foresee tension between paid and unpaid officials of a club, particularly in that situation. In fact, Wasps, for example, have effectively split into two clubs with the amateurs continuing to play at Sudbury and the professionals at Loftus Road.

L.A.:   One thing you'll always be remembered for is the two games between Wigan and Bath in 1997, which attracted a great deal of interest. What was the significance of those games?

B.A.:   They were an expression of Union going professional and there was a great deal of immediate commercial potential. I don't think there was much doubt about what would happen, that Wigan would win the League game very easily indeed and Bath would win the Union game quite comfortably. For that reason, I don't think there was any question of a series; the whole thing would be too predictable once people's curiosity was satisfied. Union is a much more specialized game than League. That means that there are a lot of things in the Union game that the League players just aren't trained to do. But it really benefits the League players because they can all run, pass and tackle whereas there are always five players in a Union team who aren't very good at those things. In the end the two games are bound to become more alike as you as you have to control the intensity of a professional Union game and try to make it more entertaining. They may even merge, eventually, but I think that is a very long way off.

L.A.: You gave up your job when Bath became a professional club. Do you have any regrets about this?

B.A.: No. To be perfectly honest, it was a feeling of relief and still is. After 27 years of teaching I felt I'd done enough. To get out of a public school staffroom after that length of time feels like a reprieve from a life sentence.

L.A.: What would you advise young players about playing full-time?

B.A.: I have advised England juniors who have asked me that they should stay in full-time education if they have the ability. The chances of being injured or of not making it in rugby are too high, quite apart from the boredom of life with nothing but rugby. The brief period of quite ordinary players going straight into full-time looks pretty bad even after three years and many of them are looking for jobs. I think most people in the game would give the same advice; the trouble is they hear a different story from agents. My own son Tony was never going to be a serious rugby player and told me so at an early age. He's an all-round chap with lots of interests and a mind of his own. At Lancaster he made only the second team at rugby, but the first team at cricket.

L.A.: Has professionalism been a bad thing in Rugby Union?

B.A.: The failure to adapt to it has been pretty bad, but the good thing about it is the opportunity to compete and fulfil potential completely for the tiny minority of players who can play at the highest level. I don't think that level is naturally club rugby; you have to remember that when I played there was no competitive club rugby, except for the Lancashire Cup, which was reintroduced during my time. So I think that there are a whole lot of minor pros who will vanish from the scene. I don't think money is much of an incentive in sport compared with natural competitiveness and ambition. I've never known a more competitive game than Boarders versus Dayboys at Lancaster Royal Grammar School with players intensely committed and people screaming on the touchline.

5

The Next Superstar ... Not!

Martin Roderick was born in 1967 in Portsmouth. He played for Portsmouth Football Club as a schoolboy and when he was 16 became an apprentice with them at £25 per week, then a non-contract professional at 17 on £40 per week and was contracted to the club before his eighteenth birthday. He played for Portsmouth for three years, mainly for the youth and reserve teams. He made one full appearance in the Football League and three in the 'Full Members Cup'. During his three years at the club Portsmouth twice narrowly missed promotion to the top division, clinching a place in the final season. He played one game for the England Youth team. Nearly all his football was played as a wide, left-sided midfield player. At the age of 20 Martin Roderick announced that he did not want a new contract and wished to pursue his education. He was admitted to Carnegie College, which was by then part of Leeds Polytechnic specializing in physical education. He played for the Polytechnic at football and represented Great Britain in the World Student Games. After graduating from there, he was admitted to the Centre for Research into Sport and Society at the University of Leicester where he gained a Master's degree. He stayed there to register for a doctorate and works there now as a telephone tutor for graduate students on distance learning programmes. With Ivan Waddington he has completed research funded by the Professional Footballers' Association on the treatment of professional players' injuries by clubs.

For most of his period in higher education Roderick played semi-professional football, appearing for Farnborough, Wycombe Wanderers, Harrogate, Shepshed, for the reserve teams of York City and Bradford City and for Kettering Town. At the age of 26, while playing for Kettering Town and studying at Leicester he contracted Hodgkin's disease, a form of lymphatic cancer. He was finally diagnosed in 1994 and successfully completed a six- months course of chemotherapy, but his football career was finished.

L.A.:   What did your parents think of you becoming a football apprentice at 16?

M.R.:   They didn't like it at all. I have two sisters, seven and five years older than myself who were classically-trained musicians with degrees and it had always been assumed that I would go to university. Then I was talking to Alan Ball (the Portsmouth manager) who was casually saying things like, 'When you're with us full time next year...', and I was thinking, 'Hang on! That's not what's expected of me.' Football managers don't understand doubts like that. He told me fairly angrily that there was no real choice because I could be a star if I put my mind to it. He kept saying, 'Do you want a Mini or a Ferrari? It's your choice.' My parents were indeed opposed, but the club invited my father in and everybody buttered him up, telling him how talented I was and how far I could go. In the end he agreed, provided I could have one day off a week to study for 'A' levels, which was pretty well unheard of. It didn't really work: I got only one pass, at a fairly low grade.

L.A.: What was it like, being an apprentice and then a player?

M.R.: There was a glamour about it, undoubtedly. The local press talked about me as the next home-grown superstar and the regional television station always seemed to show me when they did a feature on the club. I couldn't walk a mile in Portsmouth without ten people stopping to talk to me because Pompey fans knew who I was. At my Dad's golf club I moved from being a very junior member to somebody that people took notice of and dropped hints about tickets to. I particularly remember when I made my first-team debut against Fulham, retrieving the ball from a part of the terrace where I myself had stood many times and my friends chanting my name. I was sponsored by a local clothes shop and able to wear much flashier clothes than my contemporaries. In some ways my experience was an odd one because I became an apprentice the year before the Youth Training Scheme began to support football apprenticeships. There were only three of us in my year and five altogether. We had to do a lot of work and we would sometimes play in the youth team in the morning and for the reserves in the afternoon. I played for the reserves as a 15-year-old schoolboy, which would not happen now. The following year YTS kicked in and there were 15 new apprentices, which was completely different.

L.A.: But you decided to leave. That's very unusual isn't it?

M.R.: Pretty well unheard of. Everybody thought I was mad, especially as, once I'd made the decision, I was serving out my contract for the rest of the season and played the best football of my life. But I was never in any real doubt about it, even when they offered me another contract.

L.A.: The life of the young professional and the apprentice in football has received a pretty bad press in everything from TV programmes to academic theses. What was bad about it so far as you were concerned?

M.R.:   Some of it was great. I made really good friends whom I still
          see...and I used to love playing five-a-side. But there was a lot of it
          I really disliked. The banter, for example. I know everybody is
          supposed to like the banter and it is a form of humour, on the surface
          at least. But among professionals it has an edge to it which is quite
          different from a university team. For example, we had this stupid
          institution of the yellow jersey, given to the supposedly worst player
          in training after a vote. There was nothing for the best or the most
          improved, only for the worst, someone who had been nutmegged or
          missed a shot by the biggest margin. I didn't get it particularly often,
          but I did hate it. It was bad for the quality of football, making you
          avoid risk and try to be inconspicuous. There was even a stupid
          business with the quality of balls: there were about 30 balls, ranging
          from brand new to tatty and the tradition was that the best players
          had the best balls. When I remember Graham Paddon (the
          Portsmouth youth coach) it would be waving the yellow jersey or
          shouting 'Look at what you've got' about those balls.
          Of course, Portsmouth had a strong squad with a lot of players who
          made it big – Darren Anderton, Kit Symons, Brett Angell, Kevin
          O'Callaghan, Vince Hilaire – and I didn't really have much chance
          of making the first team. It was frustrating as well to see friends who
          got no opportunity at all. But it was the day-to-dayness of it all that
          got me down: cold Monday mornings, being shouted at, friends in
          tears because they feel so frustrated. Me in tears because I've come
          across some player who blotted me out of a reserve game and not
          wanting to discuss with my parents because it means they're right. I
          just came to the decision that this wasn't how I wanted to spend my
          life and these weren't the people I wanted to spend my life with.

L.A.:   Did you ever regret the decision and did you think about getting
          back into full-time professionalism?

M.R.:   No, I have never regretted it and I know plenty of my
          contemporaries would give their right arm to have a career outside
          the game. Many of the most successful are still playing, but they are
          worried about where they will be in a few years' time. One guy I
          played with now works in a garden centre. The question of going
          back did come up pretty regularly, as it does for the better players in
          semi-professional football. At Harrogate I was looked at by York
          and Bradford and there was an article describing me as an 'Anfield
          Target' – supposedly the only Harrogate player ever to be watched
          by Liverpool scouts. I played for Blackpool in the Manx Cup, but
          wasn't offered terms because the transfer of David Eyres fell
          through. I would have happily gone back once I'd got a degree and
          if I was offered the right terms, but it never happened.

L.A.:   What was it like playing for semi-pro clubs and for student teams after playing full-time?

M.R.:   My first non-League club was Farnborough and we did really well, except that I disagreed with the manager about how I should play. So he plonked me on the bench and said, more or less, 'You don't get to play until you're prepared to play my way.' I suppose I was a bit arrogant, snobbish in football terms. I thought I was a real pro, not a reject and was doing him a favour. My parents had moved to Oxford by then and it was a lousy journey to Farnborough anyway, so it was a great relief when Wycombe made me a decent offer and I was able to play the rest of that season for them. Student football was pretty easy for me, frankly, though sometimes a bit bizarre: the trials at Carnegie had coaches running all over the pitch, watching players perform close up, which is something I'd never seen in the professional game. Of course, student teams are full of people who say they've been professional footballers, but most have probably had a trial or been signed on schoolboy forms. My worst experience, I suppose, was playing a whole season for Kettering with undiagnosed cancer: no wonder I felt very unfit!

L.A.:   What about playing other sport once you'd ceased to be professional?

M.R.:   I've always played golf and my handicap is in single figures. But otherwise I only knew football from an early age. At Carnegie I took the opportunity to try lots of things, as I was doing sports science, and I enjoyed gymnastics, swimming and volleyball. I was friendly with a gymnast, Lisa Barton, and her training was an education to me: five hours' hard work a day, total dedication and a proper attention to diet. All of this in a purely amateur sport, when all the professional footballers I knew thought a couple of hours' training a day was a lot, never gave a thought to diet and would have had to list drinking as one of their main recreations. After my recovery from the cancer I did play a bit of local league football, but I'm a bit of a football snob and found it very frustrating to play at that level. I took up rugby for Oadby Wyggestonians and I've played for everything from the fourth to the first team, on the wing because I've got some pace. But I did it only for the social life and as a focus for fitness; I'm not a born-again rugby player and in my heart I think football's a much better game. I'm always competitive, though. I remember playing golf just after completing my treatment for cancer and I went into a black fury because I missed an important one-yard putt. I suppose I should have been enjoying everything in my life, even the missed putts.

L.A.:   How much did money ever matter to you as a player?

M.R.:   Not much at all. It wasn't a factor in the big decisions or a motivation on the pitch. Generally, I just accepted what I was offered, though once when I changed clubs as a semi-pro it was about four times as much as I had been getting and I nearly bit their hands off. Talented young players now have agents, of course, which changes everything.

L.A.:   How do your researches on the professional game compare with your own experiences?

M.R.:   The main recent research has focused on injuries. Strangely, given what eventually happened to me, there isn't a direct personal comparison because I was hardly ever injured – I'm a very slight figure, as you can see, and I wasn't a heavy tackler or a great header of the ball. But comparing it with what I saw I'd have to say it is more extreme: managers endanger players all the time and doctors and physiotherapists do very little to protect them. The players connive in this, subscribing to the hard-man image and always desperate to get back on the field and reclaim their place.

L.A.:   Is it fair to say, philosophically, that football clubs treat their players instrumentally rather than as human beings or as ends-in-themselves and that they are worse than other employers in this respect?

M.R.:   Yes, I think it is fair and it happens because the pressures are so intense and the time-horizon so short. Of course, if you are a young player in the circumstances I was you don't realize it at the time because you think you're going to be a superstar and everybody else hopes you're going to be one. But you do realize it a long way down the road, that when Alan Ball was screaming at you it wasn't because he cared about you. The extent to which people pick you up and drop you is something you only come to realize over time. Many players of my age say they have come to feel like a piece of meat, but things may be better nowadays with the elite players because they have the money and the agents to be much more independent.

L.A.:   And, conversely, do you feel any emotional loyalty to your previous clubs?

M.R.:   No. I am a Portsmouth fan and loyal to them, but I was before I ever played for them. I follow certain players that I played with and liked, and I like to see them do well. Also, I can think of one successful player whom I didn't think had more than a fraction of my skill and I find his success irritating.

L.A.:   Footballers often say how wonderful it is to be paid to do the thing you love. You could turn it on its head and say how terrible it is to be paid to do the thing you love. Could both be right?

M.R.:   Both are true in a sense. Making my home debut or playing for England Youth with Paul Ince, Neil Ruddock and Ruel Fox made me feel fantastic, but not being able to get into a game against Arsenal reserves made me despair. In a way, it's like being in a war – perhaps like going away to school for you – in that you think nobody can possibly understand it who hasn't been through it. I wouldn't recommend it to anybody in its traditional form unless they were able to pursue an education independently.

6

Living through Rugby's Turmoil

Stuart Lancaster was born in 1969 in Penrith, Cumbria. He was educated at St. Bees School and Carnegie College, Leeds, being awarded a bachelor's degree in sports science in 1991 and a post-graduate certificate of education in 1992. He held full-time teaching posts from 1992 to 1998 before taking a substantial leave to become a full-time player and development officer for the Leeds 'Tykes' Rugby Union team, who shared a stadium and administrative structure with Leeds 'Rhinos' Rugby League Club in a unique arrangement.

His rugby has been played at open-sided wing forward. He played for Wakefield from 1988 to 1991 and Headingley from 1991 to 1992 before that club merged with Roundhay to form a Leeds Club. Since 1992 he has played for Leeds, originally as an amateur, then as a semi-professional when professionalism was legalized and as a full-time employee of the club in 1998–99, returning to teaching and semi-professionalism in 1999–2000. Representatively, he played for the North of England Schools, for Scotland under-19s, under-21s and students (a qualification through his Scottish mother) and for the Anti-Assassins on their Australian tour of 1999.

L.A.:   You went to Carnegie: I always thought of the elite physical education colleges like Carnegie and Loughborough as pretty much professional sportsmen anyway. Is that fair?

S.L.:   Not at all. We certainly didn't think of ourselves in that way and we weren't encouraged to. It was more like an extension of school sport. There were 38 people in my year, many of whom reached a high level in their own sports, but they were mainly amateur sports in any case and a lot of people weren't competing. The college didn't put you under any pressure to compete for them: you could say it lacked ambition as an institution if you wanted to be critical. There were a couple of semi-pro footballers who were able to pay their way through college, but most people were playing a wide variety of sports and not competing intensely at any of them. As someone whose main sport was Rugby Union, I never envisaged I would be a professional sportsman.

L.A.:   So when professionalism came in 1995 you were surprised?

S.L.:   Certainly. We'd expected some changes and there were payments creeping in, but nobody expected full-blown professionalism and Rugby Union wasn't ready for it.

L.A.:   What was your first payment and how did your income from rugby develop?

S.L.:   My first payment was £50. It was in the 1994–95 season and the coach announced that he wanted us all to be put on a £50 win bonus for the Pilkington Cup tie against Stockton. We won and 15 envelopes duly appeared: technically illegal at the time. It was a one-off because we lost in the next round. When professionalism came in 1996–97 I was on £1,000 a year plus the use of a new Suzuki Swift and £75 first-team win bonus. I was disappointed with the car because I'd been expecting a Mondeo (which some members of the squad did get). In 1997–98 there was no car but £3,000 and the same win bonus. In 1998–99 when the club went full-time in order to achieve promotion my combined salary as player and development officer was £30,000.

L.A.:   For a time you must have had professionals and amateurs playing together, or at least neo-professionals and neo-amateurs. Was this a problem?

S.L.:   Yes, there was tension. You were supposed to keep secret what you were getting, but beer talks and people compare themselves. There was a rift in the club between the loyal players, who had been there before, and the imports who tended to be getting more money. The club had £2½ million pounds from the sale of the Headingley ground to the Morrison supermarket chain and they were able to use that to pay players. Eventually most of the imports left, leaving us with less talent but more team spirit and we just managed to hang on in what was then League Three.

    Later on there was the question of going full-time for a promotion push. I was the lucky one because I was given sabbatical leave by my school, but most of the first team had to face the dilemma of whether to give up their jobs and stay or leave and go to a club that wasn't full-time. The split was about fifty-fifty. As you know, we failed to get into the top league and reverted to semi-pro, with training three times a week at 5:30 pm. There's also the question of ridiculously high expectations among junior players and their parents. As development officer I was constantly with parents of lads in our under-19 and under-21 sides demanding when we were going to start paying them. Realistically I think there are only going to be 300 professional rugby players in this country and the chances of making it are minuscule, even for those who avoid injury. We did pay some junior players and I think now we were wrong to do so, even though it seems sensible to help pay a player's way through university. I even had a conversation with a school careers officer in which he said the question of qualifications didn't really matter because the lad was going to be a professional rugby player, wasn't he? I would always advise a player to get other qualifications because the chance of not needing them is extremely slim.

L.A.:   Wasn't it better in the days of amateurism when clubs were able to set up 'rugby-friendly' jobs for players which often turned into careers?

S.L.:   That worked well for some people, in small clubs as well as big ones. Unfortunately, this club doesn't seem to have been run by the sort of people who could deliver that.

L.A.:   What are the good things about being a professional?

S.L.:   I suppose the improved fitness is the main thing ... a sense of having fulfilled one's potential. You don't have to train in the evening when you're already tired, but you can concentrate on it. So I'm glad to have played rugby as well as I could have done. I think it's probably only a 5 per cent difference to being a serious amateur, but it is different. I like the flexibility, too. We have training sessions, practice sessions, physical rehabilitation sessions ... but there's space between them to get your life organized, which there isn't in teaching. It might be something as simple as going to the bank.

L.A.:   It's often said that most professional footballers are extremely unprofessional in matters of drink, diet, lifestyle and so on. What about professional rugby players?

S.L.:   We are now. I think it helps that many rugby players are from an educated background. But the first couple of years of professionalism people just carried on in the same way, drinking and eating what they wanted. It was only in 1998 that real discipline came into it. This was, of course connected with players anticipating the end of their initial three-year contract.

L.A.:   What are the disadvantages of being a professional?

S.L.:   Try a wet Monday morning in January when you've lost on Saturday or you aren't in the first team and there's nothing except rugby in your life. Perhaps the worst thing is the other sports you have to cut out of your life. I miss cricket, squash, basketball, volleyball and badminton; I could probably have been as good a cricketer as a rugby player. Even within rugby we no longer have the attractive friendly fixtures and the club won't let you play for representative and touring sides, though they did let me go on the Anti-Assassins tour of Australia as a special favour: we had a great time. It's become more grim as the financial pressure on the club has become more intense. Clubs want value for money, the cheapest possible promotion. I look forward to retiring in the sense that I'll still want to keep fit, but I'll be able to play lots of other games in my own way without any pressure. I missed teaching and the kids, as well. Also, having 13 weeks holiday, which coincide with my wife's holidays – she's also a teacher – instead of three weeks which don't coincide.

L.A.: What about being a semi-pro? I imagine it's like being an amateur, but with some money as a bonus.

S.L.: Not at all. It's much more like being a professional because you have obligations. I have to go to training three times a week and I'm fined if I'm late. I have to keep fit and I'm fined if I fail a fitness test. It's completely different from, say, college where I trained everyday, but I didn't have to. It was personal drive and loyalty that made me turn up.

L.A.: Is money actually a motivation?

S.L.: In terms of commitment to the game, but not once you're actually on the field. It isn't any different from being an amateur. On average it was ten o'clock at night after we'd won that I remembered I would get a win bonus as well. It might be different for people who make really big money.

L.A.: What's the most enjoyable rugby you've ever played?

S.L.: Undoubtedly 1997–98 when we won promotion and I was vice-captain towards the end. That was as a semi-professional. Actually, my year as a full professional was considerably less successful.

L.A.: What are your general thoughts about the future of rugby?

S.L.: As I've said, I don't think there will be the money for more than about 300 professionals in some sort of Super League. We must have an elite structure somewhat like the successful southern hemisphere countries, and it was wrong to think that we could have a vast number of club professionals like English football. Newcastle messed it all up by running a rugby club as if it were a football club; that raised everybody's expectations and created a player's market in wages which lasted about two years and then collapsed. Now everybody is trying to get success as cheaply as possible. This club is in a curious position being affiliated with a Rugby League club. Everybody in Rugby Union wants a top division club in Yorkshire, but we have in some ways to compete with a Rugby League club who treat us very generously. After all, they are one of the best in the country and we are a long way off that. They get crowds of over twenty thousand and our biggest gate is under four thousand.

L.A.: Beyond that 'Super League' level do you think the game should be ring-fenced as an amateur activity?

S.L.: Even if it's desirable, I don't think it's possible. There are always going to be ambitious clubs and individuals who will pay and you just can't police it.

First Family

Robbie Brightwell was born in Afghanistan in 1939, though his birth was registered in Rawalpindi in what is now Pakistan. Returning to England without much of an education, he was encouraged by the headmaster of his secondary modern school to take the '13 plus' examination and moved to Shrewsbury Technical College and then to Loughborough College where he studied from 1959 to 1962. His first job was as a teacher at Tiffin School from 1963 to 1966, his second as a lecturer at Loughborough from 1966 to 1972, where he also gained an MSc. He left education to become Managing Director of Adidas UK from 1973 to 1980 and then was Managing Director of Coq Sportif UK from 1980 to 1985. His later career has been as Managing Director of three companies involved mainly with fishing tackle. Robbie Brightwell's original sporting enthusiasm was football, though after an injury he concentrated on athletics. He started as a long-jumper and excelled at a variety of events, eventually settling for the 400 m. He won the championships at the European Games in 1962 and the World Games in 1964 at this event, and in the Tokyo Olympics of 1964 he came fourth in the individual event and won a silver medal in the relay. He retired from competitive athletics when he married in late 1964.

Ann Brightwell (née Packer) was born in Moulsworth, Berkshire in 1942 and qualified as a PE teacher at Dartford College. In an international athletics career which lasted from 1960 to 1964 she competed for Great Britain at seven events: all distances from 100 to 800 m, the long jump, the 80 m hurdles and the 4x100 m relay. At the Commonwealth Games in 1962 she reached three individual finals and won a silver medal in the relay. At the Olympic Games in Tokyo in 1964 she won a silver medal at her supposedly best event, the 400 m, and the gold medal for the 800 m. After the games she retired from athletics and married Robbie Brightwell. Since then she has been principally a housewife and mother, working only part-time.

The Brightwells have three sons: Gary, born in 1965, was a talented athlete not interested in competition, who runs a china and crystal business with his wife; Ian, born in 1968; and David, born in 1971, have pursued careers in professional football, both as defenders. Ian Brightwell made over 300 appearances for Manchester City between 1986 and 1998 before moving to Coventry City: David Brightwell started his career with Manchester City, but then played for a number of clubs in the lower *divisions. In 1999 he scored the other goal in Carlisle United's victory over Plymouth Argyle which preserved their league status, the winner being scored by the on-loan goalkeeper Jimmy Glass in injury time. The game was later voted to be the most dramatic in the history of football.*

L.A.: Were you ever paid for competing?

A.B.: Never. There were expenses. The first time I ever received any was when I won an English Schools Championship and we were invited for training at Lilleshall; they paid your travel expenses. One of the girls put in for the magazines she had read on the train – just a couple of magazines at about a shilling and sixpence [7½ p] each – and she got a frightful ticking off.

R.B.: I got some free shoes. On the question of expenses I once arrived late at Paddington for an international match and public transport probably wouldn't have got me there on time, so I took a taxi, but the Amateur Athletic Association refused to pay for the taxi. Rex Porter had terrible problems as a pole-vaulter because he couldn't get his pole on the tube; I think they did pay for him to be brought by taxi in the end. On the day I retired Adidas paid me £30, though that was mainly to cover a trip to Germany.

L.A.: You were both competing primarily against Russians and Americans and in both cases the athletes were, to put it politely, given more support to devote themselves to athletics. How did you feel about this?

R.B.: My personal view is that we were fools to ourselves. The British form of amateurism was largely composed of snobbery and hypocrisy. Look at the sort of athletics teams which competed for Britain between, say, 1948 and 1968: apart from some of the middle-distance runners they were mainly middle class, university-educated people who could support themselves. I used to look on the American and Soviet teams as more democratic than us. I could never see anything wrong with supporting excellence in athletics as you do in the arts and other activities; they did it, we didn't.

A.B.: When we competed with the Soviet athletes we were much more interested in gender and drugs issues. As a woman, it was a question of whether we were really competing on equal biological terms more than the kind of support they had.

R.B.: With the rise of East Germany, the concern was with drugs. There was a joke among my generation of athletes to the effect that the Soviet athletes ran as if their lives depended on it because if they didn't come up to expectations they had to sleep with Tamara and Irina Press.

L.A.: Did you ever regret retiring so early?

A.B.:   No. We planned to retire, win or lose. We were looking forward to
           getting on with the rest of our lives – teaching, getting married,
           having a family. I was married at the end of the year in which I won
           a gold medal and gave birth to Gary the following October. Of
           course, if I'd come along a generation later I'm sure I would have
           stayed longer and made more of a career out of athletics. But it was
           good to retire at the top; I don't think I would have enjoyed being
           an athlete in decline. And I had given it my best shot. I trained with
           men and twice a week I trained three times a day. So I don't think
           being professional would have made me a better athlete. My
           training was very different from today's athletes: I used to run 600-
           m bursts, not the long distances that they do now. Robbie trained
           even harder than I did. But I don't think that for any serious athlete
           money is a real motivation, though it might have kept me in the
           sport longer. We were very professional in many ways, even though
           we weren't paid.

R.B.:   I agree. I don't even think winning is the real motivation. Fear of
           failure, of defeat, is the thing that really drives you. Look at the face
           of an athlete who wins a big race: relief is the first thing that you see,
           relief that they haven't blown it, let themselves down.

L.A.:   Was your athletics career of material benefit to you?

A.B.:   I did a couple of ads when I retired, a one-off for Heinz baked beans
           and a three-year contract with Bovril. It wasn't big money, but a
           little nest egg that carpeted the house. It would have been against all
           regulations, of course, if I'd still been competing.

R.B.:   I couldn't deny, even if I wanted to, that my status as an athlete was
           extremely useful in my career, especially at the beginning. It was a
           great help in dealing with people, an excellent talking point to start
           a relationship. That lasts about five or six years, then you're reliant
           on your other talents.

L.A.:   Am I right in thinking that you both approve of the
           professionalization of athletics?

R.B.:   I do think that the concept of amateurism was naïve and that
           excellence should be supported. But having said that, nobody could
           be happy about the state of athletics or its current image. If people
           think it is infested with drugs, which they do, then it is very difficult
           to sell athletes as heroes or an athletic contest as a fair contest. We
           have to get rid of drugs if we possibly can.

A.B.:   That needs far more rigorous policing of the situation. You get the
           impression from a distance – which we are, nowadays – that most of
           the time they just want to sweep the problem under the carpet.

R.B.:   The problem is not just drugs, but has to do with the pride and
           honour of being an athlete. For example, in our day being an

international athlete, representing Great Britain, was the most important thing in the world and I get the feeling that that isn't true any more. There's also a problem because athletics is so bound up with the Olympics: they are the natural pinnacle for an athlete, like major championships are in golf and tennis. My own opinion is that the Olympics could be and should be a tremendous force for good in the world, but now they've become too big, there are too many sports and the commercialization is too overt. We have to have values in sport, whether it is professional or amateur. Professionalism doesn't mean you have to cheat or lack loyalty. Look at golf: I don't know much about it myself, though my sons love it, but highly paid professionals seem to be able to maintain sporting standards in golf. I think the only solution is much more emphasis on competitive sport and the values of sport in the educational system.

A.B.: There's definitely a lack of prestige about the sport now when you compare it with our day. I think it's bottomed out, though, and has much more chance now that David Moorcroft is directing UK Athletics.

L.A.: Have you competed in sport at a more relaxed level after you retired?

A.B.: We did run the London Marathon together when we were about 40 and we did it in three and a half hours. But the difficulty is that you're tempted to start taking it really seriously, training hard, comparing times and so on. We didn't really want to get into that.

L.A.: Let me change tack and question you, not as athletes, but as the parents of professional footballers. People say some pretty critical things about the life of the professional footballer, especially about the one-dimensional nature of his life and the lack of preparation for what happens when his playing days are over. What have been your impressions?

A.B.: I think Ian and David have both had immensely enjoyable and reasonably rewarding careers. It hasn't come easily to either of them and you have to put up with a lot of disappointment and unfair treatment in the course of a career, but you probably have to do that whatever you do. It is worrying that it is such a short career. David stayed on at school and took 'A' levels and he is about to graduate with a degree from Central Lancashire University. On the other hand, Ian has had more rewards from the game.

R.B.: I think professional football is an intensely competitive, unremitting hard life. It's a very competitive environment, but you can enjoy it, with the right attitude. In many respects its much harder than athletics: athletes don't do anything comparable to playing 60 games a year often when you're not fully fit and athletes don't have thousands of people shouting and criticizing every move they make.

A.B.:   I would add that I wouldn't have ever wanted to play in a professional team game. Its too subjective, you're too dependent on somebody's opinion and whether you fit in. As an athlete your time is absolute, objective; you can prove yourself beyond anybody's opinion of you.

L.A.:   One last question. You were both very famous when you were quite young, but that fame didn't involve money or a career as it would be expected to now. What are the advantages and disadvantages of being famous like that, or of having been famous?

A.B.:   It was neither a great problem nor a great advantage for me. If you live a normal life in a normal town it all fades fairly quickly and is very seldom mentioned. We haven't tried to stay famous or remain connected to athletics. I think the thing that lasts and is important is self-esteem, knowing that you were capable of working hard and achieving something.

R.B.:   As I said, it was useful to me for a few years, but I agree that the thing that lasts is your own knowledge of what you achieved. People have to be quite old to remember who I am now.

8

The View from Indianapolis

The National Collegiate Athletic Association is the body which regulates and administers major intercollegiate sport in the United States. It was formed in 1906 after an initiative by President Theodore Roosevelt, stimulated by a spate of injuries and deaths in college football largely arising from the use of the 'flying wedge' formation. Originally the Intercollegiate Athletic Association of the United States, it became the NCAA in 1910. Its function of overseeing the organization of leagues and conferences was expanded in 1921 when it began to organize its own championships, which it now does in 22 sports. The number of member organizations expanded steadily in the second half of the twentieth century from approximately 400 in 1950 to just under a thousand in 1999. About a third of a million young people compete annually under NCAA auspices.

Despite running sport which attracts more than ten times as many live spectators as professional sport in the United States and the existence of huge television coverage, the NCAA regards itself as an organization which is running amateur sport. Its list of purposes includes 'To encourage its members to adopt eligibility rules to comply with the satisfactory standards of scholarship, sportsmanship and amateurism.'[1] The general principles of amateurism in the NCAA manual begin with the statement, 'Only an amateur student-athlete is eligible for intercollegiate athletics participation ...'[2] The manual goes on to ban 'pay', listing six categories of remuneration which are forbidden under this heading and 11 forms of illicit expenses.[3] College athletes may not compete for prize money, for example, nor may their scholarships be made dependant on sporting performance; any income from promotional activities arising out of an individual's fame and success is to accrue to the institution, not the individual.

I visited the new, purpose-built headquarters of the NCAA in Indianapolis shortly after the Association moved there in 1999. (The premises were so new, in fact, that they had not been completed.) I talked to three people:

Bill Saum is responsible for implementing policy on agents and gambling for the NCAA, having been previously involved in the enforcement of eligibility rules. He was educated at Ohio State University and qualified as a schoolteacher before becoming a graduate assistant football coach.

*Although he had not played (American) football after high school, he went
on to work as a football coach at Heidelberg College, Defiance College and
Bowling Green State University before moving to the NCAA.*

   *Lisa Dehon was educated at the University of Kansas. She qualified as a
lawyer and worked as an assistant district attorney for four years before
moving to the NCAA, where she was first an enforcement representative
investigating the validity of eligibility programmes before becoming
specifically concerned with student-athlete reinstatement. She ran as a track
athlete and was crowned 'homecoming queen' at her high school.*
*Jane Jankowski was educated at Wartburg College in Iowa where she played
basketball and softball. She worked as a news and sports reporter for
several years, originally in Illinois and then with the* Detroit Free Press. *She
is press officer for the NCAA.*

L.A.:   I suppose that I come to this conversation as an Englishman with the
        prejudice that you aren't in any genuine sense involved in amateur
        athletics at all. After all, the sport you run is a huge commercial
        operation and the individuals competing receive substantial benefits.
        Historical scholarship tends to argue that the true amateur principle
        never really took root in the USA and certainly never crossed the
        Appalachians. British athletes of my generation often equate
        American athletes with Soviet athletes in the sense that both were
        well supported and, in effect, able to train full time. This is said both
        as an allegation of 'shamateurism' and in admiration of an effective
        system. What are your reactions to this?

L.D.:   From the very beginning the NCAA has tried to regulate college
        sport in the interests of sportsmanship, good conduct and no pay as
        such. The principle, which everybody agrees with, is that sport
        should be an avocation, not a vocation.[4] The sums of money accrued
        by participants in college sport are very small compared with those
        in major league professional sport. But the emphasis on what we
        mean by amateurism has changed. The regulations largely focused
        on the acceptance of money in various categories and we are tending
        to deregulate in these areas. For instance, our rules are becoming
        less stringent about whether an athlete has ever been paid preschool
        or whether he can win prize money or be paid at the semi-
        professional level in his sport in the vacation, say, and more
        concerned with other aspects of amateurism.

B.S.:   We will always hang on to the educational aspect of our aims. The
        NCAA believes in student-athletes and we have many rules and
        regulations designed to ensure that the athlete is fully integrated into
        the student body. For instance, there used to be the institution of
        athletic dorms where the sports scholars lived apart, like a separate

caste. We got rid of those in the 1990s. We also have a lot of policy and regulation designed to get graduation rates as high as possible.

L.D.: The big issue is eligibility. It amounts to asking, 'Are you really an appropriate person to be on an educational scholarship?' There's the question of initial eligibility, which is to do with educational attainment and scores on entrance exams. Then there's the question of continuing eligibility, a series of benchmarks designed to ensure that athletes cannot practise or compete unless they are participating properly in educational programmes.

J.J.: We're currently facing a lawsuit in which four African-Americans are claiming that the eligibility rules operate in effect in a discriminatory way.

L.A.: Do the rules work? When I was at Stanford in the 1970s there seemed to be a series of continuing stories which involved girl reporters on the *Stanford Daily* dating the star footballer and establishing that he couldn't really read or write.

J.J.: There were a number of national scandals in that period and afterwards which showed that some institutions were effectively hiring the best athletes irrespective of educational considerations. There were cases of people who were virtually illiterate. There were huge debates and some people felt that college sport was losing its soul and becoming just a version of professional sport. But we have tried to redress that, particularly with a package of reforms in 1986.

B.S.: I think you have to understand how people look at college sport. American society has embraced all forms of athletics as a major entertainment and college sport is the biggest element in this. On Saturday, I'm going to Ohio State versus UCLA. There'll be a capacity crowd of 90,000 people there, many of whom are alumni or relatives of alumni. There'll be the cheerleaders and the band and I'll look at them and think that they were in class yesterday. But it's also true that the players were in class yesterday, with very few exceptions.

J.J.: There will be 200,000 people watching college football in Greater Indianapolis in the coming weekend, which is a problem for the Colts who won't even fill their stadium ...[5]

L.A.: I heard the announcement, which means the Colts game won't be on live television in the region.

J.J.: ...and you have to remember as well that there are whole areas of the country where there is no pro sport. I'm from Iowa which has no full professional sports teams, so college sport is what people focus on.

B.S.: If you compare the colleges with the pro clubs you have to note that the colleges are older and stay where they are. The fans are much more a community. Pro fans are interested in excellence; they have to believe they're watching something world class. But college fans are much more likely to be devoted to their team even when they know it's way off the standard of being national champions. There's much more of a community of fans.

L.A.:   What about the allegation that the college system in some respects exploits athletes? That is, they look at college as the antechamber to professional sport, but a thousand colleges into 30 teams doesn't go and most of them are pushed out into the world being good at one thing, but not good enough. I suppose you could call this '*Hoop Dreams* Syndrome', though the movie *Hoop Dreams* was about high school basketball players.

J.J.:   The proportion of sports scholars who become professional is just under 1 per cent.[6]

B.S.:   Though I would say, realistically, that most Division One basketball players believe they're going to make it as a pro and the coaches encourage them in this belief even though the hard statistics – which we present to them very clearly, along with a lot of information and advice – tell them that they're probably not. That isn't an evil deception, its more in the nature of things: an athlete has to believe subjectively that he can go to the very top, even though the objective facts and probabilities suggest that it's unlikely.

L.D.:   I think criticism is valid in so far as individuals don't graduate. The current figures show a slightly higher proportion of sports scholars graduating than the rest of the student population.[7] If they do then there're a lot of advantages: you have your education paid for and you're employable because there are people who know who you are and even hero-worship you. Also, we're talking all the time about basketball players and footballers; there are a lot of scholars in minor sports for whom professionalism is not an option and whose main gain probably is in developing the self-discipline to be a serious athlete while gaining an education.

B.S.:   All that has to be contrasted with the bad publicity we get when it's discovered that some school has given a scholarship to some kid who can't read or write, or a college hero gives a totally inarticulate interview, or a former scholar gets into trouble with the law. Of course, our problems moved on to a bigger scale when college sport became a major aspect of TV.

L.D.:   You often hear those who did make it to the pros saying that the college days were the best, that there was something very special about playing for their college, because of all the loyalty and the passion that people feel towards the institution and because their success in sports was to do with their community and projecting their college or university.

L.A.:   I note that the amateurism issue is linked in the way the NCAA is organized with the gambling issue. How much of a problem is gambling?

B.S.:   It's certainly a problem. Our surveys show that about 25 per cent of sports scholars bet, most of them illegally, but only about 4 per cent bet on their own games, which is a more serious issue.

L.A.:   Finally, what was your view of the similarities and differences between your system and the systems run by the communist regimes?

B.S.:   As I understand it, what happened in the Soviet Union was that quite young children were taken away to sports academies and encouraged to concentrate entirely on becoming a world champion in their sport. I can understand how a European might look on that as similar to our system, especially as most European countries don't have a link between sport and higher education, but from our point of view it is completely different. They didn't have the link to education and the college as a community and enterprise that we have and they didn't have the idea of sport as an avocation.

There is an appropriate symbolism to visiting Indianapolis while researching a book on amateurism. Not only is the headquarters of the NCAA (now) there, but it is the heartland of the American way of sport, in the Midwest, beyond the Appalachians, a territory where the amateur ethos never really had roots, according to much scholarship. Indiana is also the home of Notre Dame University, the 'Fighting Irish' institution which probably did more than any other single college to establish the intensity, popularity and competitiveness (and, in a sense, the professionalism) which flavours American college sport.

I went to Indianapolis in the belief that the American college system was primarily a form of shamateurism in much the same way as the Soviet sports system was a form of it. I was likely to have such prejudice, not only because I was English but because of my own experience of the American system was at a very grand institution and in the 1970s. Having said that, the NCAA, through its documents and the three people I interviewed, went a long way to convince me that there are important features of the college system which make it in some respects part of a continuing amateur tradition: these features include the 'avocation' principle and the maintenance of the link with education, as well as the image of the alumnus/fan, the player and the institution being part of some permanent, rooted community. These features make it essentially different, at least, from Soviet sport and from American professional sport. American college sport, arguably, is highly commercialized in style but it is not ultimately constrained by the commercial principle and it has features of which Thomas Arnold and Pierre de Coubertin would approve.

However, that view is not the view that one meets in the bars and on the streets of Indianapolis, where it is much easier to start a conversation about amateurism and college sport than about the presidency. The popular view is that the amateur principle is dead and that college sport is essentially corrupt and shamateur. There are, though, reasons for suspecting the popular view: it is probably more influenced by the publicity given to the most notorious cases and the most dubious institutions rather than by the way in which the system works for the majority of its participants. And it is certainly more concerned with the narrow consideration of money than with the broader ethics which might be thought to define the spirit of amateurism. There is also a popular view that college sport 'exploits' student-athletes. Competitors who play in the 'final four' of the national basketball championships are watched by tens of millions of spectators on television, shouted at by coaches who are paid hundreds of thousands of dollars and accrue valuable prestige for their institutions while being rewarded only at the level of an academic scholarship. This argument assumes, of course, that the players are in one sense real amateurs.

As journalistic luck would have it, the taxi driver who took me to the airport was a former sports scholar, a footballer for the University of Indiana. He expressed a rugged scepticism about the continued existence of the amateur principle and about the direction the college system was taking. On the other hand, he himself had graduated, majoring in history ('Otherwise my parents would have killed me'), though he did wish that he had done more academic work. He now owned his own fleet of taxis, but regarded his brief appearances in front of 72,000 people as the highlights of his life. As an interviewee his articulacy did not let the NCAA down.

9

Amateur and Fantasist

Lincoln Allison was born in West Hartlepool in 1946. He was educated at Lancaster Royal Grammar School and at University and Nuffield Colleges in Oxford. Since 1969 he has been employed at the University of Warwick where, at the time of writing, he is Reader in Politics, Director of the Warwick Centre for the Study of Sport in Society and South Asia Liaison Officer. He has also held visiting posts at Stanford (California), Melbourne (Australia), Chulalongkorn (Thailand) and Tblisi (Georgia) and lectured at more than 50 universities across the globe. He is author or editor of a dozen books and more than 700 articles, his outlets ranging from newspapers and popular magazines to academic journals.

He represented his school at Rugby Union, athletics and shooting and his college at rugby, football, rowing and athletics. Other rugby teams he played for include an Oxford University second team, the Old Lancastrians, Warwick University, Durham City, Leamington, Stanford Business School and Old Leamingtonians. However, most of his sport has been football and cricket played for staff teams at the University of Warwick. He continued to play amateur league football until the age of 40 and cricket into his 50s. In 1987 he became chairman of the University of Warwick Staff and Graduate Cricket Club and in 1994–95 was involved in negotiations for the establishment of a Saturday league in which they now compete. (During the writing of this book the cricket club won its first Saturday League Championship while the football club collapsed.) He took up tennis at the age of 46 and is a member of the Leamington club, the oldest in the world. He has supported Burnley Football Club since 1953 and is now a shareholder in the club.

He is married to Ann, a keen tennis player. They have three sons who are all more talented than himself at sport, having between them attracted the interest of representative or professional teams in football, cricket, athletics, basketball and rugby.

> Why should I not publish my diary? I have often seen reminiscences of people I have never heard of, and I fail to see – because I do not happen to be a 'Somebody'– why my diary should not be interesting. My only regret is that I did not commence it when I was a youth.
>
> Charles Pooter
> *The Laurels,*
> *Brickfield Terrace,*
> *Holloway*[1]

It is a moot point whether or not I went to a 'public school'. Lancaster Royal Grammar School was a 'voluntary aided' school with the unusual mixture of about 600 day-boys and 300 boarders. I was a boarder from 1957 to 1964. But there is no doubt in my mind that I attended one of the sort of institutions which defined 'organized games' for the world. We had house matches, dorms, prefects, 'colours', 'prep', 'tuck', beatings, 'lights out', midnight feasts and even a system of 'notches' (unique to the school, so far as I can tell) which recorded minor offences and which virtually guaranteed the more unruly (such as myself) a weekly beating. The headmaster for my first four years, R.R. 'Joss' Timberlake, had been a pupil at rugby before the First World War and gave us immediate connection with Tom Brown and the very origins of modern games. The *modus vivendi* of the English boarding school actually changed little between 1900 and 1960; the world described in stories in the *Captain* magazine was, superficially at least, very much the world we inhabited.

Consider, then, our sports. The school was successful in sport and its fixture lists for rugby and cricket comprised the big northern public schools – Rossall, Sedbergh, Stonyhurst, St. Bees, Giggleswick, Merchant Taylor's – as well as the major grammar schools, such as Leeds and Manchester. The tradition has continued: even during the writing of this book 'LRGS' made national sports news by beating Charterhouse in the final of the national 'colts' cricket championship of 1999. Sport was the most important thing in our lives; I was encouraged to include this personal profile by Brian Ashton's comment that the most competitive atmosphere he had known was actually at school where we played together in the same house and school teams. We trained or played virtually every day; in fact, Sundays usually consisted of a house rugby training session in the morning followed by a game of football in the afternoon.

In short, we were in certain respects as much like professional sportsmen as anybody can be except, possibly, a professional or an American college sports scholar. Our teams were selected on merit: you were picked, dropped or injured, never merely 'unavailable'. We knew our moves and set pieces. We were thoroughly disciplined and did not drink or smoke. On certain occasions – the house final and matches against the more famous schools, for example – the crowds who watched us would have excited the envy of many clubs in the Scottish Football League. Our games were sometimes reported in the *Manchester Guardian* and the *Daily Telegraph*.

But there is one respect in which I would guess or assert – it is certainly impossible to prove – that the spirit of our play was quite different from the characters in *The Captain* who seemed to be living in the same institutions and playing the same games. For when we proudly trotted down the steps at Memorial Field, buoyed by the sound of the nails in our boots clacking on the concrete steps, so proudly smart that we even whitened our bootlaces, we were imitating an example which was to be found for some at Turf Moor, home of Burnley Football Club, and for others at Central Park, home of

Wigan Rugby League Club. A generation or two earlier the public school was its own paradigm. By our time it was, among other things, an opportunity to see yourself as a professional athlete. It is also important to note that the public school sport of Thomas Arnold, Sir Henry Newbolt and *The Captain* (or, for that matter, of R.R. 'Joss' Timberlake) was a kind of didactic instrument, a preparation for the real heroism of the imperial frontier and the battlefield. For us, in the age of nuclear weapons and rock 'n' roll, it was an end-in-itself. What really mattered was whether you kicked the last-minute goal to win the game; whether you saved your rival's mother from a runaway horse was of less importance.

Our attitude to real professional sport was probably varied and certainly complex. We aspired to amateur success: a rugby, cricket or athletics blue was probably the achievement the school would make the most of. (We were a much less classy outfit on the river). Professional sport was not frowned upon; the attitude was probably more that we were above it. When a boy who was a couple of years above me, Alan Spavin, played in the FA Cup Final for Preston North End against West Ham United in 1964 there was interest and some pride, but it was not terribly important. When my study-mate Stuart Westley played as a professional batsman/wicketkeeper for Gloucestershire there was some relief that he 'sensibly' decided to give it up and pursue his career as a solicitor.

Boarding school sport, then, given the historic role of the institution, was, in my experience, strangely professional. University was marginally less so. Club rugby, in those days, was almost farcically amateurish, with little serious training and teams changing chaotically because of such trivia as weddings and holidays. I am reliably informed that even the top club teams, even in the 1970s, did little that would be recognized as serious training in other sport. My own excursions into club rugby usually involved getting a game with the kinds of team where the numbers were made up by ancient Welsh schoolteachers who were reputed to have played in Welsh trials but who could now barely break into a run.

My real amateur career began at the age of 23, devoting myself to two games, cricket and football, for which I had neither the technique nor training. Whereas sport at boarding school, and even university, had every possibility of material gain – prefectoral privileges, better references, even better food – this real grown-up amateurism was pursued at a cost to career and relationships. Forget the football, I have played more than 600 one-day games of cricket for the University of Warwick Staff: that is 600 days of my life or three working years. The consolations have been in lifelong friendships, in the personal, sensuous moment of delivering a ball which is flighted in such a way that the batsman never makes up his mind what to do and finally acts as if he were a lunatic, and in the perfect sweep or cover drive played by a friend or son. Every single player I know would have a different account of the purpose and ethics of the game and the place of competition, but all would agree to some extent with Lord Tennyson that the ultimate purpose of the game involves some moral meaning or self-knowledge. Certainly, this level of amateurism does not involve prestige nor attention. You write your own press reports and there have been several occasions when I noted that the crowd consisted literally of two men and a dog. On one away ground we were for many years watched by an elderly married couple, who were inevitably christened 'Sid and Doris Bonkers'.[2]

Normally, with amateur sport of this kind, the great advantage of its amateurism is that you can walk away from it. On Monday morning, after a good weekend, you might permit yourself a little smile at the memory of the shrewd fielding change which produced the vital wicket, but if things went badly you can forget it and get on with your work. An exception to this is the 'tour' where you play cricket for five successive days and nothing else matters. That institution captures some of the curiously professional spirit of life at boarding school where the banter can have a nasty edge (as Martin Roderick suggested) and failure is not something you can walk away from. But success, too, can give a sharper, more concentrated satisfaction. I sometimes feel that the absurdly large amount of sport I have played in my life has all been to try to capture the elusive spirit of that euphoria which descended on us in the changing rooms of the Memorial Field Pavilion, like *charisma* upon the apostles, when we won our first house final. If so, I have come closest to it on the cricket tour.

Finally, there is the perception of amateurism and its opposites as a father. It is gratifying to have sons who all share one's enthusiasm and psychologically easier if they surpass you rather than have to live up to you. The world of the boarding school seems weird and risible to them, their sporting education having taken place primarily in clubs. What is difficult, and can be depressing, is when they reach the level of dealing with professional coaches whose job it is to define ten or a hundred failures for every success. When a favourite expedition to the fair has to be abandoned because of an important trial or training session, when you feel the lad has played so many games and come to take it so earnestly that there is no joy left, when the coach has offered nothing but 'technical' advice which is, in effect, criticism, the world of the true amateur seems extremely attractive. I am also inclined to believe that our pseudo-professionalism, with its institutional intimacy and intense loyalty is more satisfying than their pseudo-professionalism with its long car journeys to rigorous coaching sessions and games played with team-mates whose names you do not know.

PART III

The Future of Amateurism

The Future of Amateurism

The origins of this book lay in irritation, not at the demise of amateurism, but at the reaction to its decline, the too easy acceptance of its irrelevance to the future; there was also some triumphalism. One should not be too upset nor too impressed by such facile assumptions about the irrevocability of history. There was much dancing on the graves of capitalism, religion and even nationalism during the twentieth century, but all are still with us and social science is now modest enough, for the most part, to admit that we have no idea which of them will be prospering in the year 2100.

It is the same with amateurism, though in considering its future we cannot avoid returning to the question of which sense of amateurism, whose sense of amateurism we are talking about. It is difficult to believe that there will be much of a future for the negative and technical senses of amateurism, operated at different times in the twentieth century by the Amateur Rowing Association and the International Olympic Committee. They were the product of a narrow view which has now disappeared. For the same reason, the purely social definitions, those which equated amateur with gentleman and gentleman with a precise stratum in a particular society, are unlikely to be revived, since their context has also disappeared. Amateurism continues to survive in the banal senses that the vast majority of sporting competitors will continue to compete without pay and that an 'amateur' stage constitutes a kind of apprenticeship in a number of sports, including golf and horse-racing. But there remain much more important, though much less clear, amateur ideals the cultural habitat of which may be much broader. The idea of sport being practised for the love of the thing or by 'all-rounders' with other developed talents and capacities or with an overriding ethic that its purpose is 'above' mere consumption or entertainment has existed at most times and in most places where sport has existed and remains effective yet. Indeed, some would insist that at least some of these ideas are part of the definition of sport.

It is generally agreed to be myth, though, that the definitive attitude of amateurism was a lack of competitiveness or expertise. According to the real historical record it was only ever non-sportsmen who expected sportsmen not to care whether they won or not, if this could ever be imagined as a coherent attitude. The image of C.B. Fry, the legendary English cricketer, footballer, athlete and candidate for the throne of Albania who 'effortlessly' broke the world long-jump record during the 1908 Olympic Games, must be compared to the cricket coaching columns which Fry actually wrote (for money) for *The Captain* magazine which he also edited. These encouraged the young towards relentless practice and the perfection of technique. It was the amateur aspiration, according to most serious amateurs, to compete fairly, but above all to fulfil one's potential, 'to do one's best'. Instead of Vince Lombardi's 'Winning...is the only thing' the amateur code sees winning as a desirable by-product of not letting yourself down. But there may be times when you can do this and lose honourably.

I have lost count of how many times I have been asked to comment on the 'decline of the Corinthian spirit' in situations where the questioner assumed that there was once in modern sport a carelessness about victory and defeat which has now disappeared. The dictionary acknowledges two meanings of Corinthian: 'from Corinth' and 'amateur'. Greek Corinthians were never amateurs and English Corinthians always wanted to win.

The Root of All Evil

The claim is that money (or its absence) is not part of the essential definition of amateurism in its most ethically significant sense. However, it would be wrong to infer from this that money was not important. Its causal importance for the spirit of amateurism, in most circumstances and for most people, is enormous. Perhaps the difference lies in the gap between what St. Paul actually says to Timothy about money and how that is popularly misquoted. In the New English Bible translation it reads, 'The love of money is the root of all evil things, and there are some who in reaching for it have wandered from the faith and spiked themselves on many thorny griefs.'[1] The popular version is simply that money is the root of all evil, whereas the 1582 translation of the Latin Vulgate, the Douai Bible, used by many Roman Catholics, refers to 'the desire for money'.

Consider a club rugby player of good standard, but below international level. He plays for his club for nothing until the game becomes professional. Then he is offered a three- year contract which pays him £100 for each week of the season, plus a number of bonuses, including one of £100 for every time he plays for the first team and they win. Training is intensified, but it remains an evening event so that players such as himself can continue with their 'day-jobs'. How is he to regard the money? He might rationally say to himself,

> This is a bonus, a payment for doing something that I would do anyway. I'm not going to worry about a further contract nor am I going to care about whether other people are getting more or less than myself.

Still less am I going to become reliant on the money. Initially, I'm going to save it, since I was perfectly capable of living on my existing income though my wife and I may dip into it later for things we would otherwise not be able to afford, such as luxurious restaurant meals and extra holidays.

This would be the best of both worlds, a situation of amateurism-with-money in which the player retains his freedom and integrity while piling up money in the bank. But it does seem a largely unrealistic aspiration, since most people, at least according to the anecdotal evidence, become dependent on the additional income. Dependence can take several forms: the player might build the additional income into his expenditure or he might see his status as being defined by the continual receipt of the income or he might even become psychologically dependent on the continual accumulation of money. In any of these cases his well-being or self-esteem will become wrapped up in the negotiation of a new contract and his sport ceases to be an extra, an other, in life, but part of work. Money as an institution, an apparent substance which is both a means of exchange and a store of value, has got many ways of getting you, whether as spendthrift, miser or conspicuous earner. Of course, the power of money to change one's relationship with an activity is not confined to sport. Something of the same dilemma occurs in the entertainment industry, where the term 'day-job' originated. For that matter, the academic with a newspaper column finds himself in a similar position, which in that case might make the difference between really free speech and the attempt to please an editor, an owner or a market. After all, as The Preacher says in a biblical passage less often quoted or misquoted, 'The table has its pleasures, and wine makes a cheerful life, and money is behind it all.' (The King James translation says 'money answereth all things.')[2]

However, it is not impossible that very large amounts of money might emancipate a sportsman to something recognizable as the amateur spirit. On a beautiful afternoon in the spring of 2000 I saw a performance by Ian Wright as a football substitute which was quite unforgettable in this respect. Burnley were in 'the comfort zone', 2–0 up at home. It was a surprising anomaly that he played at all: he was 36 years old had won virtually every honour in the game including 31 caps for England and was a multimillionaire who had already been the subject of 'This Is Your Life' on television and had his own 'chat' show. It had become commonplace to remark that players of his status no longer bothered to eke out a career in the lower divisions. Yet, there he was, a substitute in a second division game.

When he had been on the field for five of his ten minutes a teammate hit the Reading crossbar. Spotting his opportunity, Wright nipped into the goal area and flicked the ball into the net. It was an ordinary goal with relatively little meaning. What made the moment extraordinary was his reaction to scoring and the crowd's reaction to him. He ripped off his shirt, raced to the halfway line, threw himself on the ground and beat it in sheer exuberance. We leaped to our feet, with a great roaring, laughing cheer which recognized that his expressions of joy were far more important than his goal. In fact, as if to prove the point, he behaved in a quite amateurish way for the rest of the game, waving and smiling at the crowd and the manager. The atmosphere was like a revivalist meeting: wealth and ambition offered no motive for that goal; but what it did mean was that he still wanted to do it and to do it for us. Wright is no saint – he has a particularly poor disciplinary record – and this was no demonstration of some pure amateur spirit of sport-for-sport's-sake. But it was in its context, a demonstration of the pure joy of scoring goals (or catching catches or breaking tapes) which is the more realistic idea of the core of amateurism. At the very least it was the joy of a man past the fear of failure which Simon Barnes earlier defined as the nature of professional sport. It is to be contrasted with the joyless resentment of the failed pros I had shared a field with five miles away and three decades earlier. It illustrates one of the many paradoxes of amateurism.

Another of the many paradoxes of the meaning of amateurism is that a process of intensified commercialism must, in a sense, increase the level of amateurism. Consider the following transition: initially, there are 5,000 professional footballers, the majority of the revenue to pay their wages comes from customers in the stadium and their average income is three times that of the average for full-time employees in the economy as a whole. Then the nature of the revenue changes so that now there are 1,000 players, the revenue to pay them comes mainly from global television rights and their average income is 30 times that of the national average. In some respects we could argue that the whole situation is much more amateur in that there are 4,000 players who are not paid any longer, but also 1,000 who are paid so much that they do not have to worry about the future: they can afford to enjoy their football and have to worry much less than their predecessors about pleasing their employers. There is some evidence that the latter effect really does work: by the late 1990s football managers were frequently complaining that it was difficult to discipline or control players who were already multimillionaires. But it is difficult to see this change as really increasing amateurism. The highly paid players are under tremendous pressure from their fame and importance which cancel out in some respects (though not in all) the liberating effects of their financial security and the unpaid players become non-players or moneyless professionals.

Assertions of the ethical dangers of money are, of course, not uniquely Christian: indeed, the idea of money as the root of all evil is a much more constant theme of Buddhism and Hinduism. One of the most popular and successful of twentieth-century Indian gurus, Pandit Shriram Sharma

Acharya, always insisted on the fundamental principle that 'Talent' and 'Art' should not be sold for money:

> There is one commodity which has created its place ahead of [literature, poetry and art]. It is called MONEY. These days the importance of money is very great. All arts have fallen at its feet and have subordinated themselves to it. By offering its temptation, anyone can be controlled whether he is a singer, musician, painter, actor, poet, literateur, journalist, religious leader or a politician. With it, they can be made to dance like puppets or it can be said that all arts are selling their virtue for the sweet smell of money. Talents are purchased with money and they willingly surrender themselves to dance to its tune like the gaily decorated prostitutes.[3]

However, it is only fair to remark that this unworldly view of talent rests most easily on a base of worldly security. The Indian businessman who introduced me to the works of the guru casually referred to his lending a member of his family £10 million and even the Pandit himself refers to his own possession of 'ancestral wealth'.[4]

Amateurism as a Social System

Apart from the proposition that the 'Corinthian spirit' as commonly perceived is a myth, there is probably no greater consensus on the subject of amateurism in sport than in the belief that the transition from amateurism to professionalism in both track and field athletics and Rugby Union was mismanaged and misunderstood. In each case, after all, they led to widespread acrimony and bankruptcy. In both cases there seems to have been an over-simple assumption that the principle of action could be changed and yet the activity continue almost exactly as before. In some respects amateurism functioned as a system, a complete whole in which the parts were interconnected, the workings of each a necessary condition of the workings of every other and of the whole.

The theory of social and political systems in this sense is an ancient one, at least as old as Plato's and Aristotle's understanding of city-states as bodies politic, analogous to living organisms. In Walter Bagehot's seminal work *The English Constitution* the different 'elements' perform separate functions but cannot operate without each other. The dignified elements (of which the monarchy is the prime example) serve to create and sanction authority which the efficient elements (a prime example being the Cabinet) exercise to implement policy.[5] Twentieth-century theories of social and political systems such as those of Talcott Parsons and David Easton have been more complex and less elegant, with their language of dysfunctions, eufunctions, sub-systems and homeostatic mechanisms, but the essential theory is the same.[6]

Thus we can conceive of the amateur regime within which the club, the committee, the national association and so on were part of a single system. The amateur and voluntary principles were also part of the system, not necessarily special or unusually fundamental parts, but parts nevertheless. The symptoms of systematic breakdown were financial collapse, the resignation of established officials, the almost complete impasse in Rugby Union between the leading clubs and the national unions and what seems to be generally agreed to be the highly disruptive influence of agents in both sports. However, this is not a real systematic collapse like the breakdown of the Soviet Union in the same period. More moderately, we must just say that amateurism had some systematic tendency; to some extent its working fitted the ideal type or model of a system. Its breakdown involved bankruptcy, anger and a certain amount of chaos, but life went on.

Perhaps it is too demanding to ask why participants did not understand these systematic tendencies, since there was also a failure to appreciate them in the much more complete systematic breakdown of the Soviet Union. But I think it is useful to distinguish two levels of misunderstanding. First is the simple failure to acknowledge any systematic properties of institutions which leads to the naïve belief that a good idea or practice can be transported anywhere, an arm, so to speak, taken off one body politic and stuck on another. Equally, failure to recognize systematic qualities might allow the belief that in circumstances of breakdown the broken institutions can simply be replaced by rational alternatives. One might think that this *naïveté* would only be found among a wholly uneducated sector of society were it not clearly the case that influential economists involved in institutions of global governance strongly believed that a 'big-bang' collapse of the Soviet Union would produce a healthy capitalist development, notwithstanding Adam Smith's insistence that functional markets require (what is now called) 'infrastructure' for transport, education, defence, financial stability and the enforcement of contracts. All of these were collapsing in the Soviet case. So it is hardly surprising that many people also believed that payments could be introduced into sport and the whole thing carry on as before.

The more sophisticated form of error is a mistake about what kind of sub-system the amateur system was within the social system. Amateur sport existed not as a simple sub-system, like parties with the political system, but as a kind of ring-fenced world of its own which was to some degree separate from the rest of the social system, but also in large part symbiotic with it, yet at the same time sometimes dysfunctional with respect to it. In its exclusion it was like the ancient clannishness, what Edward Banfield called the 'amoral familism' which is found in such societies as Sicily and Georgia.[7]

These institutions serve to feed and protect individuals and act as bulwarks against the state, but they also prevent society and individuals from flourishing. Amateur sport, as I have argued, constituted a much more positive part of civil society analogous in some ways to religious and artistic institutions.[8]

The sophisticated error, then, was in believing that amateur sport could be absorbed into a commercializing society in the same way that other institutions were. From the election victory of Mrs Thatcher in Britain in 1979 until the end of the century, there was a wholesale demolition of constraints and limitations on the operation of commercial principles. This process did not end, but continued to accelerate after her loss of power in 1990. It was not just that the 'natural monopolies' were privatized; universities were forced to compete and attract funds, quasi – and crypto – market structures were forced upon schools and hospitals. Previously there had even been an entire day of the week, Sunday, in which commercialism was suspended, but that too disappeared. Only a few institutions such as the BBC and some of the designations in the Town and Country Planning system retained their immunity to the spread of commercial practices due largely to the conservative anti-commercialism within the Conservative Party.

There are many ways in which the extension of the commercial principle was bound to infringe upon the autonomy of amateur sport: freer markets in land (and therefore pressures for the sale of sports grounds) and in television rights are obvious examples. But the system had greater bulwarks of independence than those parts of the state, such as educational institutions and utilities, which were commercialized or privatized. It also did things differently: a former division of a nationalized industry adapts more easily to becoming a monopolistic private company than does an amateur club to being a competitive company. On the whole the industry can modify its objectives, reducing its workforce and raising prices, wages and salaries. That is a small revolution, welcome to many of those who have power within the organization compared with the introduction of money into institutions which minimized and ring-fenced its use. And it must be emphasized again that it is completely erroneous to equate the spread of commercial principles with a 'rolling back of the state'. On the contrary, from the point of view of amateurism and civil society the introduction of commerce is the introduction not only of the massive and necessary regulative powers of the state but also, often, of the state's redistributive functions.

A Game with Three Sides: Amateurism, Professionalism and Commercialism

A normal opposite of amateurism is 'professionalism': one dictionary definition has it that to be an amateur is to practise something as a pastime rather than as a profession, and in ordinary language the more usual dichotomy is between amateurism and professionalism. Yet I have argued as if the opposite of amateurism were commercialism, with professionalism a quite different phenomenon from commercialism. It is now necessary to explore this triangular relationship between partial opposites which are, at the same time, ideal types of society, principles and way of doing things within a given society which have a tendency to form systems. We may imagine, as an ideal type, what a fully amateur society, a fully professional society and a fully commercial society might be like: But we can also observe the same person in a real society acting professionally, commercially and as an amateur within the same day or the same hour.

Commerce is relatively easy to define: the primary meaning of the word is that it consists of financial transactions. Commercialism, then, is a belief in the efficacy or propriety of financial transactions or a tendency for such transactions to be the dominant form of social relations. A commercial society is one in which a relatively high proportion of arrangements are on a commercial basis.

Professionalism is a much more difficult concept. The word comes from the verb to profess, meaning to avow one's faith and gives rise to the idea of a 'professor' with as full a commitment to an academic subject as one could imagine. The core of the root of the concept is the idea of a vocation or calling. But the idea of a body of people called to perform a role in society has also taken on many features which do not follow directly from this core. The typical profession:

- institutes and controls qualifications which pose barriers to entry to the profession;
- has a code of ethics intended to define proper conduct for its members and to secure their acceptance by the rest of society; and
- consists of a hierarchy of ranks and titles.

In many respects to organize an activity professionally is the opposite of allowing it to develop commercially. Perhaps the most obvious case is entry into the activity: the commercial model of a market requires that people should be able to enter and leave an activity as easily as possible, while professions often require long years of training and difficult qualifications. At the beginning of the twenty-first century most societies demonstrate a particularly strong contrast between law and computer technology. It is usually difficult to practise law without years of training, approved qualifications and membership of a professional organization. Different branches of the computer industry, by contrast, contain firms set up by 16-year-olds and self-taught enthusiasts.

For several generations now there have been well-developed theories of competition between the professional and the commercial model of society. James Burnham's reform of Marx to acknowledge 'the divorce between ownership and control' was an important theme in the 1930s while 20 years later Michael Young constructed an anti-utopian vision of professional society as 'meritocracy'.[9] Thirty years on from that Harold Perkin's account of professional society was a much fuller description of the nature of professionalism as such and its tensions with commercialism.[10]

In this account professionalism can form an alternative basis of society. Merit, rather than birth or money defines status. Acquired qualifications become the most important badges of rank. Because this is so, almost every activity that can possibly do so aspires to professional status: rat-catchers become rodent operatives, croupiers and cocktail waitresses have appropriate certificates and so on. The nature of property changes so that rights of tenure to one's job and pension rights become more important than landed property or direct share ownership. The shape of society is different; it is no longer stratified but a complete set of vertical columns. As Perkin puts it:

> It is not a class society in the traditional sense of a binary model with a small ruling class exploiting a large underclass, but a collection of parallel hierarchies of unequal height, each with its own ladder of many rungs. In this way the inequalities and rivalries of hierarchy come to predominate over those of class.[11]

During the Cold War, versions of the theory of professional society were invoked to explain and predict the evolution of a common social structure on both sides of the Iron Curtain. Communism and capitalism were to 'converge' into a form of society run by specialized, technical elites according to such writers as Aron and Rostow.[12] The French '*technocracie*', the Soviet '*apparat*' and the American 'revolving door' between corporate management and government would eventually become the same kind of social leadership. Professional would speak unto professional, as old ideological decisions became increasingly formal and dignified, counting for little in the real world of careers and organizations. This view did not envisage governments such as Mrs Thatcher's coming into power to attack the professions in the name of commerce; nor did it envisage the Cold War being won so emphatically by one side in the name of commerce.

How Bad Is It To Be a Professional?

It is often a compliment to be called professional and the compliment works as noun, adjective and adverb. But there are also derogatory senses of professional: it has long been common to refer to prostitution as 'the oldest profession' and law as 'the second oldest profession', with the added comment that lawyers are worse because prostitutes sell only their bodies. If we want to say that someone is remorseless in pursuit of his own interest or simply in making a nuisance of himself we call him a 'professional scrounger' and a 'professional agitator'. In sport the notion of a 'professional foul' signifies moral dubiety, an image extended in Tom Stoppard's play of that name.[13] Derogation of members of the professions for their charlatanism and extreme self-interest is nothing new. Ben Jonson's *Volpone* contains a stream of anti-lawyer and anti-doctor jokes as the heirless Volpone pretends to be dying and the doctor and the lawyer try to have his will altered in their favours. Jonson's contemporary and friend Shakespeare has the rebel Jack Cade in *Henry VI*, Part II condemn to death anyone who can read or write, starting with the lawyers.[14] His character has almost nothing in common with the historical Jack Cade and one suspects that Shakespeare gave him his virulent sentiments because the groundlings would enjoy listening to them.

These are merely examples of hostility to particular professions, formulated in a period in which professionalism was far from sufficiently dominant that we would talk about a professional society. But as such a society does develop, the professions acquire additional features which outsiders might suspect. Professionals take over from both amateurs and commercial entrepreneurs. The direct take-over from amateurs is most complete in diplomacy, politics and administration, where the 'all-round man' with a classical education and no technical or specialist qualifications is superseded by the careerist and the 'professional' politician who knows no other job. The replacement of the entrepreneur takes place in the structure of companies where real control of most companies (and especially of large, established companies) falls into the hands of Masters of Business Administration whose careers have begun as salaried managers rather than as risk-takers. Arguably, there is also a tendency for many professions to lose their amateur human values and to detach themselves from their clients. Doctors, teachers, lawyers and bank managers can less and less be seen as specialist members of communities whose real expertise lies in their ability to make important human judgements, but are increasingly bound by rules and procedures, seeking above all 'to keep their noses clean'. In a series of comments on medicine, for example, the late Petr Skrabanek accused doctors of systematically retreating from the role of attempting to cure individual patients to a position in which they are more specialist, more highly paid and much more concerned with screening and monitoring patients than with curing them.[15]

Professions start by acting as guilds, setting up barriers to entry. They develop this process by creating increasing specialisms – a commercial lawyer, an allergy doctor, a sixth-grade teacher. In economists' terms they constantly 'seek rent', setting up artificial tolls to individual progress in society which are sources of income for them without a corresponding increase in society's product. You need a doctor's certificate for this, a lawyer's signature for that and a degree from a set of professors even to get a half-decent job.

Perhaps the defining feature of professionalism is its moral ambiguity. Whose interest, ultimately, does the professional serve? Most would claim, surely, that their actions ultimately serve the interests of society. But this is a difficult claim to believe given the other calls on their loyalty. These include the interests of the profession itself and (a separate call) the ethics of the profession, the Hippocratic Oath, or the barrister's duty not to obtain a conviction by deception. There are also the particular clients, for those professionals who have them and the expectations of loyalty to the organization you work for. It is all a great deal more complicated than trying to maximize profits.

It is reasonable (if indecisive) to believe that all these factors constrain professional behaviour. If we apply the actions of public choice theory and assume, as economists do, that rational self-interest is going to outweigh (or redefine) all of the above we can generate a kind of 'career theory' in which the individual professional is driven primarily by his own desire for career success. This may generally prove compatible with supporting the interest of the profession as a whole and will only rarely tempt him to flout professional ethics. The choice between career and client may occasionally be a tricky one. But the outstanding characteristic of professionals is their almost total lack of any loyalty to the organizations they work for, or, in a larger sense, to place or community. The professional academic will take his prestige and his research grants to a rival university which offers him more money or an easier life; he will do it without a qualm and he will expect no criticism for it. The professional local government officer will go to the other end of the country for the sake of preferment and a great deal further than that if his skills are transferable. In each case they are acting in the traditions of the lawyer and the mercenary soldier who will serve every master and opposite causes. In each case they leave behind amateurs, students and local politicians, who have abiding loyalties to institutions, places and communities. In a professional society this difference of behaviour is so fully accepted that it is not questioned.

Professionalism in Sport?

Given this description, a reasonable reaction might be to demand 'what on earth has this got to do with sport?' Professional sports make some pretensions to the trappings of professionalism with coaching certificates and a spurious language of technicality. These go farther on the European continent than they do in Britain: Franz Beckenbauer, as *de facto* manager of the West German national football team which won the World Cup in 1990, had to work nominally alongside a qualified coach because he himself did not have the appropriate qualifications. But such pretensions are normally as thin as they are predictable. In most sports competitive ability is the only entry requirement. The question of a professional ethics remains deeply ambiguous. People talk of a 'model professional' as a player whose conduct on and off the field fits the general norms of society well. These include fairness, politeness and the ability to give a pleasant interview. Sir Bobby Charlton, Trevor Brooking and Gary Lineker are perhaps the most famous model professionals in English football. But a 'professional foul' is cheating in the interest of one's team, something that Acton was alleged to have done in 'Acton's Feud' and which the Corinthian Casuals insisted no gentlemen would ever do. 'Model professionals' are famous precisely for not committing 'professional fouls'.

I am referring here to football and, on statistical grounds at least, need make no apology for doing so: at the time of writing there are many more professional footballers in the English Premiership alone than there are competitors making a living in golf, tennis and boxing combined in the whole of Europe. Martin Roderick commented on how much more professional an amateur gymnast seemed than the professional footballers with whom he had trained and played. Indeed, much of the evidence suggests that English professional footballers have generally been gloriously unprofessional in much of their conduct. It would often be more accurate to call them atavistically gladiatorial rather than professional. Duncan Stewart's research into alcohol in sport supports the comments of many Italians who have played in England and suggests an attitude to drinking and a level of consumption of drink which would seem to be more rational for a gladiator who must salute Caesar and die on the morrow rather than a highly-paid, modern, games player.[16] At one point a player tells him of a famous manager berating three of his players for not drinking enough! The place of footballers in society is concomitant with this; generally, they have possessed the fragile glamour of the circus artiste and the popular singer. Thus we are not surprised when they demonstrate short-time horizons and even self-destructive instincts more than the solid status of the professional. But it is also true that in some respects professional footballers are typical professionals. They have the same sense of being a type apart, pursuing a uniquely significant activity, as do other professionals. The most chilling aspect of this, in Andrew Parker's account, is the description of a coach mocking and discouraging his apprentices from pursuing their education because it might weaken their resolve to 'make it'.[17] Professional footballers have the same clashes of interest and ethical dilemmas as other professionals: the game, the profession, the club and the self all exert claims. The most powerful claim of all must be the exigencies of the individual career, especially given its fragility and short length. Professional footballers can instantly transfer their allegiance with their registrations and proudly don the jersey and wave the scarf the instant the transfer is complete, just as academics will change the description 'University of X' to 'University of Y' on their article in a prestigious journal the moment their paymaster changes. We are no longer shocked by such behaviour, but perhaps we ought to be.

Even so, professionalism in sport remains only the minor dimension of the decline of amateurism: the more comprehensive opposing force remains commercialism.

The Sportsman's Dystopia

Let us try to consider the idea of sport operating on a purely commercial basis. From the outset this is a very problematic conception. One reason that it is so difficult is that most of what we know of sport has been formed by the amateur hegemony. According to one argument, a purely commercial sport might be inconceivable because what would sell best would not be worth considering as sport at all. Unconstrained by ideas of fairness and purity of achievement, it might be a comic melodrama between good and bad in which it is arranged that the popular favourite wins – something like professional wrestling, in fact. We would be entitled to say that it was not sport, but a popular entertainment in the form of a sport.

In a purely commercial transaction a person is either a buyer or a seller, a consumer or a producer. This purity may not be achieved in real life, but some kinds of transaction are much closer to it than others. At a rock concert people who pay to go in may be fans and believers, their relationship to the band may have many dimensions beyond consumption and they are, as an audience, partly producers themselves of what it is they are consuming. Watching a film in a cinema is therefore a much more purely commercial act than attending a rock concert for most people.

In the same way, it is difficult to conceive of a purely commercial university. Even if you can manage to fit 'learning' into the conceptual pigeon-hole of 'consumption', universities are traditionally committed to advancing knowledge on all fronts irrespective of whether that knowledge has public benefits or not, and even where it has public benefits, whether or not those benefits are, or ever could be, sold by their producers. In its educational function one dimension of the role of a university system is to grade people. Universities thus resemble regulatory bodies rather than companies, and absurdity and tension arise from the truism that people will not pay happily to be graded lowly.

In existing society people attend stadiums for reasons which cannot be put under the heading of 'consumption', unless that term is stretched well beyond its meaning in other contexts. They are there to admire and to participate in an important sense; if they support football clubs they are there as part of an indefinitely long story which binds a kind of community together. In many sports, but perhaps especially rugby and cricket, they are there as part of a great chain of sporting being which links the most humble participants to the most exalted who share a sense of shared tastes and values. The club dinner and the guest appearance of the Great Man are an important part of this chain.

Thus the insistence of the Institute of Economic Affairs and its sympathizers on the Conservative back benches during any policy debate about football that it is an entertainment and should be treated as such is one of those true, but trivial statements whose narrowness misses many points. It is in this conceptually difficult context that the idea of a fully commercial sport should be explored. What is it that people would buy when they are consumers in a sporting transaction? The most obvious answer is spectacle, the typical product of the circus. This generates what John Hoberman has called in a number of works 'the performance principle'. It is the Olympic slogan – *Citius, Altius, Fortius* – without the Olympic ideals. In caricature we might say that commercial sport would necessarily be a kind of freak show where we paid to see the extremes of human physical achievement. But we would also have to include in the category of pure consumption those motives which were directed towards status. Since much consumption is essentially 'conspicious' and the goods and services are 'positional' in Hirsch's sense (their supply limited by their very nature), we must allow these motives to fall under the heading of pure consumption. The season ticket at Melchester Rovers and the skiing holiday in Klosters can be part of a consumption portfolio which also includes drinking Margaux and eating in restaurants awarded three rosettes in the *Michelin Guide*.

The performance principle suggests an interesting speculation about drugs. Consider the possibility of the full legalisation of all possible substances which enhance athletic performance. The Olympic 100 m is a competition between biological machines, the products of rival drug companies, just as Formula One car races are at least as much competition between rival technologies as between individual performers. But would it sell? As spectacle, it would be better than anything we have had so far and there would be a considerable technical interest. Yet it would all – according to the orthodox, if rather hysterical, legacy of the amateur ethos – consist of 'cheating'. It would certainly be far removed from the 'Roger Bannister' image of athletics, when the competitors were gallant young men who fitted training into their other careers.[18]

I confess to not knowing the answer: the question when raised in a conference on the future of athletics which I chaired generated much passion and divided the audience almost equally. But at this point we must admit that speculation about the shape of a purely commercial sport cannot get very far without making assumptions about the range of tastes in society. We could treat taste as essentially universal and assume, for instance, that human nature creates an eternal desire for spectacle. On this basis we could assume that a purely commercial sport would have the essential properties of the Roman arena which specialized in extremities of spectacle and the absence of moral aspiration or constraint. (Modern scholarship has, if anything, enhanced our view of the extremities of the arena.)[19] Such sports science fiction films as *Rollerball* and *The Running Man* assume that human beings in the twenty-first century will be essentially the same as they were in ancient Rome.

On the other hand, there are at least two arguments which would suggest that we should assume that tastes differ substantially between societies.[20] The first is the thesis of the 'civilizing process', a complex argument, it must be conceded, but one which has the implication that modern sport has been successful precisely because we no longer have a taste for the kind of cruelties that went on in the Roman arena or in the several animal-baiting activities which were common in England up to the 1830s.[21]

The other factor to be taken into consideration is simply that there may be substantial differences between national cultures in ways which radically affect sporting perceptions and tastes.[22] One common theme of this argument points to a contract between a Germanic tradition which admires a purely physical prowess and an English tradition in which character (or 'bottle') and teamwork are the admirable qualities in sport. This was a theme of the *Kulturkampf* conducted in late nineteenth-century Germany in defence of the 'purity' of the German gymnastic tradition and against the increasing popularity of English organized games, which were associated with crowds, rowdy behaviour and gambling. At a later stage the same sort of difference of culture was apparent in the attitudes of East German coaches to the Anglophone condemnation of drug regimes for athletes as reactionary and hypocritical. In these respects the United States appears to have considerable German as well as English influences and there is an important difference of sporting culture between the two countries.[23] English people, in my experience, do not share with Americans their sense of wonder at the sight of a 350 lb man who can run the 100 m in under 11 seconds. Correspondingly, Americans find it hard to comprehend a standing ovation for a number 11 batsman (who after all is not very good at batting), whose only achievement is to survive for half an hour against hostile bowling without scoring. In this respect, even the enhanced division of labour which would seem to be part of a fully commercial conception of sport may be doubted because it is precisely the lack of division of labour – bowlers having to bat in cricket, defenders having to take penalties in football or stout prop forwards finding themselves in space with the ball in rugby – which appeals to a certain English taste for a drama of mettle put to the test.

There must also be some doubts about the economic basis of a fully commercial sport which might evolve in the twenty-first century. What, for example, would be the predominant source of revenue? It is easy to say that television will become increasingly important and 'bums on seats' correspondingly less so. But there are at least two other sources of revenue which might be bigger than television. The first is gambling, which already dominates the finances of some sports (such as horse racing). Gambling also dominated the pre-amateur commercial sports of cricket and pugilism; the institution of amateurism was to some degree a revolution against gambling. (In most East Asian societies gambling is the main focus of the interest in sport.) It is a strange contingency that the most commercial society on earth, the United States, has what Scitovsky calls 'the Puritan Ghost' which, allied to the legacy of organized crime, has relegated gambling to relatively small and shadowy parts of American society.

The other source of revenue which may be potentially bigger than the others combined cannot be described in or by a single word. It is the existence of sport as a prestigious adjunct to other commercial activities. Several figures were quoted at the end of the twentieth century to suggest that sport was the sixth biggest industry in the European Union, the eleventh in the United States and the twenty-second in the world. As statistics these are fairly hopeless, being on vague and different bases, but it is clear in all cases that watching sport live is a small part of the total and what matters is a huge and ill-defined range of sports-related transactions including holidays, advertising, clothing, health products and services and, above all, forms of sponsorship. Increasingly, organizations from national and city governments to financial and manufacturing companies want to be associated with sporting success.[24] Perhaps the reality of commercial sport will be its treatment as a favourite child of corporate power; maybe the paradoxical consequence of that will be that they will virtually pay the spectators because the image of a full stadium is extremely important and the revenues to be gained from charging for admission very unimportant.

Ambiguity, uncertainty and paradox seem to be the consequences of speculating about the nature of a maximally commercialized sport. The Roman arena might provide some clues as to what it could be like. We can certainly say that in most respects sport in the United States is closer to a model of full commercialism than are other sporting realities. There even seems to be the development of a kind of gladiatorial code in American sport as there was in Rome, where the elite consumers are fascinated by the glamour of the gladiators, but would not want their children to be one. (Of course, in the United States this perception has a racial dimension which is irrelevant to my current theme.)[25]

It also seems undeniable that global and British sport have moved towards a more fully commercial model. This is evident in many respects, most of which have already been covered here, but there is a particularly interesting body of writing about the changing nature of the experience of watching football in England. There is a range from the best seller, of which Nick Hornby's *Fever Pitch* is the most prominent, to Steve Redhead's academic development of the concept of 'fandom' and its decline.[26] The general theme of these accounts is that the true fan is being replaced by the consumer. True fans stand on terraces, they shout and sing and sometimes fight; they talk of the club as 'we' or 'us' and measure their lives in remembered results; they get as much misery as joy from the whole thing. They are (and this is my comment rather than a theme of the writing) dedicated amateur sportsmen and sportswomen who happen to occupy the terraces rather than the playing surface.

But true fans are being replaced by consumers who sit in comfortable, safe seats and for whom the whole experience does not transcend life, it is a mere part of one pattern of consumption. In a foretaste of the change, Colin Ward wrote in 1989:

Somewhere, in a place called Utopia, is a football stadium which is covered

all round, is all seated and has a sheltered picnic area. Families go there on a Saturday afternoon with their best clothes on and watch football in reverential silence. Every week the stadium is packed and there is no booing, racism or fighting amongst fans...When a goal is scored a polite ripple of applause breaks out. This is the Utopia of politicians who know nothing about football and still less about football fans.[27]

This politician's Utopia differs in several crucial respects from the commercial El Dorado. For example, 'reverential silence' will not sell anything: the real sound of commercial sport is the munching and slurping of comestibles combined with music and shouted commentary which are intended to excite the crowd. I confess to a particular shock (which may have directed the whole course of this argument) on attending my first baseball game. The bases were loaded, a 'slugger' walked out to bat. It was the equivalent of the last hope batsman going to the wicket in a major cricket match. But whereas what happens in such circumstances in a major cricket match is a sense of tension and a low murmur which approaches silence, what happened at the baseball game is that *the organ played*! It is the lack of reverence for what is going on which seems to typify the commercial in sport.

At the beginning of the 1980s I wrote a prophetic account of the future of football in an essay which turned out to be an uncommercially early example of the expression of fandom:

> Never again will [football] have the kind of place in society that it did at the height of the old working-class culture. But it will survive, rules will be changed, the stadia will be modernized; it will turn itself into a family entertainment like American sport with peanuts and popcorn and probably dancing girls. Many of us will dislike the change, but there seems little point in regretting a process that is as deeply rooted in the major direction of society as was the original evolution of modern football. But I hope that in the clean bright world where there are only family seats and no terraces, the old atmosphere will survive.[28]

Most of this came to pass in the 1990s, though it is debatable whether 'the old atmosphere' survived. On the other hand, it did generate a counter-culture of the determined and self-ascribed fan with his 'fanzines' and earnest niche in the high culture. It is parallel in some ways to the emergence discussed earlier of a 'post-industrial' counter-culture in American sport. During the 1990s crowds at rugby's Varsity Match and at lower division and non-league semi-professional football actually went up contrary to what one would expect from any prior theory of commercialization. It is likely that any pure commercialization of sport would be accompanied by a reaction. If so, and given its ambiguities and paradoxes, 'pure commercialization' may be a chimeric nightmare for the sportsman. A more subtle possibility would pose a greater threat.

A Clearer and More Realistic Nightmare

For more than a hundred years the adjective most closely associated with commercialism in England has been 'brash': Wiener's classic account of English anti-commercialism draws on a deep well of books, sermons and newspaper leaders which express disapproval of brash commercialism, though his account does conflate commercialism with industrialism.[29] Actually, I think there is a great deal of evidence that English people like brash commercialism in its place – which may be Blackpool or the United States – but are seriously fearful of its capacity to destroy their institutions and landscape which are important to their culture.

Thus the frontal assaults of Brashcomm are likely to be repulsed and relegated to the margins of the culture. We will continue to want to do things in the best possible taste, to condemn all drug use (however unrealistically) as cheating and we shall stick as far as possible to traditions like the FA Cup.

The All-England Lawn Tennis Championships are likely to be marked by white clothes and strawberries and the absence of fireworks and lasers for the indefinite future. This is how commerce works for an anti-commercial people. There will be more technically amateur participants in sport than ever before.

However, much of what I have argued suggests that they will tend to be unpaid crypto-professionals rather than true amateurs. This is well established in football and a clear trend in rugby and cricket. (But not, to be fair to the complexity of human affairs, in athletics where there are probably more true amateurs competing at the beginning of the twenty-first century than they were at the height of the amateur hegemony. These include 'fun runners', club athletes of no pretensions whatsoever to 'excellence' and participants in booming activities such as fell-running which exist out of the control of the athletic authorities. As signs from the above would have it, I broke from writing this section to cycle around the common near my house and saw a fairly serious 'fun run' with a most impressive range of participants of both sexes, many shapes and all ages.)

The new forms of pyramids and leagues fit into a chain of command from the government to the Sports Councils, to the National Associations, leagues and clubs. The purposes of this chain have to do with 'excellence' and 'youth development', from government down, the motive of each actor is to be seen to be pursuing the goal of national success. The net effect (as clearly illustrated by my research on cricket) is more hierarchy and instrumentality, less joy and tradition. The norms and traditions of amateur sport are continually eroded by televised professionalism. The chain of command may be strengthened, but the great chain of social being, which linked the village player to the international in rugby and cricket, is weakening.

All this happens, not because of the real market (which might in itself leave amateur sport to its own devices), but because of the imperatives of pseudo-markets established by the state. In this respect the situation in British sport is much like that in British universities, where the need for 'earned income' has done little to damage academic life, but state insistence on 'Research Assessment Exercises' and 'Quality Assurance Agencies' have caused great harm. States are in particularly dangerous form when they seek to define and promulgate 'excellence'. The freedom of the academic institution is eroded by the need to get at least as good a research grading as its rivals; the freedom of the sports club is eroded by having to compete for public money so as not to fall behind its rivals.

The dangers of the corporatist pseudo-market and the excellence agenda are thus much more profound than those of Brashcomm. The political form of the danger is something well known in British history: the perpetuation of the shells of institutions which masks their subtle and essential metamorphosis into something with a different purpose and a different ethos.

Arguments for Amateurism Reconsidered

It has been one of the basic arguments of this book that amateurism has been, and remains, in steady decline. Therefore arguments for amateurism must seek to preserve the remainder or to revive the essence, possibly in new forms. It must be remembered that the consequential and utilitarian basis of my argument is not radical like those of deep ecologists, Marxists or Islamic fundamentalists. It does not say that we should organize society on a different basis to be in harmony with nature or the Forces of History or God's Will. Utilitarianism is already the philosophical basis of what we do, especially in Britain, and most aspects of government take decisions and justify their actions on its basis. Treasury economics is a highly technical form of applied utilitarian philosophy.[30]

The general problem is that we do not understand happiness and equate it with instrumental technicalities such as 'economic growth' and 'the standard of living'. It is important in this context to take account of Scitovsky's argument that the premise of modern economic calculations is an extraordinarily crude conception of human well-being which has abandoned the serious task of philosophizing about happiness (an investigation conducted on a far more advanced level in the eighteenth century than it is now) in favour of refined mathematical constructs built on this extremely crude foundation. For the games player the bottom line may be as simple as the statement of the Namibian farmer Schalk van der Merwe during the Rugby World Cup in 1999, 'I wouldn't like to be a pro. To make rugby your work wouldn't be very nice, you don't enjoy it so much. You should play for the love of the game'.[31] It is part of the critique of orthodox economics developed by Scitovsky and Hirsch that, if he were to turn professional, he would create additional transactions in an economy and thus contribute to 'economic growth' and 'the standard of living' which we normally consider to be good things. Thus the particular arguments for amateurism which follow are applications of a general critique of contemporary Western societies from within their prevailing ideology:

Amateurs Do It Better?

Professionalism is about careers. Thus professionals, when they have important decisions to make, have too much at stake to make them well. That whole bundle of status, self-esteem and personal financial management which we call a career is a lot to have to put on the table. Professionals in any field are likely to err in the directions of caution, conformity and self-interest when compared with the amateur.

Of course, since I have insisted that it would be wrong to try to establish any particular definition of amateurism, then some stipulation is necessary of what would be an amateur for the purposes of this argument. It would be a matter of degree: a person would be an amateur to the extent that he did not need to remain or succeed in the particular role but had other sources of self-esteem. In politics it is good to have people like Lord Grey of Fallodon, whose tenure as Foreign Secretary was irksome because he really wanted to be back on his Northumbrian estate writing a book about the birds there.[32] A more modern example would be John Nott, who walked out of a television interview because he was sick of politics and wanted to return to business. In professional society there are professional politicians; there is no need to call Cincinnatus from his plough because there is a queue of ambitious shysters claiming to be able to save Rome. Career politicians, we would infer from the theory of careers, will do almost anything to survive. The professionalization of Western politics has deep roots, but it has been observed to proceed steadily since American political science noted the existence of 'new politics' in the 1960s which was less concerned with ideology and more driven by opinion polls. A person would be an amateur in any field to the extent that there are emotional counterweights and alternative sources of income to his career. In academic life we desperately need more amateurs in this sense to counterbalance the career professionals who mould their lives around the needs to score well in 'research' and 'quality' exercises and the ability to fill in the forms which secure public funding. These professionals may produce many things, but originality is never going to be one of them. Equally, excellence must elude the profit-seeker in certain fields where it can only be achieved by aristocratic and amateur methods incompatible with commerce: a good example is the superior quality of many kinds of food and wine based on varieties which yield only uncommercially small quantities.

In sport, the argument seems to apply most clearly to coaches. As a rugby player I was coached under the old system which meant, excepting a few schoolmasters, the captain of the team. The best of them were brilliant, leaders by example, capable of inculcating an unlikely mixture of joy and fanaticism. There is a sharp contrast between this and the coaches of professional football and cricket clubs with whom my sons have had dealings. They have been generally miserable, negative and incapable of inspiring any kind of team spirit. By contrast, I have seen joyful geniuses coaching mini-rugby on Sunday mornings, men who can make the imposition of extra press-ups an amusing experience. The explanation is the culture of fear: the herd of coaches who deal with youthful 'wannabes' on behalf of professional clubs are lowly in their trade, their tenure is insecure and there are hundreds of former professional players who would have been keen to take their jobs. Neither joy nor independent thought seem to flourish under these conditions.

The argument transfers less convincingly on to the field of play itself. A priori one might construct an argument that true amateurs are much more capable of panache, flair and imagination than over-coached professionals, fearful of incurring the wrath of those who select teams. Rugby players might look back to Richard Sharpe, an England player of the late 1950s and the early 1960s, whose decision-making was unreadable and who produced tactics of a brilliance not seen now. But it would be difficult to sanction this argument: in some sports the top players have enough financial security to risk brilliance without fear as professionals. In any case, most participants bear witness to the mental reality that once you are on the playing surface, against an opponent, in front of a crowd, the business of amateur or professional status is almost entirely irrelevant: the double negative need not to underachieve is paramount. Amateurs can be gripped by fear as much as professionals. A counter-example to Sharpe would be David Campese, who played for Australia in the 1980s and the 1990s. 'Campo' notoriously wrote 'professional rugby player' in his passport long before Rugby Union legalized professionalism and sought a living playing the game in continental Europe. Yet no player in the history of the game has possessed quite the cheek and outrageous brilliance of 'Campo'; nor has any, at the highest level, matched his amateurish errors. (A curious contrast of unpaid excellence and richly rewarded mediocrity is to be found in televised quiz programmes: at the highest level, in 'Mastermind', 'Mastermind India' and 'University Challenge', they are strictly amateur, whereas rich rewards may be gained at a much lower level, such as in 'Who Wants To Be a Millionaire?')

Part of this argument must be an exploration of the difference between amateurism and professionalism as epistemologies and philosophies of education. The amateur view, which was the only one in the eighteenth century and still prevailed in most of the nineteenth, is that knowledge is a seamless whole. You cannot understand politics without knowing history and law and considering the theories of the philosophers, economists and sociologists. To consider the nature of the universe requires knowledge of physics, philosophy, mathematics and theology. Professional knowledge, by contrast, is defined by its boundaries. One has one's 'field' and digs deep in it, defending it against the outside and disciplining oneself not to leave it. You can be a physicist without knowing anything of the ideas of Descartes or Kant or a lawyer who has never heard of Justinian or Montesquieu.

Without wishing to oversimplify or exaggerate the point, it is clear that our conception of knowledge has, in this sense, become more professional. The world of the traditional Oxford college, with the fellows each having his own discipline, who meet and talk at dinner is now a fading anomaly in the world of specialized academic departments. It is also clear that, whatever the advantages of professional knowledge, amateur knowledge has a spirit of joy and a breadth of vision that also carry huge utilitarian gains.

Amateurism Is Good Commercialism

Both Rugby Union and athletics have had severe financial problems since admitting professionalism. We must not forget the simple fact that, *ceteris paribus*, as the economists would say, running an industry where the labour is free is a jolly good idea. It is an especially good idea when the alternative is a competitive chasing after that non-substitutable labour which has the marketable mark of the champion upon it. But there is another aspect of the economics of amateurism which is important. Arguably, heroes and characters are much more natural and genuine products of amateurism than of professionalism. Lionel Tennyson, ignored and underrated as a batsman, yet hammering the top Australian bowlers, Roger Bannister, collapsing over the line, Richard Sharpe, beating man after man until even he does not seem know in which direction he is going to turn next: the unpredictable and heroic images of amateurism cannot easily be duplicated by mere jobbers. It does seem that the public in many cases preferred its rugby players and athletes to be also doctors and teachers.

The Meaning of Life Argument

In moving from amateur to professional and/or commercial milieux, people commodify their labour and to some extent are alienated from it. These terms have been used throughout the history of Marxism and are still in use today; indeed, a plausible Marxist account of capitalism in the early twenty-first century is that the process of commercialization–commodification continues apace and there is still a long way to go before the system will reach its end and collapse, notwithstanding that Marx and Engels thought revolution was imminent in 1848.

But in Marxist thought observations about commodification are left as analytical remarks and implicit comparisons with a different ('fully human') society. We are entitled to ask, as Mill did of sexual inequality, 'What's wrong with commodification?' Sometimes to commodify is good: exchange relationships increase wealth and freedom. Selling anything, including one's labour, is better than giving it away, all other things being equal.

It is tempting to say that what is wrong with commodification, when it is wrong, can best be expressed in a kind of sub-Kantian language: the difference is between doing things as means and doing them as ends. We all understand, *in extremis*, the difference between travelling to get from *A* to *B* and travelling for the joy of it. But the distinction, a difficult one in many instances, becomes incoherent in most sporting cases. In competitive amateur sport we play to win the championship. But we establish the championship and compete in it so as to be able to play: the means–ends distinction collapses into circularity. In any case the best description of the motivations of amateur and professional sportsmen seems to be success defined as a complex interplay between potential, fulfilment, self-esteem and the esteem of others. A particular form of status is more important than money on any field of play. Is that more of an 'end' than having money? The question does not seem to be answerable.

The distinction which works and which has ethical importance is Scitovsky's between comfort and culture. Comfort goods remove fears, pains, irritations and so on; cultural goods give meaning to life. Many things that we do (such as having a family meal) combine elements of comfort and culture; some (such as sitting in a traffic jam or working at a badly paid and unpleasant job) offer neither. It is typical of an intense cultural experience for any individual that:

- he creates it or contributes to it in some way;
- this gives a sense of achievement;
- the achievement was always in doubt;
- it will be remembered and be a source of satisfaction indefinitely; and
- it creates a bond between the person and either other people or a particular terrain or both.

The abiding flavour of culture, in this sense, is its authenticity, the sense of life having a real and natural meaning. Clearly, sport in certain societies is a particularly real source of such meaning, whether it is playing a part in a great cricket match or climbing a mountain or jumping out of a plane. It is not necessary that the match be of a particularly high standard, nor the mountain Everest, nor the jump the hardest. Let us remember that Hirsch uses the word romance in a way which is parallel to Scitovsky's concept of culture. One important aspect of people when they act as cultural or romantic beings is that we cannot distinguish what they do as production or consumption; it is both and more than both.

The distinction between amateur and professional experiences is by no means the distinction between cultured and comfortable experiences, but the two are related. Money does tend to change relationships and make instrumentalists of people. Even though some people – sportsmen, actors, perhaps even the occasional academic – may be able to transcend the effects of money and gain true romance from their profession, most people are going to find it in their amateur capacities. The full commodification of life, which makes watching a football team mere consumption and running a rugby club mere production, must exclude romance.

The Argument from Civil Society

In the Good Society commerce is practised freely, but treated with contempt. That is, it is practised freely within a large and well-defined area, but there are limiting borders of commercial activity: there are times, places and activities where it has only a subsidiary part to play or no part at all. Hirsch's *reductio ad absurdum* of the indefinite application of the commercial principle is sex, which, in its broadest ramifications, may be a candidate for the most important of all human activities.

But there is also an important argument to consider about politics, about the collective basis for our individual well-being. If society moves towards hyper-commercialism, resources of time and effort are squeezed at both ends: we work increasingly hard in order to consume increasingly hard. There are longer hours at work, but also more hours to be spent in the shop and the restaurant. Both are able to expand because amateur and domestic activities have declined.[33] Why should *homo mercis* join a political party or be a member of the cricket club committee? It is easy to show that in a naturally self-interested commercial society people would not engage in political activity.

Hyper-commercialism in this sense is only an abstraction and possibly an incoherent one because the political infrastructure which supported it would collapse. The movement towards it is anything but complete. On the other hand, it is a movement. Brought up in a land of pubs and clubs, I have been surprised and depressed while researching this book by the extent to which most of the rest of the world lacks this structure of civil society, but also by the degree to which it has declined in England.

What Is To Be Done?

What should a person who believes in the amateur principle – in a range of senses – support or prescribe for the twenty-first century? There is an acute logical problem if that person is a theorist of society. What such theorists do nowadays – it was different in the seventeenth and the eighteenth century – is to analyse society, where analysis is at least partly causal. Thus, they are likely to draw a picture of the direction in which society is heading which is full of endemic, systematic trends. The danger is that your account of why existing society works as it does and why it must change in the ways that it is changing is so thorough that it leaves no space for prescription or action. Extreme versions of this problem are to be found in those Marxists influenced by Antonio Gramsci, whose crypto-functionalist account of capitalist society demonstrates how every part – from the electoral system to the judiciary, to popular culture – has its role in keeping the system in being.

You may be reduced to believing that nothing you could ever say could make any difference or, if it did, it would only be to add further support to the system. The logical conclusion may be to invite a leading capitalist to comment and then close your once revolutionary magazine down – this is exactly what Martin Jacques did with *Marxism Today* in 1991–92, the capitalist being Sir John Harvey-Jones.[34]

Much 'theory' thus contains little in the way of overt ethics and even less in the way of prescription. There are implicit comparisons between the real social systems we observe and fully human societies or Enlightenment values, but little in the way of outrage or recommendation. 'Critical theory' does not criticise anything in the normal sense of the word and the later developments of Marxism prescribed only that you sit around universities with a rather superior look on your face and analyse society. Feminist theories, including feminist theories of sport, offer remarkably little account of what would constitute a fair treatment of women in sport or how we should attempt to achieve it; these debates are largely precluded by the transcendent nature of the 'patriarchy' which is analysed.[35] It is all too easy, if you theorize in this way to become morally impotent.

A further problem you face if you want to say what should be done is the question of prescription. Who should do what it is you think ought to be done, the candidates being (at least) individual people, governments and other institutions? I assume the primacy of individual belief, an assumption denied to those who see beliefs as the determined consequences of social structures. The major changes of the second half of the twentieth century, such as the rise of feminism and environmentalism (or even more contentiously, the decline of socialism) are not initiated or controlled by the state or the political elite. Society does change through books being written and by good arguments in the public bar. A book can play a part in making people look at the world differently and thus in changing the world (or in preventing it from changing or in slowing its changes).

But, of course, there are effects which only states can achieve. The classic public choice theories of the 'Tragedy of the Commons' and the 'Free Rider' are sufficient to create a large role for the state. In the Tragedy of the Commons, the common is overgrazed to the point of ecological destruction and there is nothing any individual can do about it, because his own choice not to graze his animals will only make it easier for self-interested others to graze theirs.[36] Only an authoritative, collective action – something state-like, in other words – which controls access or parcels out the common to individual owners can preserve the land. A version of the 'Free Rider' problem says that the trams could be run more efficiently and make a profit to reinvest if we did not have to employ anybody to sell tickets or collect fares, if people just paid. But some people will ride free and this corrupts the will of those who pay, so that the only solution is an authoritative system. A sporting parallel is to be found in 'the spirit of the game', a self-regulating set of norms without which some games would degenerate into anarchy: it has been conventionally thought within the game that this is particularly true of Rugby Union. The professional foul rides free on the spirit of the game.

So far as individuals are concerned the project of amateurism should be part of the maximization of personal autonomy. One dimension of this is the discovery of the fallacy of prosperity which consists in the recognition expressed in economic terms, that consumption and work-for-consumption show inevitably diminishing returns. (A more familiar way of putting this would be to cast doubt on the value of 'material goods' compared with goods such as family, cricket club and landscape. But most 'material' goods are not, in fact, material and the use of the term tends to obfuscate.)

It is true that when people live in dire material poverty (as is currently true, in my own bitter experience, in much of the former Soviet Union) to offer them amateur institutions (as Isaiah Berlin said of offering liberty to the starving) is to mock their condition.[37] But the situation in many countries in the twenty-first century promises to be beyond dire material poverty, and cultural goods, things of the spirit, should be increasingly important. That happiness lies in developing one's own range of talents and relationships is something which has been argued from Hume and Rousseau to Mill and Marx and, in our own day, Maslow. Few people disagree with it, but most people act as if it were not true. Capitalism remains a necessary condition of the good life, but it is certainly not a sufficient condition.

For clubs, the prescription must also be that they guard their autonomy. Cultivate independent sources of income, join no pyramids, maintain your traditions, put yourself in a position where you have to accept no directions, protect yourself from the allied forces of commerce and the state, neither of which is evil in itself, but both of which have a tendency to dominate.

It is more difficult to prescribe what the British state should do. A wish list might start with the Governance of Sports Act 2010, which declares, in effect, that the sovereign power of Parliament will protect the autonomy of British sporting institutions and traditions so that (for example) it would be illegal for an English football club to participate in a foreign competition if such participation interfered with its involvement in the FA Cup. It would also create powers to limit media control of sport. The reason for starting with such a nationalistic theme is simply that in sport more than almost any other sphere public decisions are made by global forces so any attempt to restrain commercialism must start with nationalism.

However, it is difficult even to imagine a real government, as opposed to a wish-list government, going very far to institute that sort of nationalism, which seeks to preserve what is best in national tradition, and to eschew the crass nationalism which concerns itself with the 'excellence' of national sporting performance. It is extremely difficult to fight against forces which are based on international and global markets – remember that it was the migration of English footballers to Italy which led to the abolition of the maximum wage in English football, which was, in some respects, the beginning of the end of amateur hegemony. In order to do so a state would have to attempt, at least in some respects, the level of autonomy previously only attempted by Myanmar, Albania and North Korea, with generally disastrous results.

But government could at least cease to interfere in sport and where it does interfere it should do so on the basis of criteria concerned with what is actually valuable in sport. Previously, governments have had sports policies based on health policy or the rather patronizing 'Sport for All' (which seemed to consist of trying to get Muslim ladies into swimming pools and extolling the virtues of 'plucky cripples')[38] and furthering 'quality' or 'excellence'. Government should confine its role to financial assistance (from non-tax sources such as the Lottery) for capital projects which help foster a sense of community and to preserve sporting traditions.

Cheer Up, It May Never Happen

We have no idea what the world will be like by the end of the twenty-first century. All the social scientists and social theorists, the makers of utopias and dystopias, have got it wrong so far. For much of the twentieth century the growth of *étatisme* was assumed, but it reversed in the last quarter of the century. The Malthusian expectations of world impoverishment which were so prevalent as late as the 1970s proved wildly incorrect, at least as a guide to the medium term. The leisure age of under-employment and state welfare, so widely expected in mid-century, never arrived. On the grand scale, nobody expected the revival of Christianity in the first half of the nineteenth century and few people expected the revival of capitalism which occurred in the second half of the twentieth.

It is important in considering proposals and prescriptions to remember that social systems are not really systems, but mere tendencies; they generate no inexorable laws. The forces of history, with their bullying language of 'progress' and 'modernization', are not so forceful if you stand up to them. The period from which we should draw inspiration in this respect is the one which gave rise to modern sport, the second half of the nineteenth century. In the 1840s, by the unanimous account of its literary and philosophical observers, urban England was a ruthless commercial world with little or no time for leisure; its traditions (and especially its sporting traditions) were in terminal decline. It was variously expected to experience revolution, social breakdown or a hardening and rationalizing of the soul. Stern religious belief was seen by many as the only antidote to its ills. Yet by 1900 that society had 'reinvented' itself as a world of pigeon-fanciers, Sunday School cricket leagues, brass bands, music halls, football fans, competitive gardeners and so on. Indeed, the place Orwell described in 'England Your England' is very much a product of that period, at least in its specific institutions and practices. It must remain the inspiration for a future belief in amateurism.

Perhaps the twenty-first century will be a new golden age of amateurism. Prosperous human beings in a free and stable society tend to rediscover the best things in life, the things which give it meaning: love, landscape and sport, all of which involve romance, in the sense it has been discussed here. These things are, if not quite free, then potentially available to everybody and free from commercial constraints. The cultural memories of sportsmanship, community and the ideal of a gentleman (and of a lady) have deep roots which will not be eradicated. The fear of the eradication of ancient cultural values which was so much part of the theory of totalitariansim and so clear an aim of Mao Zedong's 'cultural revolution' or Pol Pot's regime have receded. The vast improvement in the technologies of recording and transmitting information enhance individual autonomy and not the power of the state; they give us access to our identity and our past rather than homogenize us.

It is difficult to imagine sport's surviving the century without some important legacy, at least, of the amateur ideal. Commercialism must be modified by idealism if sport is to prosper. The requirement is parallel to that of Baron de Montesquieu in his insistence that only mixed and moderate government could survive.[39] Just as monarchy is modified by democracy in the most stable regimes, so capitalism is modified by Christianity and democracy. In sport, the 'performance principle' must be modified by honour and friendship. Sometimes one senses in contemporary sports commentary a yearning for a true hero whose excellence of performance is combined with the metaphoric shining armour of a true gentleman. Pele, Sir Garfield Sobers and Sir Bobby Charlton were such men. Who is to say that there will be no more? A revival of sportsmanship and amateur ethics will fall into an historical pattern of cyclical reactions to hyper-commercialism since 1714.

In so far as we merely consume things, then their future is of no interest. We might finish the last bottle of the '45 port or the last ever Beluga caviar with a certain consumer relish because nobody would ever taste them again. We might even clap especially warmly with enjoyment on the last night of a theatrical production, because life goes on and there will be other productions. But where experiences have real cultural meaning, their termination would have the opposite effect. You could not look at a favourite landscape knowing that it was going to be destroyed by development tomorrow or next year without the pleasure being annihilated. The meaning for us exists because we are part of that landscape and because it will be there indefinitely, as it was in the past. As with Burke's account of the constitution, the culture is a contract between the generations. What is true of landscape is also true of a game or a football club. One might, as an Englishman, watch and enjoy a Spanish bullfight as an interesting curiosity, precisely because the abolition of bullfighting was imminent. But people are devastated by the thought that their football club might not be there in the future.

Those economic utilitarians who see human beings as primarily consumers do not understand the social nature of time. Jeremy Bentham (a bachelor) rigorously stipulated that legislation takes no account of the unborn, while Lord Keynes fatuously remarked that in the long run we shall all be dead. But, I do have a hope that, at some time in the second half of the twenty-first century, my grandson will play cricket with my great-grandson and see the latter take the winning catch in a game that matters hugely to those on the field of play, but to no one else. It is not impossible.

Chronology of Amateurism in British and Olympic Sport, 1863–1995

The Establishment of Amateurism, 1863–95

1863:   Establishment of the Football Association.

1866:   John Graham Chambers founded the Amateur Athletic Club with a membership mainly of City of London men with backgrounds in the ancient universities; the primary purpose is to hold a series of athletic contests, including boxing, in association with the University Boat Race.
The National Hunt Committee recognizes a category of amateur riders who must be licensed as such.

1867:   The eighth Marquis of Queensberry endowed a series of challenge cups for amateur boxers.

1871:   The Rugby Football Union formed.

1872:   The FA Challenge Cup is contested for the first time by 14 amateur teams with players from predominantly public school backgrounds; the final is won by The Wanderers, beating the Royal Engineers 1–0.

1880:   Amateur Boxing Association and Amateur Athletic Association founded.

1882:   Amateur Rowing Association founded with the specific intention of excluding manual workers from the sport; Hillsdale Boat Club (Michigan) refused entry to the Henley Royal Regatta.

1883:   Although professionalism is not yet recognized in Association Football, the FA Cup is won by Blackburn Olympic, who beat the Old Etonians in the final, 2–1 after extra time; the Olympic players are predominantly working class and allegedly professional.

1885:   The FA recognized professionalism, though with strict limitations on wages and dividends.

1888:   Football League formed.

1890:   National Amateur Rowing Association formed, with a less strict
          definition of amateurism than that of the ARA.

1891:   The penalty kick is introduced into professional football; the
          Corinthian Casuals, a predominantly public school and amateur
          club, announced a policy of refusing to score from penalty kicks.
          FA Amateur Cup instituted.

1893:   FA Amateur Cup launched.

1894:   Baron Pierre de Coubertin hosts a Paris Conference with
          representatives from 13 nations; the rules of amateurism are
          defined and it is agreed to hold a modern Olympic Games in
          Athens in 1896.

1895:   Rugby split over 'broken time' payments for players; professional
          Rugby League is largely confined to Lancashire and Yorkshire,
          while the strictly amateur Rugby Union code holds sway over the
          rest of the game.

Amateur Hegemony, 1895–1961

1896:   First Modern Olympics in Athens: there were representatives of
          12 nations, though the dominance of the USA was immediately
          apparent with victories in nine of the 15 track and field events
          (there had been several attempts to revive the Olympic Games in
          the nineteenth century with at least four in each of Greece and
          England; the Athens games of 1870 were probably the most
          successful).

1900:   Paris Olympics overshadowed by the Paris Exhibition.

1907:   Amateur Football Association formed by southern opponents of
          professional football.

1908:   London Olympics. Nineteen nations compete, but the event was
          dominated by the British and the Americans and by wrangling
          between them over ethics and qualifications (the St. Louis games
          of 1904 had been virtually an all-American event).

1912:   The Stockholm Olympics: the number of competitors doubled and many sports historians have seen Stockholm as the real establishment of the Olympic movement; but it was also notable for the victories of the native American Jim Thorpe in the pentathlon and the decathlon; his gold medals were subsequently withdrawn because he was paid to play baseball.

1913:   Formation of the International Amateur Athletic Federation.

1921:   J.H.B. Kelly, the Olympic sculling champion, was barred from the Henley Royal Regatta because he had worked as a bricklayer.

1924:   First Winter Olympics in Chamonix, France.

1931:   Cyril Tolley, twice British Amateur Golf Champion, awarded £1,000 in a libel action against Fry's, the chocolate maker, because an observer of their advertisement might infer that he had accepted money for the use of his name and thereby compromised his amateur status.

1932:   France barred from the Five Nations Rugby tournament because of alleged club professionalism (restored in 1945).

1936:   The Henley stewards refused entry to the Royal Regatta to the Sydney Police crew, who were *en route* to the Berlin Olympics.

1951:   The Soviet Olympic Committee formed, reversing previous Communist Party policy which eschewed the Olympics and the idea of amateurism as 'bourgeois'.

1952:   Soviet 'amateurs' compete for the first time at the Helsinki Olympics, coming second to the USA in the medals table. After the games the American Avery Brundage was elected President of the IOC. Brundage was a man for whom amateurism was 'a humanitarian religion – it, like the golden rule, stands for the right against the wrong. No philosophy, no religion preaches loftier sentiments.' Brundage was instrumental in rescinding the medals Jim Thorpe won in 1912; he described professional athletes as 'performing monkeys' and conducted constant and unsuccessful campaigns to 'clean up' or abolish the Winter Olympics.

The Decline of Amateurism, 1961–95

1961:   Abolition of the maximum wage in Association Football, then

£20 per week. The Fulham Chairman Tommy Trinder and the Burnley Chairman Bob Lord announced that they would pay Johnny Haynes and Jimmy McIlroy £100 per week (Lord had previously been an opponent of abolition). They were defiant gestures as a more commercial labour market in the game would duly condemn both clubs to lower-division football for most of the rest of the century.

1962:   Abolition of the amateur category in first-class cricket and the end of annual matches between 'Gentlemen' and 'Players' which had taken place since 1806.

1964:   'Match of the Day' football highlights began on BBC2 television, the first regularly televised football.

1967:   The Lawn Tennis Association announced the abolition of the 'amateur' category.

1968:   The International Lawn Tennis Federation categorized players into 'amateurs', 'registered players' and 'contract professionals'. Rod Laver returned to Wimbledon for the first time since winning the men's championship as an amateur in 1962 and won the first 'Open' championship.

1972:   After the Munich Olympics Avery Brundage retired and was replaced by the Anglo-Irish peer Lord Killanin (né Michael Morris). Killanin was to spend most of his time in office dealing with the issue of political boycotts of the games; but his attitude to amateurism was considered 'flexible' and 'pragmatic' and he accepted the principle that athletes should be compensated for the opportunity cost of their participation.

1974:   The FA Amateur Cup was held for the last time; it was to be replaced by a 'Vase' where eligibility is defined by the (minor) status of the club rather than by the amateur principle.

1975:   Final deletion of the word 'amateur' from FA rules.

1976:   The Montreal Olympics lost money on such a scale that the city was still paying the debt into the new century.

1977:   The Australian media owner Kerry Packer signed more than 400 players for his 'World Series Cricket' because of his frustration at being unable to bid for the television rights of existing games. In

Greig v. *Insole* the High Court in England found that the International Cricket Council and the Test and County Cricket Board were in restraint of trade in attempting to ban Packer's players from earning a living in English county cricket.

1978: A compromise was effected between Packer and the cricket authorities. It left the game with more competition for television rights, higher wages and a minor competition called the World Series.

1980: After the Moscow Olympics the Spanish–Catalonian aristocrat Juan Samaranch was elected President of the IOC. He aspired to make the games a world championship in all sports and had little interest in strict interpretations of the amateur principle. He was inclined to allow individual sports to implement their own principles of amateurism.

1983: The IOC accepted a proposal from the International Amateur Athletics Federation that athletes should be allowed to earn money which should be placed in a trust fund controlled by their national associations or federations; the athletes should have access to the money either when they 'needed' it or at the end of their careers.
The IOC (posthumously) returned Jim Thorpe's medals to him.

1984: The IOC accepted the principle that professional ice hockey players could compete in the Winter Olympics provided they had not played in the National Hockey League.

The Los Angeles Olympic Organizing Committee under its chairman Peter Ueberroth succeeded in making a large profit from the Games by adopting a strategy of maximizing the revenue from television and sponsorship. Los Angeles had no rivals in bidding for the games and there was considerable opposition to the bid within California. The games were dubbed 'the first private enterprise games' and considerably strengthened the case of those who argued that sport should be run on fully commercial principles. They also created fierce competition to hold future games.

1988: Steve Royle, the (professional) Director of Rowing at Oxford University, said before the Boat Race, 'We are completely professional, only there's no money in it. We're not amateurs, we're sportsmen.'

1989:   The Football League completed a three-way deal with
           Independent Television (ITV), the British Broadcasting
           Corporation (BBC) and British Sky Broadcasting for the showing
           of live games and recordings. Football's television revenue,
           previously a fraction of its income, leapt to £74 million (the
           revenues would increase a further tenfold in the next decade).
           Graham Kelly moved from the Football League to take over as
           Chief Executive of the Football Association.

1992:   The top division of English Football clubs broke away to form the
           FA Premier League to exploit their earning potential more fully.

1995:   The International Rugby Board voted to declare Rugby Union an
           'open' sport.

A Note on the Theoretical Difficulties of Factual Statements

A 'theorist' has certain difficulties in constructing a chronological table
which consists of statements which purport to be facts. It is not (for this
theorist, at least) a problem with the concept of facts: facts occur when there
are an overwhelmingly agreed conventions governing the concepts we use
(as there are on dates and places) and also on the rules of evidence. It is a
fact that the Battle of Hastings took place in 1066 and it is also a fact that
the first modern Olympics took place in 1896. Facts exist; they are a source
of great joy, perhaps especially for 'theorists'.

    The difficulty lies in the selection of facts. In constructing this table I
have tried to limit my selection to events which were of direct relevance to
amateurism and the amateur hegemony. Thus among the Olympic Games
Stockholm (1912), Montreal (1976) and Los Angeles (1984) seem to me to
be extremely important, whereas Antwerp (1920), Berlin (1936) and
Munich (1972) were not in themselves important to amateurism. The
histories of American 'Major League' sport, of winter sport and arguably, of
Association Football, could be said to consist of an undermining of the
amateur ethos, but only certain discrete events are relevant. I have also
included some events because they were significant indicators of the
condition of the amateur ethos rather than important to it: these include, for
example, the statement made by the Oxford Director of Rowing in 1988 and
the movement of Graham Kelly to the Football Association in 1989.

Appendix II

The Concept of the Amateur and of Amateurism

Definitions

From the Oxford English Dictionary, *1933, Vol.1 (Note there is no mention here of payment as such.)*

Amateur
1. One who loves or is fond *of*; one who has a taste for anything.

1784 *Europ. Mag. 268.* The President will be left with his train of feeble Amateurs. 1797 BURKE (T). Those who are the greatest amateurs or even professors of revolutions. 1801 MISS EDGEWORTH *Irish Bulls* xiv. (1832) 266 The whole boxing corps and gentlemen amateurs crowded to behold the spectacle. 1817 CHALMERS *Astron.* Disc.i. (1852) 40 The amateurs of a superficial philosophy. 1863 MRS. ATKINSON *Tartar Steppes* 89 I am no amateur of these melons.

2a. One who cultivates anything as a pastime, as distinguished from one who prosecutes it professionally; hence, sometimes used disparagingly, as dabbler, or superficial student or worker.

*c.*1803 REES *Amateur*, in the Arts, is a foreign term introduced and now passing current amongst us, to denote a person understanding, and loving or practising the polite arts of painting, sculpture, or architecture, without any regard to pecuniary advantage. 1807 *Edin. Rev.* X. 401 It was not likely that an amateur...should convict these astronomers of gross ignorance. 1827–39 DE QUINCEY *Murder* Wks. 1862 IV. 15 Not amateurs, gentlemen, as we are, but professional men. 1882 *Boy's Own Paper* IV. 807 Our amateurs are improving, and the interval between them and the professionals is growing beautifully less.

b. Often prefixed (in apposition) to another designation, as *amateur painter, amateur gardener.*

1863 BURTON *Bk. Hunter* 101 Amateur purchases do not, in the long run, make a profit. 1866 GEO. ELIOT *Felix H.* 38 He's a sort of amateur gentleman.

3. Hence *attrib.* almost *adj.* Done by amateurs. Cf. *Amateur gardener* with *amateur Gardening*.

1848 MARIOTTI, *Italy* II. iii. 84 Not merely a subject for amateur discussion. 1849 SIR J. STEPHEN *Eccles. Biogr* (ed. 2) I. 442 The evening closed with amateur dramaticals. 1862 HELPS *Organiz. Daily Life* 64 The getting-up of an amateur play. 1882 *St. Nicholas* II. 717 Amateur Newspapers. 1882 *Boy's Own Paper* IV. 415
Amateur running records.

Amateurish
Such as characterizes an amateur rather than a professional worker; having the faults or deficiencies of amateur work.

1864 MISS BRADDON *H. Dunbarr* III.i.6 Fond of pictures, in a frivolous amateurish kind of way. 1865 DICKENS *Mut.Fr.* I. X. 72 He goes in a condescending amateurish way, into the city. 1868 *Pall Mall G.* 19 Sept. 12 As a work of literary art it is what painters call 'amateurish.' 1881 *Athenum* No. 2810, 310/3 Written in a more amateurish style.

Amateurishly
In an amateurish manner.

1882 *Jrnl. Educ.* No. 155. 171 Those…who dabbled amateurishly in useful work.

Amateurishness
The quality of being amateurish; the appearance of being an amateur, and not a professional worker.

1865 *Pall Mall G.* I May II Making allowances for a certain amateurishness which time will cure. 1881 *Standard* 9 May, The amateurishness of the gentleman and the self-consciousness of the lady.

Amateurism
The characteristic practice of an amateur.

1868 *Tomahawk* 5 Dec., Amateurism is the curse of the nineteenth century. 1882 *Field* 7 Oct. 506 [Either] to keep within the bounds of honest amateurism, or turn professional.

Amateurship
The quality or character of an amateur; *a.* of being fond of, having a liking for, something; *b.* of dabbling in matters for which one has no professional training, dilettantism.

1834 DE QUINCEY *Caesars* Wks. 1862 IX. 106 The cool and cowardly spirit of amateurship in which the Roman…sat looking down upon the bravest of men…mangling each other for his recreation. 1834 MISS EDGEWORTH *Helen* II. 2 Horace [thinking] most of himself and his amateurship 1875 HAMERTON *Intell. Life* iii. v. 100 Napoleon III indulged in…a dangerous kind of amateurship. He had a taste for amateur generalship.

From the Concise Oxford English Dictionary, *1995 edition*

2: *amateur* [n. 1.] a *a person who engages in a pursuit* (e.g., an art or sport) as a pastime rather than as a profession b derog *a person who does something unskillfully or amateurishly.* 2. (attrib.) *for or done by amateurs* (amateur athletics). (foll. by of a person who is fond of a thing)
amateurism n. [French, via Italian *amatore* from Latin *amator –oris* 'lover,' from *amare* 'love']
amateurish/amttris/ adj. Characteristic of an amateur, esp. derog, one who is unskilful or inept; amateurishly adv. amateurishness n.

Declaration of Amateurism

'The game is an amateur game. No one is allowed to seek or receive payment or other material reward for taking part in the game.'

['Rugby Union Football' in Tony Pocock (ed.), Official Rules of Sport and Games 1992–93, *Kingswood Press, 1992, p.727. Rugby Union was at this time the only sport which defined and required amateurism in its own rules or laws* per se *though some bodies of rules (for example, athletics) referred to other definitions of eligibility which referred to amateurism and often (for example, archery) referred to a distinction between amateur and professional competitors.]*

In a definition of professionalism issued in 1900 the Rugby Football Union said that proscribed professional activities included:

Asking, receiving, or relying on a promise, direct or implied, to receive any money consideration whatever, actual or prospective, any employment or advancement, any establishment in business, or any compensation whatever for playing football or rendering any service to a football organisation; training or loss of time connected therewith; time lost in playing football, or in travelling in connection with football, expense in excess on the amount actually disbursed on account of reasonable hotel or travelling expenses.

An Amateur Must Be...

'...an officer of Her Majesty's Army or Navy, or Civil Services, a member of the Liberal Professions, or of the Universities or Public Schools, or of any established boat or rowing club not containing mechanics or professionals... [He] must not have competed in any competition, for either a stake or money, or entrance fee, or with or against a professional for any prize; nor ever taught, pursued, or assisted in the pursuit of athletic exercises of any kind as a means of livelihood, nor have ever been employed in or about boats, or in manual labour; nor be a mechanic, artisan or labourer.'

[*Declaration on amateurism of 10 April 1878 by the committee on the subject, established by leading London boat clubs and chaired by Francis Playtord. This is often claimed to be the first definition of amateurism.*]

Implications of Amateurism

'The amateur derives pleasure from the contest;
The activity is freely chosen;
The process is every bit as important as the outcome;
The motivation to participate comes from the intrinsic rewards from the activity rather than the extrinsic reward of money and fame;
Because there is a love of sport for its own sake, there is a climate of sportsmanship...'

[*D. Stanley Eitzen*, 'The Sociology of Amateur Sport: An Overview', *International Review of the Sociology of Sport*, 24, 2 (1989), p.95]

Principles of Amateur Organization in Sport

'[These were:]

1. the creation of 'fair' competition by establishing common rules;

2. the avoidance of excessive violence and injury by disciplinary codes which, for example, outlawed 'hacking' (the deliberate kicking of opponents);

3. to encourage participation; most amateur bodies placed much more stress on playing than on spectating; in some amateur sports, notably Rugby Union, spectators were scarcely tolerated.

4. to exclude from competition those who profit financially from sport; originally this was designed to exclude those who were at an unfair advantage because of their occupation; for example, a waterman or a swimming teacher; it was only when the commercial possibilities of sport became obvious around 1880 that the systematic payment of players became an issue;

5. abolition of gambling; opposition to the use of sport for betting was an important aspect of amateurism that contrasts starkly with earlier aristocratic attitudes; the Amateur Athletic Association prosecuted competitors in 1880s for betting and the Football Association continued to oppose all forms of gambling, including the 'football pools' up to the 1930s, by which time betting on football matches had become almost a national institution...'

[From Richard Holt, 'Amateurism and its Interpretation: The Social Origins of British Sport', *Innovation*, 5, 4 (1992). This is a description of the principles which governed amateur organizations at their establishment and for some considerable time, rather than a summary of the principle of amateurism]

Excerpts from the Regulations of the National Collegiate Athletic Association in the United States [Bylaw, Article 12. Amateurism]

12.01 GENERAL PRINCIPLES
12.01.1 **Eligibility for Intercollegiate Athletics**. Only an amateur student-athlete is eligible for intercollegiate athletics participation in a particular sport.
12.01.2 **Clear Line of Demarcation**. Member institutions' athletics programs are designed to be an integral part of the educational program and the student-athlete is considered an integral part of the student body, thus maintaining a clear line of demarcation between college athletics and professional sports.
12.01.3 **'Individual' vs. 'Student-Athlete'**. NCAA amateur status may be lost as a result of activities prior to enrollment in college. If NCAA rules specify that an 'individual' may or may not participate in certain activities, this term refers to a person prior to and subsequent to enrollment in a member institution. If NCAA rules specify a 'student-athlete,' the legislation applies only to that person's activities subsequent to enrollment.
12.01.4 **Permissible Grant-in-Aid**. A grant-in-aid administered by an educational institution is not considered to be pay or the promise of pay for athletics skill, provided it does not exceed the financial aid limitations set by the Association's membership.

12.01.5 **Compliance with Legislation for Emerging Sports.** Beginning with the 1995–96 academic year, a member institution sponsoring an emerging sport for women (see 20.02.5) shall comply fully in that program with all applicable amateurism legislation set forth in Bylaw 12. (*Adopted: 1/10/95*)

12.02 DEFINITIONS AND APPLICATIONS
12.02.1 **Individual.** An individual, for purposes of this bylaw, is any person of any age without reference to enrollment in an educational institution or status as a student-athlete.

12.02.2 **Pay.** Pay is the receipt of funds, awards or benefits not permitted by the governing legislation of the Association for participation in athletics.

12.02.3 **Professional Athlete.** A professional athlete is one who receives any kind of payment, directly or indirectly, for athletics participation except as permitted by the governing legislation of the Association.

12.02.4 **Professional Athletics Team.** A professional team is any organized team that:

   a. Is a member of a recognized professional sports organization.
   b. Is directly supported or sponsored by a professional team or professional sports organization (see also 12.6.1.1);
   c. Is a member of a playing league that is directly supported or sponsored by a professional team or professional sports organization (see also 12.6.1.1); or
   d. Has an athlete receiving for his or her participation any kind of payment, directly or indirectly, from a professional team or professional sports organization (see also 12.6.1.1).

12.02.5 **Student-Athlete.** A student-athlete is a student whose enrollment was solicited by a member of the athletics staff or other representative of athletics interests with a view toward the student's ultimate participation in the intercollegiate athletics program. Any other student becomes a student-athlete only when the student reports for an intercollegiate squad that is under the jurisdiction of the athletics department, as specified in 3.2.4.4. A student is not deemed a student-athlete solely on the basis of prior high-school athletics participation.

12.1 GENERAL REGULATIONS
An individual must comply with the following to retain amateur status. (See Bylaw 14 regarding the eligibility restoration process).

12.1.1 **Amateur Status.** An individual loses amateur status and thus shall not be eligible for intercollegiate competition in a particular sport if the individual:

   a. Uses his or her athletics skill (directly or indirectly) for pay in any form in that sport;

b. Accepts a promise of pay even if such pay is to be received following completion of intercollegiate athletics participation;

c. Signs a contract or commitment of any kind to play professional athletics, regardless of its legal enforceability or any consideration received;

d. Receives, directly or indirectly, a salary, reimbursement of expenses or any other form of financial assistance from a professional sports organization based upon athletics skill, or participation, except as permitted by NCAA rules and regulations;

e. Competes on any professional athletics team and knows (or had reason to know) that the team is a professional athletics team (per 12.02.4), even if no pay or remuneration for expenses was received; or

f. Enters into a professional draft or an agreement with an agent (see also 12.2.4.2.1).

12.1.1.1 Prohibited Forms of Pay. 'Pay' as used in 12.1.1 above includes, but is not limited to, the following:

12.1.1.1.1 Salary, Gratuity or Compensation. Any direct or indirect salary, gratuity or comparable compensation.

12.1.1.1.2 Division or Split of Surplus. Any division or split of surplus (bonuses, game receipts, etc,).

12.1.1.1.3 Educational Expenses. Educational expenses not permitted by the governing legislation of this Association (see Bylaw 15 regarding permissible financial aid to enrolled student-athletes).

12.1.1.1.3.1 Educational Expenses from Outside Sports Team or Organization. Educational expenses provided to an individual by an outside sports team or organization that are based in any degree upon the recipient's athletics ability [except as specified in 15.2.5.5 and 15.2.5.7-(I)], even if the funds are given to the institution to administer to the recipient. (*Revised: 1/10/95*)

12.1.1.1.3.1.1 Educational Expenses – US Olympic Committee. An individual (prospective student-athlete or student-athlete) may receive educational expenses awarded by the US Olympic Committee pursuant to the applicable conditions set forth in 15.2.5.7. (*Adopted 4/15/97*)

12.1.1.1.3.1.2 Educational Expenses – US National Governing Body. An individual (prospective student-athlete or student-athlete) may receive educational expenses awarded by a U.S. national governing body pursuant to the applicable conditions set forth in 15.2.5.7. (*Adopted 4/15/97 effective 8/1/98*)

12.1.1.1.4 Expenses, Awards and Benefits. Excessive or improper expenses, awards and benefits (see Bylaw 16 regarding permissible awards, benefits and expenses to enrolled student-athletes).

12.1.1.1.4.1 Cash or Equivalent Award. Cash, or the equivalent thereof (e.g., trust fund), as an award for participation in competition at any time, even if such an award is permitted under the rules governing an amateur, non-collegiate event in which the individual is participating. An award or a cash prize that an individual could not receive under NCAA legislation may not be forwarded in the individual's name to a different individual or agency.

12.1.1.1.4.2 **Expenses/Awards Prohibited by Rules Governing Event.** Expenses incurred or awards received by an individual that are prohibited by the rules governing an amateur, non-collegiate event in which the individual participates.

12.1.1.1.4.3 **Expenses from Outside Team or Organization.** Expenses received from an outside amateur sports team or organization in excess of actual and necessary travel, room and board expenses, and apparel and equipment (for individual and team use only from teams or organizations not affiliated with member institutions, including local sports clubs as set forth in 13.12.2.4) for competition and practice held in preparation for such competition. Practice must be conducted in a continuous time period preceding the competition except for practice sessions conducted by a national team, which occasionally may be interrupted for specific periods of time preceding the competition. (*Revised 1/10/90, 1/10/92*)

12.1.1.1.4.4 **Unspecified or Unitemized Expenses.** Payment to individual team members or individual competitors for unspecified or unitemized expenses beyond actual and necessary travel, room and board expenses for practice and competition.

12.1.1.1.4.5 **Expenses from Sponsor Other than Parents/Legal Guardians or Non-professional Sponsor of Event.** Actual and necessary expenses or any other form of compensation to participate in athletics competition (while not representing an educational institution) from a sponsor other than an individual upon whom the athlete is naturally or legally dependent or the non-professional organization that is sponsoring the competition.

12.1.1.1.4.6 **Expenses for Parents/Legal Guardians of Participants in Athletics Competition.** Expenses received by the parents or legal guardians of a participant in athletics competition from a non-professional organization sponsoring the competition in excess of actual and necessary travel, room and board expenses or any entertainment expenses, provided such expenses are made available to the parents or legal guardians of all participants in the competition. (*Adopted: 1/16/93, Revised: 1/11/97*)

12.1.1.1.5 **Payment Based on Performance.** Any payment, including actual and necessary expenses, conditioned on the individual's or team's place finish or performance or given on an incentive basis, or receipt of expenses in excess of the same reasonable amount for permissible expenses given to all individuals or team members involved in the competition.

12.1.1.1.6 **Preferential Treatment, Benefits or Services.** Preferential treatment, benefits or services because of the individual's athletics reputation or skill or pay-back potential as a professional athlete, unless such treatment, benefits or services are specifically permitted under NCAA legislation. (*Revised: 1/11/94*)

12.1.1.1.7 Prize for Participation in Institution's Promotional Activity. Receipt of a prize for participation (involving the sue of athletics ability) in a member institution's promotional activity that is inconsistent with the provisions of 12.5 or official interpretations approved by the Management Council.

12.1.1.2 Use of Overall Athletics Skill – Effect on Eligibility. Participation for pay in compensation that involves the use of overall athletics skill (e.g., 'superstars' competition) constitutes a violation of the Association's amateur-status regulations; therefore, an individual participating for pay in such competition is ineligible for intercollegiate competitions in all sports. (See 12.5.2.3.3 for exception related to promotional contests.)

12.1.1.3 Road Racing. 'Road racing' is essentially the same as cross country or track and field competition and cannot be separated effectively from those sports for purposes of Bylaw 12. Therefore, a student-athlete who accepts pay in any form for participation in such a race is ineligible for intercollegiate cross country or track and field competition.

12.1.1.4 Exceptions to Amateurism Rule.

12.1.1.4.1 Exception for Insurance against Disabling Injury or Illness.

12.1.1.4.2 Exception for Institutional Fund-Raising Activities Involving the Athletics Ability of Student-Athletes.

12.1.1.4.3 Exception for USOC Elite Athletic Health Insurance Program.

12.1.1.4.4 Exception for Training Prior to Collegiate Enrollment.

12.1.1.4.5 Exception for Developmental Training Programs.

12.1.1.4.6 Exception for Family Travel to Olympic Games.

12.1.1.4.7 Exception for Payment of Initial-Eligibility Clearinghouse Fee.

12.1.1.4.8 Exception for Camp Sponsored by a Charitable Foundation Funded by a Professional Sports Organization.

12.1.1.4.9 Exception for Receipt of Free Equipment and Apparel Items by a Prospective Student-Athlete.

12.1.1.4.10 Expenses for Participation in Olympic Exhibitions.

12.1.2 Amateur Status if Professional in Another Sport. A professional athlete is one sport may represent a member institution in a different sport. However, the student-athlete cannot receive institutional financial assistance in the second sport unless the student-athlete:

    a. Is no longer involved in professional athletics;

    b. Is not receiving any remuneration from a professional sports organization;

c. and has no active contractual relationship with any professional athletics team. However, an individual may remain bound by an option clause in a professional sports contract that requires assignment to a particular team if the student-athlete's professional career is resumed.

12.1.2.1 Professional at Later Date. If the individual later becomes involved in professional athletics while still a student-athlete with remaining eligibility, the individual would be considered to have violated the principles of ethical conduct per Bylaw 10, thus rendering the individual ineligible for intercollegiate competition.

[*From* 1999–00 NCAA Division I Manual, *National Collegiate Athletic Association, 1999, pp.71–5. It is instructive to compare the length and complexity of these regulations, produced in a highly legalistic and litigious context, with the simplicity of the Rugby Union document*].

Appendix III

Amateurism in Verse

There is a poetic dimension to amateurism, illustrated by the following three pieces written during its heyday. *Vitaï Lampada* ('The Torch of Life') reads now (as it did to some people when it was written) as a risible account of the relation between sport and empire. Lionel Tennyson's jolly piece expresses the admiration of the amateur skipper for his professional colleagues and the final selection is one of several in which Sir John Betjeman captures the atmosphere of the autonomous amateur club at the height of its importance. Sir John's admiration was usually directed towards the sportswoman rather than the sportsman.

Sir Henry Newbolt

Vitaï Lampada

There's a breathless hush in the Close to-night –
Ten to make and the match to win –
A bumping pitch and a blinding light,
An hour to play and the last man in.
And it's not for the sake of a ribboned coat,
Or the selfish hope of a season's fame
But his Captain's hand on his shoulder smote –
'Play up! play up! and play the game!'

The sand of the desert is sodden red, –
Red with the wreck of the square that broke; –
The Gatling's jammed and the Colonel dead,
And the regiment blind with dust and smoke.
The river of death has brimmed his banks,
And England's far, and Honour a name,
But the voice of a schoolboy rallies the ranks:
'Play up! play up! and play the game!'

This is the word that year by year,
While in her place the School is set,

Every one of her sons must hear,
And none that hears it dare forget.
This they all with a joyful mind
Bear through life like a torch in flame,
And falling fling to the host behind –
'Play up! play up! and play the game!'

[From: Henry Newbolt, *Collected Poems 1897–1907* (Nelson, 1907), pp. 131–3]

Lionel, Lord Tennyson

On the Ashes Victory of 1928–29

Now here's a health from o'er the sea,
A word of greeting o'er the foam,
In England's hour of victory,
To those who bring the Ashes home.
Sydney, Melbourne and Brisbane know
What England knows who sent them forth,
How gallantly, come weal or woe,
They played the greatest game on earth.
Their names a mighty book would fill
And furnish many a powerful rhyme,
Our lordly Hobbs' classic skill
Mellowed but not subdued by time,
Our giant captain's cheerful grin,
The grin that masks a leader's guile,
Duckworth whose hands hold fast as sin,
Geary who bowls you with a smile.

Stubborn Sutcliffe's Yorkshire bat,
Broad and big as a great barn door,
Hendren quick on his feet as a cat,
Hammond's slash for an offside four,
Larwood's swift and terrible ball,
The fasts of Tate with their lift and fire,
The courage of Jardine cool and tall,
The craft of White which cannot tire.

Their great achievements and their praise
Henceforth shall furnish history's page,

How for the space of seven long days,
In one stern fight they did engage:
And how, defying even fate,
They fought and turned the game again,
Therefore from those who watch and wait,
A health to Chapman and his men!

[From: Lionel, Lord Tennyson, *Sticky Wickets* (London: Christopher Johnson, 1950), pp.79–80; written in 1929]

Sir John Betjeman

A Subaltern's Love-song

Miss J. Hunter Dunn, Miss J. Hunter Dunn,
Furnish'd and burnish'd by Aldershot sun,
What strenuous singles we played after tea,
We in the tournament – you against me!

Love-thirty, love-forty, oh! weakness of joy,
The speed of a swallow, the grace of a boy,
With carefullest carelessness, gaily you won,
I am weak from your loveliness, Joan Hunter Dunn.

Miss Joan Hunter Dunn, Miss Joan Hunter Dunn,
How mad I am, sad I am, glad that you won.
The warm-handled racket is back in its press,
But my shocked-headed victor, she loves me no less.

Her father's euonymus shines as we walk,
And swing past the summer-house, buried in talk,
And cool the verandah that welcomes us in
To the six o'clock news and a lime-juice and gin.

The scent of the conifers, sound of the bath,
The view from my bedroom of moss-dappled path,
As I struggle with double-end evening tie,
For we dance at the Golf Club, my victor and I.

On the floor of her bedroom lie blazer and shorts
And the cream-coloured walls are be-trophied with sports,
And westering, questioning settles the sun
On your low-leaded window, Miss Joan Hunter Dunn.

184

The Hillman is waiting, the light's in the hall,
The pictures of Egypt are bright on the wall,
My sweet, I am standing beside the oak stair,
And there on the landing's the light on your hair.

By roads 'not adopted', by woodlanded ways,
She drove to the club in the late summer haze,
Into nine-o'clock Camberley, heavy with bells
And mushroomy, pine-woody, evergreen smells.

Miss Joan Hunter Dunn, Miss Joan Hunter Dunn,
I can hear from the car-park the dance has begun.
Oh! full Surrey twilight! importunate band!
Oh! strongly adorable tennis-girl's hand!

Around us are Rovers and Austins afar,
Above us, the intimate roof of the car,
And here on my right is the girl of my choice,
With the tilt of her nose and the chime of her voice,

And the scent of her wrap, and the words never said,
And the ominous, ominous dancing ahead,
We sat in the car park till twenty to one
And now I'm engaged to Miss Joan Hunter Dunn.

[From: The Earl of Birkenhead (ed.), *John Betjeman's Collected Poems* (London: John Murray, 2nd edn, 1962), pp. 105–7]

Notes

SERIES EDITOR'S FOREWORD

1. *The New Shorter Oxford English Dictionary* (Oxford: Clarendon Press, 1993), pp.62–3.
2. Quoted in *The Oxford Dictionary of Quotations* (Oxford University Press, 1996), p.256 (16).
3. G. Lacy Hillier was a late nineteenth-century advocate of cycling as the ultimate amateur pleasure. I am grateful to Andrew Ritchie, a doctoral student at IRCSSS, University of Strathclyde for details of Hillier. The description of Hillier's defence is also Ritchie's. It could not be bettered. 'Canute-like' because at the very moment he was writing professional cycling was going from strength to strength and entering a time of successful expansion.
4. Editorial, *The Bicycling News and Tricycling Gazette*, XXII, 22 (28 May 1892), p.1. I owe this reference to Andrew Ritchie.
5. Ibid.
6. See, for example, J.A. Mangan, 'Aggression and Androgyny: Gender Fusion In and Beyond Sport in the Post Millennium', *Revue Française de Civilisation Britannique*, X, 4 (2000), pp.131–40.
7. Roger Scruton, *England: An Elegy* (Chatto and Windus, 2000), p.vii.
8. Ibid., p.58.
9. Norman Davies, *Europe: A History* (Oxford University Press, 1996), pp.5–6.
10. See Jeffrey Richards, for example, on this point in 'The English Gentleman: Playing the Game', *The Listener*, 6 May 1982, p.16.
11. See J.A. Mangan, 'Imitating their Betters and Disassociating from their Inferiors: Grammar Schools and the Games Ethic in the Late Nineteenth and Early Twentieth Centuries', *Proceedings of the 1982 Annual Conference of the History of Education Society of Great Britain* (Leicester, 1983).
12. See J.A. Mangan, *Athleticism in the Victorian and Edwardian Public School: The Emergence and Consolidation of an Educational Ideology* (Frank Cass, 2000), passim.

PART I: CHAPTER 1

1. See Appendix II for a range of definitions.
2.   From Art more various are the blessing sent
   Wealth, commerce, honour, liberty, content
   Yet these each other's power so strong contest
   That either seems destructive of the rest.
   Where wealth and freedom reign contentment fails
   And honour sinks where commerce long prevails.
   Oliver Goldsmith, 'The Traveller', from *Collected Works*, Vol. IV, ed. Arthur Freidman (Oxford University Press, 1966), p.252; first published 1764.
3. Edmund Burke, *Reflection on the Revolution in France* (1790; Penguin, 1986), p.170.

4. The fullest development of this concern is in Adam Smith, *An Enquiry into the Nature and Causes of the Wealth of Nations*, Vol. II, Bk 5, Pt I, pp.182–98, ed. E.R.A. Seligman (1776; Dent, 1962).

5. Harriet Taylor, *Enfranchisement of Women*, published jointly with John Stuart Mill, *The Subjection of Women* (Virago, 1985), p.27.

6. Norman Angell, *The Great Illusion* (Heinemann, 1910).

7. See Ch. 2.

8. The first of several notes in the tradition of the eponymous Anglican vicar who begins his sermon 'As I was on my way here tonight...'; as I was writing this I was waiting at the bus stop when three young women dressed in the tracksuits of the University of Warwick Women's Rugby Club passed me. One of them was saying, 'It was great. Bev and Sue and Lauren all stuck their arses out of the window.' I wanted Harriet Taylor to have been there to share the moment.

9. For a broad survey of the relevant 'contextualizing' theory see Grant Jarvie and Joseph Maguire, *Sport and Leisure in Social Thought* (Routledge, 1994).

10. The work which brings together much of the achievement of British sports historians is Richard Holt, *Sport and the British: A Modern History* (Oxford University Press, 1989).

11. The best known of these works is Jennifer Hargreaves, *Sporting Females: Critical Issues in the History and Sociology of Women in Sport* (Routledge, 1994).

12. Mill, *The Subjection of Women*, see n.5, p.146; first published in 1869.

13. Almost none! An honourable exception is Eugene A. Glader, *Amateurism and Athletics* (West Point: Leisure Press, 1978). At the time of writing the only other book with 'Amateurism' in its title was about a style of literary critism: see Naomi Lebowitz, *The Philosophy of Literary Amateurism* (University of Missouri Press, 1994).

14. See Ch. 5.

15. The stated basis of the argument in Robert Nozick, *Anarchy, State and Utopia* (Blackwell, 1974).

16. W.B. Gallie, 'Essentially Contested Concepts', *Proceedings of the Aristotelian Society*, 56 (1955–56), pp.167–98, is the original of this argument.

17. George Orwell, 'England Your England' in *The Penguin Essays of George Orwell* (1940; Penguin, 1994), pp.140–1.

18. There is a fascinating book to be written by someone on the cultural geography of amateurism. This is not it, though it does contain some relevant remarks, especially about the United States, Japan, South Africa, Thailand and the (former) Soviet Union.

19. It seems near-universal that the great statements about sport are both misquoted and misattributed. The version quoted here is from the title page of Brian Glanville (ed.), *The Footballer's Companion* (Eyre & Spottiswoode, 1962). But the passage by Camus included in the book does not contain this statement. What it does say is '... what I most surely know in the long run about morality and the obligations of men, I owe to sport. I learned it with RUA' (p.352; this is from an article in *French Football* in 1957 and the RUA was the sports club of the University of Algiers). What seems to be the case is that there is no definite version of the statement, in that it is not included in any of Camus's major works, but that he said something similar on several occasions in interviews and journalism, variously attributing his ethical education to sport in general, football or the RUA in particular. The first occasion I have come across was in an interview in 1953.

20. Frances Hutcheson, *Inquiry into the Original of Our Ideas of Beauty and Virtue* (John Derby, for William and John Smith etc., 1725), Treatise II, unnumbered pp.It is, of course, normally attributed to various passages by Jeremy Bentham about half a century later, but Bentham was merely quoting Hutcheson.

21. See Lincoln Allison (ed.), *The Utilitarian Response* (Sage, 1990) and Allison, *Ecology*

and Utility (Cassell, 1991).

22. See John Stuart Mill, 'Bentham', in *Utilitarianism* (*London and Westminster Review*, August 1838; ed. M. Warnock, Fontana, 1962), pp.78–125.
23. Samuel Brittan 'Choice and Utility', in Allison (ed.), *The Utililitarian Response*, pp.74–97.
24. Robert Goodin, 'Government House Utilitarianism', in ibid., pp.140–60.
25. Lincoln Allison, *Environmental Planning: A Political and Philisophical Analysis* (Allen & Unwin, 1975) and *Ecology and Utility*.

CHAPTER 2

1. Richard Holt, 'Amateurism and Its Interpretation: the Social Origins of British Sport', *Innovation*, 5, 4 (1992), p.20.
2. See especially, Lincoln Allison (ed.), *The Politics of Sport* (Manchester University Press, 1986), pp.1–26.
3. See Appendix I.
4. Ronald A. Smith, *Sports and Freedom: The Rise of Big-Time College Athletics* (Oxford University Press, 1988), p.168.
5. Quoted in David C. Young, *The Olympic Myth of Greek Amateur Athletics* (Ares, 1984), p.24.
6. I am indebted to Pierre Lanfranchi for this observation.
7. Quoted by Eric Halladay in 'Of Pride and Prejudice: the Amateur Question in Nineteenth-century Rowing', *International Journal of the History of Sport*, 4, 1 (1984), p.47.
8. Andrew Strenk, 'Amateurism: Myth and Reality', in Jeffrey Segrave and Donald Chew (eds), *Olympism* (Human Kinetics Books, 1981), p.57.
9. Fred Swainson, 'Acton's Feud, a Public School Story', *The Captain*, 3 (1900), pp.58–516.
10. D. Stanley Eitzen, 'The Sociology of Amateur Sport: an Overview', *International Review of the Sociology of Sport*, 24, 2 (1989), p.95.
11. Brian Dobbs, *Edwardians at Play, Sport 1890–1914* (Pelham, 1973), p.161.
12. From a poem called 'Alumnus Football' published in 1941. Quoted in the *Oxford Dictionary of Quotations* (4th edn, 1992), p.540. Rice was an American journalist, but the stanza is often attributed to the English poet W.E. Henley including, famously, by Alan Bennett in 'Take a Pew', the spoof Anglican sermon which was part of the 1961 satire *Beyond the Fringe*. The misattribution is understandable since Henley was a High Tory and an English patriot who might well have expressed such a sentiment. The style is quite close to that of Henley as well. Compare these lines from his most famous poem, 'Invicta':

    It matters not how straight the gate,
    How charged with punishments the scroll,
    I am the master of my fate;
    I am the captain of my soul.

Henley's expression of an almost existential version of agnosticism and a belief in freedom is a far more complex sentiment than that of Rice. But from my point of view it is ironic as well as symbolic that the two most famous statements to the effect that there are more important values than winning were both made by Americans and are both commonly attributed to Europeans.
13. See Ch. 18, vv. 23–7.
14. Sir Henry Newbolt, *Collected Poems 1897–1907* (Nelson, 1907), p.131. See Appendix III.
15. The first serious biography was Bernard Darwin, *W.G. Grace* (Duckworth, 1934).

16. Quoted in Young, *Olympic Myth*, p.62. See also Richard D. Mandell, *The First Modern Olympics* (University of California Press, 1976).
17. See Eric Dunning and Ken Sheard, *Barbarians, Gentlemen and Players* (Oxford University Press, 1979), pp.203–31.
18. The Bolton club's problems are discussed in Halladay, 'Of Pride and Prejudice', p.45.
19. Quoted in Smith, *Sports and Feedom*, p.165.
20. Alexis de Tocqueville, *The Old Regime and the French Revolution* (1856; Anchor Doubleday, 1983), pp.83–4.
21. Martin Wiener, *English Culture and the Decline of Industrial Spirit, 1850–1950* (Cambridge University Press, 1981).
22. Hippolyte Taine, *Notes on England* (1872; trans. Edward Hyams, Thames & Hudson, 1957).
23. Swainson, 'Acton's Feud', p.62.
24. See Marie-Thérèse Eyquem, *Pierre de Coubertin: L'Epoque Olympique* (Paris: Calmann-Levy, 1966).
25. For the author's own account of this strain of political thought see Lincoln Allison, *Ecology and Utility* (Cassell, 1991), pp.26–59.
26. Young, *Olympic Myth*, pp.115–33.
27. H.W. Pleket, 'Games, Prizes, Athletes and Ideology', *Arena*, 1, 1 (1976).
28. Avery Brundage, 'Why the Olympic Games', in US Olympic Committee, *Report on the Games of the XIVth Olympiad, London, England* (New York, 1948).
29. John P. Mahaffy, 'Old Greek Athletics', *Macmillan's Magazine*, 36 (1879), pp.61–9; E. Norman Gardiner, *Athletics of the Ancient World* (Oxford University Press, 1930).
30. Young, *Olympic Myth*, p.84.
31. John A. Lucas, *Future of the Olympic Games* (Champaign, IL: Human Kinetics Books, 1992), p.2.
32. Ibid., p.5.
33. Earl R. Anderson, 'Athletic Mysticism in the Olympics', *The Gamut* [Cleveland State University], 2 (Winter, 1981), p.85.
34. Karl Marx, 'History', from *The German Ideology* (1846), quoted from Lewis S. Feuer (ed.), *Marx and Engels: Basic Writings on Politics and Philosophy* (Fontana, 1969), p.295.
35. See John Hoberman, *The Olympic Crisis* (New York: Caratzas, 1986); Vyv Simson and Andrew Jennings, *The Lords of the Rings: Power, Money and Drugs in the Modern Olympics* (Simon & Schuster, 1992).
36. This has been a consistent theme of Riordan's analyses of Soviet sport. See Jim Riordan, 'Elite Sport Policy in East and West', in Allison (ed.), *Politics of Sport*, pp.66–89.
37. For the complete package of the Olympian international ideology which associated disarmament, peace, sport, Olympianism and friendship to the Soviet Union one should look no further than the life and work of Philip Noel-Baker (1889–1982). Noel-Baker was a man of quite astonishing distinction: Olympic silver medallist, Member of Parliament, winner of the Nobel Peace Prize and member of the International Olympic Committee. He also seems, in retrospect, to this reader at least, to have been quite astonishingly silly. See Philip Noel-Baker, *Man of Sport, Man of Peace, Collected Speeches and Essays* (ed. Don Anthony) (Sports Editions, 1991).
38. George Orwell, 'The Sporting Spirit', in *The Penguin Essays of George Orwell* (1945; Penguin, 1994), pp.321–3.
39. See the more 'revisionist' writings of Jim Riordan, including *Sport, Politics and Communism* (Manchester University Press, 1991).
40. I am indebted to John Sugden for this contrast. See his *Boxing and Society: an International Analysis* (Manchester University Press, 1996), pp.131–71.
41. See Lincoln Allison, 'The Olympics and the End of the Cold War', *World Affairs*, 157, 2 (1994), pp.92–7.

CHAPTER 3

1. W.E.H. Lecky, *Democracy and Liberty* (1896; Indianapolis, IN: Liberty Classics, 2 vols, 1981). Lord Salisbury's essays on 'The Reform Bill', 'The Conservative Surrender' and 'The Programme of the Radicals' are to be found Paul Smith (ed.), *Lord Salisbury on Politics* (Cambridge University Press, 1972).
2. See especially Samuel Brittan, *The Economic Consequence of Democracy* (Temple Smith, 1977).
3. Francis Fukuyama, *The End of History and the Last Man* (Penguin, 1992).
4. See especially Le Corbusier, *Vers une Architecture* (1923); translated as *Towards a New Architecture* (Architectural Press, 1987).
5. Ihab Hassan, 'The Critic as Innovator: the Tutzing Statement in X Frames', *Amerikastudien*, 22, 1 (1977).
6. For the classic account see R.W. Malcolmson, *Popular Recreations in English Society, 1700–1850* (Cambridge University Press, 1979). The author's own accounts of traditional sport and the process of modernization are to be found in Lincoln Allison, 'Batsman and Bowler: the Key Relation in Victorian England', *Journal of Sport History*, 7, 2 (1980) and 'Association Football and the Urban Ethos', *Stanford Journal of International Studies*, 13, 2 (1978), the latter reprinted in John D. Wirth and Robert L. Jones (eds), *Manchester and São Paulo, Problems of Rapid Urban Growth* (Stanford University Press, 1978).
7. For a summary of the alternative view see Neil Tranter, *Sport, Economy and Society in Britain 1750–1914* (Cambridge University Press, 1998), Ch. 2.
8. Sir Henry Newbolt, *Collected Poems 1897–1907* (Nelson, 1907), pp.131–4. See Appendix III.
9. The author's report was incorporated into David Moorcroft, 'Paper for the European Athletics Development Project, 2nd Workshop, Stockholm, 17–19 March 1999'.
10. Men of business in Elizabeth Gaskell, *North and South* (1855) and Charles Dickens, *Hard Times* (1854).
11. Lincoln Allison, 'If the Price Is Right', *New Statesman*, 17 November 1995; see also Ray Simpson, *The Clarets Collection 1946–1996* (Burnley Football Club, 1996), pp.63–5.
12. Fred Inglis, 'The State of Play: Capital, Sport and Happiness', in Lincoln Allison (ed.), *Taking Sport Seriously* (Aachen: Meyer & Meyer, 1998), pp.155–72.
13. The political dimensions of that movement are examined in Lincoln Allison, 'Sport as an Environmental Issue', in Lincoln Allison (ed.), *The Changing Politics of Sport* (Manchester University Press, 1993), pp.207–32.
14. Peter McIntosh and Valerie Charlton, *The Impact of Sport for All Policy, 1966–1984* (Sports Council, Study 26, 1985), pp.125–6.
15. Jill Matheson, 'Participation in Sport', *General Household Survey* (HMSO, 1987), p.9.
16. Jeff Achey, 'Access Denied', *Climbing* (1 November 1998), p.77.
17. See, for example, Paola Feher, Michael C. Meyers and William A. Skelly, 'Psychological Profile of Rock Climbers: State and Trait Attributes', *Journal of Sport Behaviour* (21 June 1998), pp.167–80.
18. J.-F. Lyotard, *The Postmodern Condition* (1979 [in French]; Manchester University Press, 1984).
19. See Peter J. Beck, *Scoring for Britain: International Football and International Politics, 1900–1939* (Frank Cass, 1999).
20. The best known case of the strong thesis is Kenichi Ohmae, *The End of the Nation State* (New York: Free Press, 1990) and *The Borderless World* (Fontana, 1995).
21. Most notably Paul Hirst and Graham Thompson, *Globalisation in Question* (Polity,

190 *Amateurism in Sport*

1996).
22. See Steve Greenfield and Guy Osborn, 'Oh To Be in England?', *Cricket Digest* (Autumn 1997), pp.8–11.
23. See Lincoln Allison, 'The Government and Governance of Sport', *Politics Review* (September 1998), pp.28–31.

CHAPTER 4

1. Antonio Gramsci, *Prison Notebooks [Quaderni del Carcere]*, ed. Quentin Hoare and Geoffrey Nowell-Smith (Lawrence & Wishart, 1971).
2. Bob Lord, *My Fight for Football* (Stanley Paul, 1963), pp.134–5.
3. See Bharat Ahluwalia, 'Running Cricket into the Ground', *Outlook*, 40, 7 (28 February 2000), pp.46–52.
4. See Jack Williams, 'Part of the Mainstream? Asian Contributions to the English Game', *Cricket Digest* (Autumn 1997), pp.17–20.
5. Department of Education and Science, *Report of the Committee on Football* (HMSO, 1968), p.100.
6. Richard Holt, *Stanmore Golf Club, 1893–1993, a Social History* (Stanmore Golf Club, 1993).
7. *Britain in the World of Sport* (Birmingham University, 1956).
8. Sir John Wolfenden, *Sport and the Community: Report of the Wolfenden Committee on Sport* (Central Council for Physical Recreation, 1960).
9. See Barrie Houlihan, *The Government and Politics of Sport* (Routledge, 1991) and *Sport, Policy and Politics, a Comparative Analysis* (Routledge, 1997); John F. Coghlan and Ida M.Webb, *Sport and British Politics since 1960* (Falmer Press, 1990); John Hargreaves, 'The State and Sport', in Lincoln Allison (ed.), *The Politics of Sport* (Manchester University Press, 1986); and David Pickup, *Not Another Messiah, An Account of the Sports Council, 1988–93* (Edinburgh: Pentland, 1996).
10. Benny Green (ed.), *The Wisden Book of Cricketer's Lives, Obituaries from the Wisden Cricketer's Almanac* (Wisden, 1986), p.vii.
11. See J.A. Mangan, *The Games Ethic and Imperialism* (Harmondsworth: Viking, 1986), Ch. 7.
12. See Duncan Campbell, 'Breaking the Law Is Big Business', *Guardian Weekly* (18 April 1999), p.23.
13. Learie Constantine, 'Foreword', in John Kay, *Cricket in the Leagues* (Eyre & Spottiswoode, 1970), p.12.
14. A version of the results is published in 'A Curate's Egg. How Healthy Is Grass Roots Cricket?', *Cricket Digest* (Autumn 1997), pp.2–4.
15. Gordon White, 'Civil Society, Democratization and Development (1): Clearing the Analytical Ground', *Democratisation*, 1, 3 (1994), p.378.
16. John Urry, *The Anatomy of Capitalist Societies: Economy, Civil Society and the State* (Macmillan, 1981), p.12.
17. Ernest Gellner, 'The Importance of Being Modular', in John A. Hall (ed.), *Civil Society: Theory, History, Comparison* (Polity, 1995), p.32.
18. David Robertson, *The Penguin Dictionary of Politics* (Penguin, 1986), p.44.
19. Larry Diamond, 'Towards Democratic Consolidation', *Journal of Democracy*, 5, 3 (1994); reprinted as 'Third World Civil Society Can Promote Democracy', in Jonathan S. Petriken (ed.), *The Third World, Opposing Viewpoints* (San Diego: Greenhaven, 1995), pp.151–9.
20. See Philip Mosely, 'Balkan Politics in Australian Soccer', in J. O'Hara (ed.), *Ethnicity*

and *Soccer in Australian Society* (Sydney University Press, 1994) and Wray Vamplew, 'Soccer in Australia: a Lost Cause', in Lincoln Allison (ed.), *Warwick Working Papers in Sport and Society* [University of Warwick Centre for the Study of Sport in Society], 4 (1995–96).

21. See Lincoln Allison, 'The Concept of Civil Society in Georgia, Thailand and South Africa', *South African Journal of International Affairs*, 4, 2 (1997) and 'Sport and Civil Society', *Political Studies*, 46, 4 (1998).

22. Lee Gruzd, 'Back on the Field: the Changing Political Role of Sport in South Africa 1988–95', MA thesis, Witwatersrand University (1995), p.21.

23. David C. Wilson, 'New Trends in the Funding of Charities', in Alan Ware (ed.), *Charities and Government* (Manchester University Press, 1989), pp.55–81.

24. R.J. Butler and D.C. Wilson, *Managing Voluntary and Non-Profit Organisations, Strategy and Structure* (Routledge, 1990), p.161.

25. See Richard Titmuss, *The Gift Relationship: From Human Blood to Social Policy* (Penguin, 1970).

26. See Graham Leach, *The Land of Altruism?* (Institute of Directors, 1999). In line with the 'neo-liberal' outlook of the Institute, Leach tends to blame the 'welfare state' for the decline. While wishing to insist on the complexity of any causation involved, I would stress that this is incompatible with my own explanation.

27. Wilson, 'New Trends', p.74.

28. Chris Hann, 'Philosophers' Models on the Carpathian Lowlands', in Hall, *Civil Society*.

29. House of Lords. [1931] AC 333; 100 LJKB 328; 145 LTI; 47 TLR 351. See Cecil A. Wright, *Law of Torts* (Butterworths, 3rd edn, 1963), pp.968–71.

30. Ibid., p.969.

31. Ibid., p.970.

32. Judgment of the Court of Appeal, 11 February 1988 by Lord Justice O'Connor, Lord Justice Lloyd and Lord Justice Nicholls, *The Times*, Law Reports, 19 September 1988.

33. In *Nordenfelt* v. *Maxim Nordenfelt Guns and Ammunition Company* 1894 AC 535. Quoted in Simon Gardner, Alexandra Felix, John O'Leary, Mark James and Roger Welch, *Sports Law* (Cavendish, 1998), p.230.

34. Ibid.

35. *Greig and Others* v. *Insole and Others*, 1977 G.No.2246 *World Series Cricket Pty Ltd* v. *Same*, 1977 J.No.4876. See Gardner *et al.*, *Sports Law*, pp.231–3.

36. See G. Haigh, *Cricket War: the Inside Story of Packer's World Series Cricket* (Melbourne: Text Publishing Co., 1993).

37. Quoted from the *Daily Telegraph*, 22 June 1999, p.39. There are naturally considerable ambiguities in the question of what counts as watching a cricket match on television (how many minutes or hours? Whether live, highlights or news reports, etc.).

38. Ferdinand Tonnies, *Gemeinschaft und Gesellschaft*; trans. Charles P. Loomis as *Community and Association* (Routledge & Kegan Paul, 1955).

CHAPTER 5

1. Correspondence quoted in 'The triumph of de Coubertin's Worldwide Philosophy' in Philip Noel-Baker, *Collected Speeches and Essays* (Sports Editions, 1991), p.108.

2. In an essay entitled 'Contradictions of Modern France', *Fortnightly Review*, 63 (March 1898), p.352. Quoted in Richard D. Mandell, *The First Modern Olympics* (University of California Press, 1976), p.64.

3. The character appeared in a variety of boys' comics produced by the Dundee firm D.C. Thompson & Co. from the 1930s to the 1980s, including *The Rover* and *The Wizard*.

4. See his obituary, *Daily Telegraph*, 27 March 1999, p.25.

5. J.K. Galbraith, *The Affluent Society* (Hamish Hamilton, 1958); E.J. Mishan, *The Costs of Economic Growth* (Staples, 1967); Tibor Scitovsky, *The Joyless Economy* (Oxford University Press, 1976); Fred Hirsch, *Social Limits to Growth* (Harvard University Press, 1976).

6. Kenneth Boulding, *Economic Analysis* (Hamish Hamilton, 1948), p.29.

7. Hirsch, *Social Limits*, pp.15–26.

8. Ibid., pp.71–116.

9. Lincoln Allison (ed.), *The Changing Politics of Sport* (Manchester University Press, 1993), pp.219–22.

10. Hirsch, *Social Limits*, p.23; Staffan Lender, *The Harried Leisure Class* (Columbia University Press, 1970).

11. John Stuart Mill, *Autobiography*.

12. General, but not complete, agreement. There were 'neo-liberal' and 'new-right' thinkers in the 1980s who were prepared to argue, privately at least, for the ideological superiority of prostitution over other forms of sex, but they have mostly recanted and it would serve no purpose to name them.

13. Hirsch, *Social Limits*, p.97.

14. E.F. Schumacher, *Small is Beautiful: A Study of Economics as if People Mattered* (Blond & Briggs, 1973).

15. Hirsch, *Social Limits*, p.101.

16. I make no claim to the originality of this image. A football fan like this, played by John Thompson, was a regular feature of *The Fast Show* on BBC Television in 1998.

17. William Morris, *News from Nowhere* (1890; Routledge & Kegan Paul, 1970).

18. Quoted in the *Daily Telegraph*, 24 July 1998, p.38.

19. Ibid., 25 October 1997, p.19.

20. Garry Nelson (and Anthony Fowles), *Left Foot in the Grave, a View from the Bottom of the Football League* (Harper/Collins, 1997). The quotation from Simon Barnes is on the cover.

PART II: CHAPTER 1

1. Quoted from 'I Couldn't Be an Obese American', Alice Thompson's interview with Olga Korbut, *Daily Telegraph*, 20 July 1999, p.17.

2. See James Riordan, *Sport, Politics and Communism* (Manchester University Press, 1991).

3. Jim Riordan, 'The Strange Story of Nikolai Starostin, Football and Laventi Beria', *Europe–Asia Studies*, 46, 4 (1994).

4. Translated from Nikolai Starostin, *Futbol's kroz gody* (Moscow: Sovetskaya Rossiya, 1989), p.128 by Riordan and quoted in 'The Strange Story', p.688.

5. See for example, John Sugden, *Boxing and Society* (Manchester University Press, 1996), pp.131–71.

6. See Hiroyuki Ishii, 'A Cross Cultural Analysis of the Emergence of Professional Rugby Union in England and Japan', MA thesis, Warwick Centre for the Study of Sport in Society, 1999; the references to M. Murao, *Supo-tu Seisin* (The Sporting Spirit) (Tokyo: Chuo art Syuppan, 1997) translated by Ishii.

CHAPTER 2

1. There are a number of literary products of this devotion, most notably Hallam

Tennyson, *Alfred Lord Tennyson: A Memoir by His Son* (Macmillan, 2 vols, 1897).

 2. Benny Green (ed.), *The Wisden Book of Cricketers' Lives* (Queen Anne Press, 1986), pp.881–2; *The Times*, 7 June 1951; *Who Was Who 1951-60* (Adam & Charles Black, 1961), p.1074; Lionel, Lord Tennyson, *Sticky Wickets* (Christopher Johnson, 1950). There is no entry on Tennyson in the *Dictionary of National Biography.*

 3. *Sticky Wickets*, p.10.

 4. Ibid., p.167.

 5. See ibid., p.169.

 6. Ibid., p.173.

 7. Ibid., pp.79–80 (the complete poem is included in Appendix III).

 8. Ibid., p.154.

 9. Ibid., p.161.

10. Ibid., p.169.

11. There have been many accounts of this story including a fictionalized television film and several documentaries. For a succinct and clear account see Green, *The Wisden Book*, pp. 493–4, 935–6.

12. Ibid., p.493.

13. *Sticky Wickets*, p.167.

14. Albert Camus, with a rather different outlook on life from Lionel Tennyson's, described this tension as '... we had to play "sportingly" because that was the golden rule of the RUA and "strongly", because, when all is said and done, a man is a man. Difficult compromise! This cannot have changed I am sure.' Camus, 'What I Owe to Football', originally in *France Football*, quoted by Ian Hamilton (ed.), *The Faber Book of Soccer* (Faber, 1992), p.93.

15. *Sticky Wickets*, p.128.

16. See Edward Banfield, *The Unheavenly City: The Nature and Future of Our Urban Crisis* (Boston, MA: Little, Brown, 1970).

17. See *Sticky Wickets*, pp.154–66 and Peter Wilson, 'Did Bradman Snub Lord Tennyson? Accused of Rudeness', *Sunday Pictorial*, 30 May 1948.

CHAPTER 3

 1. There is an autobiography which takes Moorcroft's story up to 1984, shortly before the Los Angeles Olympics: Dave Moorcroft (with Cliff Temple), *Running Commentary* (Stanley Paul, 1984).

 2. Ibid., pp.144–51.

CHAPTER 4

 1. Bath was regarded as an extreme case of the 'rugby friendly' job. In the early 1990s, the Johnson Group, chaired by Malcolm Pearce, a lifelong Bath supporter, employed 16 of their players; see Sarah Edworthy, 'Future Looks Shipshape for Bristol', *Daily Telegraph*, 19 September 1998, p.54.

 2. There is an interesting and growing body of writing on the sociology and managerial problems arising out of the interaction of voluntary and commercial sports organizations; see for example, N. Thibault, T. Slack and B. Hinings, 'Professionalism, Structures and Systems: the Impact of Professional Staff on Voluntary Sport Organizations', *International Review for the Sociology of Sport*, 26, 2 (1991), and J. Lyle, 'The Exercise of Power: the Relationship between Professional Officers and Volunteers in National Governing Bodies of Sport', in Scottish Centre Research Papers in Sport, Leisure and Society, Vol. 12 (Heriot-Watt University, 1997).

CHAPTER 5

1. See Andrew Parker, 'Chasing the Big Time: Football Apprenticeship in the 1990s', PhD thesis, University of Warwick, 1996.

CHAPTER 8

1. *The NCAA*, NCAA 15646-8/99, p.7.
2. *NCAA Division I Manual*, 1999–00, NCAA 1999, p.71.
3. Ibid., pp.72–3.
4. This distinction is often made in this context. The *Concise Oxford Dictionary* (1999 edn) lists two meanings for avocation: the first, consistent with the root in the Latin *avocare* (to call away) is a 'minor occupation'; the second simply equates avocation with vocation which, in turn, has two kinds of meaning: a 'calling' or 'strong feeling of fitness' and an employment, trade or profession especially in so far as it requires dedication.
5. The Indianapolis Colts (American) Football team, previously the Baltimore Colts.
6. The relevant facts are clearly laid out in the NCAA Professional Sports Liaison Committee, *A Career in Professional Athletics, a Guide for Making the Transition* (NCAA, 1997). Not surprisingly, the figures in the two most commercial sports are slightly higher than this: 1.9 per cent for basketball and 3.3 per cent for football.
7. The most recently available figures – for the 1992 entry – show 58 per cent of athletics scholars graduating, compared with 56 per cent of the general student body. Of course, this comparison must be put in the context that, to different degrees, many of the general student body would drop out because of inadequate financial support whereas all athletic scholars would have adequate funding. It can hardly be satisfactory that only 40 per cent of black male athletes graduated even if it is higher than the figure for black males as a whole (31 per cent). By contrast, 71 per cent of white female athletes graduated. All of these figures relate to the 310 Division One Institutions which are allowed the highest number of scholarships (for example, 85 football scholarships per institution); see NCAA Fact Sheet, *Graduation* for 1999.

CHAPTER 9

1. George and Weedon Grossmith, *The Diary of a Nobody* (1892; Oxford University Press, 1998), p.2.
2. A couple typifying British stubbornness and eccentricity, for many years featured in the satirical magazine *Private Eye*.

PART III

1. 1 Timothy 6:10.
2. Ecclesiastes 10:19.
3. Shiram Sharma Acharya, *Awake O Talented and Come Forward* (Yug Nirman Yojana, 1997), pp.6–7.
4. Ibid., *My Life – Its Legacy and Message* (Haridwar, India: Yugfirth Shanti Kunj, 1998).
5. Walter Bagehot, *The English Constitution* (1867; Fontana, 1965).
6. Talcott Parsons, *The Social System* (Routledge & Kegan Paul, 1951); David Easton, *A Systems Analysis of Political Life* (Wiley, 1965).
7. Edward Banfield, *The Moral Basis of a Backward Society* (Free Press, 1958); Lincoln

Allison, 'The Concept of Civil Society in South Africa, Georgia and Thailand', *South African Journal of International Affairs*, 4, 2 (1997).

8. In Part I and in 'Sport and Civil Society', *Political Studies*, 46, 4 (1998).

9. James Burnham, *The Managerial Revolution* (1941; Penguin, 1962); Michael Young, *The Rise of the Meritocracy* (Penguin, 1958).

10. Harold Perkin, *The Rise of Professional Society in England since 1880* (Routledge, 1989).

11. Ibid., p.9.

12. Raymond Aron, *18 Lectures on Industrial Society* (trans. M.K. Bot, Weidenfeld & Nicolson, 1967); W.W. Rostow, *The Stages of Economic Growth: a Non-Communist Manifesto* (Cambridge University Press, 1960).

13. Tom Stoppard, *Every Good Boy Deserves Favour and Professional Foul* (Faber, 1978).

14. *Henry VI*, Pt II, Act 4, Scene VII.

15. Petr Skrabenek, *The Death of Humane Medicine and the Rise of Coercive Healthism* (The Social Affairs Unit, 1994).

16. Duncan Stewart, 'Alcohol: the Ethical Dilemma', MA thesis, University of Warwick, 1997.

17. Andrew Parker, 'Chasing the Big Time: Football Apprenticeship in the 1990s', PhD thesis, University of Warwick, 1996.

18. John Hoberman, *Mortal Engines: The Science of Performance and the Dehumanization of Sport* (Free Press, 1992).

19. I am indebted to Ellis Cashmore for this speculation and to Ivan Waddington for pointing out that, when the Dutch TVM and the Italian Festina teams were expelled from the 1998 Tour de France (as a result of action by the French police and not the cycling authorities), they were treated as heroes on their return to racing by both spectators and other cyclists. However, cycling *aficionados* may not be typical of sports fans in this respect, not least because of the acceptance of the almost superhuman levels of pain and effort involved in modern competitive cycling. Arguably, the individual cyclist takes drugs (primarily the blood-enhancing EPO) in order to compete rather than in order to win.

20. It is now estimated that 23,000 men fought for their lives in Rome in the years 106–114 and that 5,000 animals died in a single day at the inauguration of the Colosseum in AD 80. See Barry Cunliffe, *Rome and Her Empire* (Bodley Head, 1978). I am indebted to my colleague Richard Beacham for accounts of his own research on the arena.

21. See Norbert Elias and Eric Dunning, *Quest for Excitement: Sport and Leisure in the Civilising Process* (Blackwell, 1986).

22. See John Hoberman, *Sport and Political Ideology* (University of Texas, 1984).

23. Udo Merkel, 'Sport in Divided Societies – the Case of the Old, the New and the 'Re-united' Germany', in John Sugden and Alan Bairner (eds), *Sport in Divided Societies* (Aachen: Meyer & Meyer, 1999); also, John Hoberman, 'Sport and Ideology in the Post-Communist Age', in Lincoln Allison (ed.), *The Changing Politics of Sport* (Manchester University Press, 1993).

24. The relationship between public authorities and commercial sports organizations is usually much closer in the United States than it is in Britain and considerable sums of public money are devoted to providing stadiums and in other ways securing the presence of 'major league' sport in particular cities. See Michael Danielson, *Home Team: Professional Sport and the American Metropolis* (Princeton University Press, 1997).

25. A theme fully explored in John Hoberman's, *Darwin's Athletes: How Sport Has Damaged Black America and Preserved the Myth of Race* (New York: Houghton

Mifflin, 1997).

26. Nick Hornby, *Fever Pitch* (Gollancz, 1992); Steve Redhead, *Post-Fandom and the Millennial Blues: The Transformation of Soccer Culture* (Routledge, 1997). See also Damian Hall, 'From Passion to Plastic: a Study of "New Football", Fandom Identities and Cultural Change', MA thesis, University of Warwick, 1999.

27. Colin Ward, *Steaming In: A Journal of a Football Fan* (Simon & Schuster, 1989), p.6.

28. Lincoln Allison, *Condition of England* (Junction Books, 1981), pp.137–8.

29. Martin J. Weiner, *English Culture and the Decline of the Industrial Spirit: 1850–1980* (Cambridge University Press, 1981).

30. This is a bald assertion of a proposition developed in my books *Environmental Planning* (George Allen, 1975); (as editor) *The Utilitarian Response* (Sage, 1990); and *Ecology and Utility* (Cassell, 1991).

31. Sybil Ruscoe, 'Rugby Too Tame for the Wild Man of Namibia', *Daily Telegraph*, 14 October 1999, p.45.

32. G.M. Trevelyan, *Grey of Fallodon* (Longmans, 1937); Edward Grey, *Fly Fishing* (Dent, 1899); Viscount Grey of Fallodon, *The Charm of Birds* (Hodder & Stoughton, 1927).

33. For the evidence of this point see Allison (ed.), *The Changing Politics of Sport*, pp.207–32.

34. This is, I hope, a fair description of the two final issues of *Marxism Today*, those of November 1991 and December 1991–January 1992.

35. This is true in my opinion of the leading British work in the genre: Jennifer Hargreaves, *Sporting Females: Critical Issues in the History and Sociology of Women's Sport* (Routledge, 1994).

36. Hardin, 'The Tragedy of the Commons', *Science*, 162, pp.1243–8.

37. Isaiah Berlin, *Two Concepts of Liberty* (Oxford University Press, 1958).

38. The phrase is taken from early press coverage of the Paralympics and has come to be used ironically by spokesmen for the disabled in describing official attitudes towards them. I am indebted to Sarah Lewis for pointing this out to me.

39. Charles Louis de Secondat, Baron de Montesquieu, *L'Esprit des lois* (1748); *The Spirit of the Laws* (trans. T. Nugent, Hafme, 1949).

Index